From Sicily to Elizabeth Street

SUNY SERIES IN AMERICAN SOCIAL HISTORY

Charles Stephenson and Elizabeth Pleck, Editors

From Sicily
to Elizabeth Street

Housing and Social Change Among Italian Immigrants, 1880–1930

DONNA R. GABACCIA
Mercy College

State University of New York Press   ALBANY

Published by
State University of New York Press, Albany

© 1984 State University of New York

For information, address State University of New York
Press, State University Plaza, Albany, N.Y., 12246

Library of Congress Cataloging in Publication Data

Gabaccia, Donna R., 1949–
From sicily to elizabeth street.

(SUNY series in American social history)
Bibliography: p.
Includes index.
1. Italian Americans—New York (N.Y.)—Social
conditions. 2. Italian American families—New York
(N.Y.) 3. Italian Americans—New York (N.Y.)—Social
life and customs. 4. New York (N.Y.)—Social conditions.
5. New York (N.Y.)—Social life and customs. 6. Sicily—
Social conditions. 7. Sicily—Social life and customs.
8. Housing—Social aspects. I. Title. II. Series.
F128.9I8G32 1984   305.8'51'07471   83-4933

ISBN 0-87395-768-7
ISBN 0-87395-769-5 (pbk.)

10 9 8 7 6 5 4 3 2 1

For all my households —
Usu fa natura

Contents

Figures   ix
Maps   x
Tables   xi
Acknowledgments   xiii
Introduction   xv
    Environment and Behavior   xvi
    From Agrotown to Tenement   xx
CHAPTER ONE: Sicilian Social Ideals in the Nineteenth Century   1
    Family and Familism   3
    Occupation and Social Class   5
    The Social Origins of Conflicting Ideals   8
CHAPTER TWO: Residential Choice in the Sicilian Agrotown   11
    The Physical Setting   13
    Choosing a House   21
    Occupation, Class and Kin   24
    House and Household   26
    Residential Mobility   32
    Summary   34
CHAPTER THREE: Everyday Life and Sicilian Society   35
    A Typical Day   37
    Activity, Time and Location   40
    Agrotown Social Patterns   45
    Summary   51
CHAPTER FOUR: Sicilian Migrants   53
    Familism and Migration   55
    The Social Organization of Migration   57
    Class and Immigrant Occupations   61

CHAPTER FIVE: Tenement Residential Patterns   6.
    Tenements   6(
    New Restraints   7∢
    New Opportunities   7!
    New Restraint or New Ideal? The Malleable Household   8(
        and the Kitchen *Salotto*
    Environmental Change and Residential Patterns in   8.
        New York
CHAPTER SIX: Everyday Life in New York   8(
    A Typical Day   8"
    Activity, Time and Location   8!
    Environmental Change and Everyday Life   9!
CHAPTER SEVEN: Immigrant Society and Culture   10(
    The Nuclear Family and American Individualism   10(
    A Family Social Cycle   10.
    The Question of Class   10!
    Social and Cultural Change   11.
Appendix A: Social Ideals in Sicilian Proverbs   11"
Appendix B: A Note on Sources and Methods   12(
Notes   13(
Bibliography   15∢
    Sicily and Migration   15∢
    Immigrant Italians   15!
    Environment and Behavior   16.
Index   16!

Figures

I–1. Sambuca di Sicilia   xvii
I–2. Elizabeth Street   xix
2–1. A *Cortile*   16
2–2. A *Cortile*   17
2–3. A Simple Sicilian House   19
2–4. A Simple House   19
2–5. A Larger Sicilian House   20
2–6. A Larger House   20
2–7. *Salotto* Wall and Ceiling Decorations   31
3–1. Men Cooking in the Countryside   41
3–2. "The Street is Their Drawing Room"   47
5–1. Rear Tenements   69
5–2. A Barracks Tenement   69
5–3. A Dumbbell Tenement   70
5–4. A New Law Tenement   70
6–1. 233–35 Elizabeth Street   88
B–1. Sicilian Naming Pattern   128

Maps

2-1. Sambuca di Sicilia in Western Sicily   15
2-2. Sambuca di Sicilia   15
5-1. Manhattan Little Italies   67
5-2. Elizabeth Street Land Use, 1905   73

x

Tables

2-1.	*Casa* Clusters	26
3-1.	Two Agrotown Families, 1900	37
4-1.	Crop, Migration, and Working Class Organization	57
4-2.	Immigrant Occupations	63
5-1.	Family, House and Partner Household	76
5-2.	Kin Clusters	79
6-1.	Two Immigrant Households, 1905	87
B-1.	Elizabeth Street Housing and Population	126

Acknowledgments

My interest in how people use space in their homes and neighborhoods originated in my own idiosyncratic and sometimes painful efforts to reach agreements about space, socializing and privacy with the members of my many households. Long before I considered writing about the relationship of environment and behavior, I lived in a surprisingly varied number of households — "extended family" ones, "malleable" ones, "nonfamily" ones, "partner" households and nuclear households — in houses, apartments and dormitories on both sides of the Atlantic. The people who lived with me at 1110 South Maple, 522 Hill, 701 Miller, 36 Stöcklestrasse, 802 Stimson, 1110 White, Mazzini 29, 345 Riverside, Pankstrasse 16, and in the Riuone Nuova taught me much about the personal and social meanings that physical space can — and almost always does — assume.

Like many books, this one has changed considerably since its first draft, evolving not only in response to my own developing ideas about the urban environment, migration and south Italian social life, but also in response to the valuable suggestions of others. My greatest debts are to Elizabeth Pleck, Louise Tilly, Robin Jacoby and William Lockwood who helped me while writing the first draft and who read and commented on the doctoral dissertation that resulted.

Many more drafts were written during three years in Berlin at the John F. Kennedy Institute of the Free University. I cannot imagine a more comfortable and supportive environment for the young scholar than the Kennedy Institute. Its excellent library never failed me; the geography department generously helped in preparing maps. Working with my German colleagues and students, I also came to appreciate, in a very personal way, how culture change occurs. Although I avoided generalizing from this experience while writing about emigration, I do know what it "feels like" to be an emigrant. For this reason I offer special thanks to Mica Ulich, Dagmar Schultz, Christiane Harzig, Heinz Ickstadt and Ekkehart

Krippendorff, as well as to my historian colleagues Knud Krakau and Willi Adams, who helped, in differing but very important ways, to ease the culture shock.

I have also enjoyed and continue to benefit from a rare combination of scholarly exchange and friendship with Jane and Peter Schneider, who first introduced me to Sambuca. There is scarcely a line in this book that does not reflect some shared conversation on one continent or the other. To their son, Benjamin, who helped choose and produce photographs from Sambuca, and to their daughter Julie, who enjoyed entertaining my son, I offer separate thanks.

Finally, without my parents, I might never have begun this book — or any book, for that matter. And without Thomas and Tamino, I almost certainly would never have finished all those revisions.

My errors are, of course, my own.

DONNA GABACCIA

June 1982

Introduction

Between 1880 and 1920, thousands of ordinary immigrants left their homes in dense south Italian settlements called agrotowns to live in urban canyons—the tenement districts so evocatively described by New York's many housing reformers. The question posed in this book is a simple one: did the exchange of "low houses, each made up of a single ground floor room, each pressed up against the next" for "boxes arranged like drawers in a bureau" affect the lives of people moving from one to another? To answer that question, the book compares the family and community lives of Sicilians in the agrotowns of western Sicily to those on Elizabeth Street, a western Sicilian tenement neighborhood on New York's Lower East Side. My decision to analyze the relationship of environment and human social behavior by comparing two similar groups of persons on two continents largely dictated the choice of western Sicilians and of Elizabeth Street for detailed study.[1]

For many Sicilians, the move from agrotown to tenement was accompanied by rapid, significant and mainly satisfying changes in a wide variety of social relationships, in and outside the nuclear family group. Many of these changes could be traced directly or indirectly to the influence of a changing housing environment. The Sicilians described in this book seem to differ from the south Italian immigrants studied by Virginia Yans-McLaughlin in *Family and Community*.[2] Old-World traditions quite unlike those of Buffalo's Italians guided their adjustment to a new environment. Sicilians preached skepticism towards most social relationships; if they glorified any social tie outside the nuclear family, it was that of friendship, not kinship. The fact that few families in Sicily could achieve their social ideals also may have made Sicilians' attitudes toward social change far more positive than Yans-McLaughlin believed was true of Buffalo's immigrant Italians. In fact, *la famiglia*—the immigrant network of close and extended kin living in several neighboring households and described in *Family and Community* as the New-World expression of Old-World traditions—appears instead to have emerged during migration to and life in a new urban environment.

Environment and Social Behavior

During the years when Italian immigrants crowded American cities, reformers and socially concerned scholars in both Europe and America firmly believed that the housing environment was primarily responsible for the living conditions of the urban poor. Low quality housing, reformers argued, caused disease; it also produced devastating social consequences in criminality, family breakdown and social disorganization. American housing reformers feared in particular the social dangers of life in tenement houses. Many of their social surveys seemed to demonstrate a correlation between social pathology and poor housing. Thus armed, New York reformers like Jacob Riis, Lawrence Veiller and Robert de Forest urged that legislators pass better regulatory laws and private investors build better houses. Better buildings would help cure the social ills of American cities.[3]

Today, few social scientists accept the early reformers' simplistic theory of material determinism. Correlations between housing quality and social patterns, social scientists now tell us, did not reflect a causative link between the two. Poverty may have influenced how people lived in tenements, but the buildings themselves did not. Historians, too, contributed belatedly to the critique of material determinism: not only did Riis and other reformers fail in identifying the origin of urban social problems, they also misnamed them. Working-class and immigrant tenement dwellers were not socially disorganized. They created neighborhoods and communities in ways that they—not middle-class reformers—deemed appropriate.[4] Historians confirmed what planners often proclaimed in the 1960's. People, not houses, create the social life typical of a given area, whether it is a city or a suburb, a Sicilian agrotown or a tenement neighborhood.[5]

Still, the notion persists that a relationship exists between environmental and social patterns. Many architects continue to see themselves as social engineers who direct and shape social behavior in the buildings that they design.[6] The very concept of city planning assumes some sort of linkage between environmental form and social behavior. Scholarly and governmental discussions of housing policy, sociologists' reports on public housing problems in the ghetto, and anthropologists' analyses of non-Western housing architecture all pay homage to the popular but hazy notion that "we shape our houses and then our houses shape us."[7]

Figure 1-1. Sambuca di Sicilia. "Approaching the city, however, the scene changes; . . . from the distance of about a mile, more or less according to the importance of the city, the traveller finds himself in the middle of an oasis of olives, almonds, grape vines, prickly pears, and, below, in the bottom of the valley, he sees the dark green leaves of the citrus gardens. Entering the city — here there are almost no villages — he must pass the long streets of low houses, each made up of a single ground-floor room, each pressed up against the next, without windows and with only a single entryway. . . . These are the houses of peasants." (Sidney Sonnino, *I Contadini in Sicilia*, Inchiesta in Sicilia, vol. 2 (Florence: Valecchi, 1974), p. 11).

Social-scientific efforts to move beyond material determinism without treating the housing environment as completely irrelevant draw on Louis Wirth's early, sensitive observations of American cities. Wirth urged his colleagues to view the urban environment as a conditioning factor "offering the possibilities and setting the limits for social and psychological existence and development."[8] Many recent studies analyze human choice in a housing environment portrayed as a system of opportunities and restraints; such studies focus on the extent to which people can achieve their housing standards and their social ideals in the housing available to them.[9] Housing can limit their efforts to achieve their goals, but even when restraints are many, people never behave in ways directly determined by the environment. Humans are never "rats" in a "housing maze." They even exercise choice when responding creatively to restraints — not all people, for example, will respond similarly when faced with an obstacle.[10] Unlike the early reformers, then, today's students of housing usually "look for what a . . . physical setting makes impossible, rather than for what it makes inevitable."[11]

Furthermore, "restraints" are not built into a house physically, as are bricks, mortar and floor boards. Instead they are *perceived*, either by residents struggling to achieve their housing and social ideals, or by social scientists observing that process. For this reason sociologists of housing often focus on what they call the "match" or "fit" or "congruence" of housing characteristics and particular groups of people, with their own unique needs, ideals and resources.[12] One person's castle can, in fact, be another person's cage.

The degree of match between available housing and a particular human group is a qualitative judgment; it cannot be measured with precise accuracy. Sociologists speak of a "good match" when people can meet their own housing standards and behave in ways that they themselves find socially desirable. A good match, in other words, imposes few perceivable restraints. In addition, goodness of match must be judged from two perspectives, which sociologist William Michelson calls "mental" and "experiential." A person, Michelson notes, can be very pleased with his house or with her social life, or with both, even when house, or social life, or both, fall far short of the person's social and housing ideals.[13] Match, then, must be judged from both these perspectives.

The match of available housing and human resources or desires is important at two critical moments: first, when individuals or families choose a residence and, second, when they attempt to use the physical world that surrounds them for their everyday work and leisure activities.

Figure I-2. Elizabeth Street. (Lindsay Denison, "The Black Hand," *Everybody's Magazine* 19 (1908): 294. "Here were myriads of human beings, stifling in boxes arranged like drawers in a bureau, with holes to look out upon the opposite boxes and the roaring 'elevated.' Those who were at home hung out of the windows in as few garments as were decent; while the long seething bare canons of brick, paving stone and asphalt were swarming with children in quest of air and amusement . . . . Hardly a tree or any green thing was to be seen—except in the far eastward vista. (Richard Watson Gilder, "The Housing Problem—America's Need of Awakening," *The American City* 1 (1909): 34.)

Guided largely by their housing ideals, individuals or families seek to achieve their housing standards in the available housing supply. In doing so, they locate themselves spatially among other individuals and families in the larger environment.[14] Unique residential patterns—household structure, social and economic clusterings, rapid or slow residential mobility—are the result. These residential patterns in turn create conditions favorable or unfavorable to residents as they seek to attain their social ideals.

The housing environment can more directly influence human social behavior through its power to restrict "what people do, with whom they do it and where they do it."[15] Choices about use of the environment for everyday work and leisure activities allow residents of differing age, sex, class and family status better or worse opportunities for interaction and for achieving their ideals through social interaction. The chapters that follow compare Sicilian residential choices and everyday lives in agrotown and tenement neighborhood to identify the influence of a changing environment on social practices in both settings.

From Agrotown to Tenement

The working hypothesis of this study was that the tenements of New York would match Sicilian needs and desires rather poorly, and that immigrants would change their social behavior as they responded creatively to new environmental restraints. New York's housing, after all, was built neither for nor by Sicilians, while Sicilians and their own ancestors had for centuries directly "shaped" the houses and streets of Sicilian agrotowns. Logically, the agrotown should have matched Sicilian resources, needs and desires far better than did the tenements.

But this was not the case. Unlike other "folk" or "vernacular" architectural forms, Sicily's agrotowns poorly reflected the housing and social ideals of their creators.[16] While allowing many Sicilians to achieve only their minimal housing standards, agrotowns imposed huge restraints on Sicilians hoping to reach their social ideals in their everyday lives. Sicilians perceived these environmental restraints quite clearly. While somewhat satisfied with their houses, many recognized and resented their social failures. They would have agreed with a sociologist's conclusion that they endured "high residential dissatisfaction." Their migration was as much a response to residential as to occupational dissatisfaction.

By contrast, the majority of Sicilians moving to Elizabeth Street quickly achieved many of their social ideals, living among the tenements much as they chose. Elizabeth Street tenements proved a relatively good match for Sicilians seeking homes there. Nevertheless, immigrants disliked their tenement homes, for they varied considerably from Sicilian housing ideals. When social and housing ideals conflicted, many immigrants ultimately compromised the former to achieve the latter.

Change in immigrant family and community life resulted when former Sicilian peasants painlessly abandoned familiar social practices in order to realize some Old-World social ideals. Within this general pattern there was, of course, considerable variation. One important group of immigrants — artisans — experienced relatively little change during migration. And women immigrants sometimes ignored Sicilian social ideals, while overcoming considerable new environmental restraints, to continue to form familiar social ties with their neighbors in the tenements.

Sicilians' changing family and community patterns were an outgrowth of Old-World traditions, yet this did not mean that Elizabeth Street's residents — like Yans-McLaughlin's immigrants in Buffalo — remained "culturally folk."[17] Immigrant social ideals soon differed from those of nineteenth-century Sicilians. One reason is that both housing and social ideals guided Sicilian immigrants in making new lives among the tenements. When these conflicted, immigrants had to choose between them to justify their behavior. Immigrants could always draw on a variety of conflicting ideals, as well as their sometimes-contradictory former habits, for guidance in the New World. As they interpreted their lives in the New World, Sicilian immigrants completely abandoned some Sicilian ideals. Others, while Sicilian in origin, assumed new and distinctively immigrant forms in the United States. Culturally, the first generation was already becoming Italian-American; indeed, the process began even before arriving immigrants first saw the tenements of lower Manhattan.

CHAPTER ONE

Sicilian Social Ideals in the Nineteenth Century

South Italians — including Sicilians — enjoy a curiously contradictory social reputation. Sometimes portrayed as fiercely competitive familists, they are deemed suspicious of outsiders — of the state or even of their own neighbors. Alternatively they are described as a passionately sociable people, always in the company of others. Skillful social architects, they build large, intricate kin groups, crime "syndicates," or "dense community networks," all seemingly with equal skill.[1]

It was Edward Banfield who opened the scholarly form of this debate about south Italian social character. In the 1950's Banfield called the residents of one south Italian town "amoral familists."[2] Because of their dedication to the interests of the nuclear family, these south Italians, according to Banfield, could not cooperate with others. Early critics accepted Banfield's label, but faulted him for describing familism as the cause rather than the consequence of grinding south Italian poverty. Others disputed the accuracy of the label itself. Banfield was accused of cultural blindness, of failing to recognize that south Italians have their own form of social morality. South Italians, these critics argued, are scarcely familistic; however, their social ties take the form of personal networks, rather than voluntary institutionalized association as in middle-class America.[3]

Banfield believed that Italians in the past were as familist as they are today, about that we know considerably less. The earliest anthropological study of Sicily, Charlotte Gower Chapman's *Milocca*, reflected field work completed in the 1920's.[4] This study and evidence from the nineteenth century do suggest, however, that Sicilian social relations have changed through time, so that contemporary anthropological accounts are of limited use to historians seeking information about immigrant backgrounds. Too much — mass migrations, two wars, fascism, and eighty years of economic change — has intervened.[5]

Except as they are deduceable from behavioral data (a tricky business, at best), the social values of southern Italians in the past remain elusive. As long as the social ideals of the past remain hazy or unexplored, historians will experience difficulty in interpreting the social experiences of south Italian immigrants. Virginia Yans-McLaughlin, Josef Barton and John Briggs all base their analyses of immigrant social patterns largely on the present-day anthropological debate.[6] Exploring the values, ideals and motives of ordinary people in the past is, of course, immensely complicated; sources are few, and they are often difficult to interpret. However, it is a necessary task, undertaken by this chapter, which examines Sicilian social ideals as reflected in a large collection of Sicilian proverbs gathered in the nineteenth century by Giuseppe Pitrè.[7]

Proverbs, like all folklore sources, must be used with some care. Folklore has an inherently conservative bias. It emerged as a field of study only when middle-class observers discovered with dismay that rural life was rapidly changing in character. In their efforts to collect and to preserve, folklorists often overemphasized and celebrated the differences between an organic peasant past and a decadent modern proletariat. In some hands, folklore became more a critique of modernism than a scientific study of society or culture.[8]

Unlike many folklorists, Giuseppe Pitrè was not overly interested in criticizing the social changes that he observed around him. Pitrè, a Palermo physician, became interested in Sicilian tales, customs and proverbs long before political unrest in the 1890's encouraged widespread and explicitly conservative interest in the "disappearing" Sicilian peasant. Compared to his colleague Salomone-Marino, Pitrè seemed a relatively sympathetic observer of the Sicilian peasant's effort to live in a rapidly changing economy. He did not, for example, indulge in bitter attacks on peasant political activism—as did Salomone-Marino and others.[9]

Pitrè's collection offers several other advantages for the student of past social values. Proverbs—"short, pithy saying[s] in frequent and widespread use"—express well-known facts, truths or lessons.[10] These lessons vary from society to society and through time, as Pitrè's comparisons of Sicilian and other proverb collections show. Pitrè collected proverbs from a variety of oral and written sources all over Sicily in the years preceding mass migration from the island. With more than 13,000 proverbs, the collection covers almost every imaginable aspect of Sicilian life, and its size guarantees that the collector had not simply selected those sentiments that matched his own evaluation of Sicilians and their culture. Pitrè did provide a lengthy introduction to his collection, and he did divide it into categories he considered logical. One can, however, ignore Pitrè's editorial work. The proverbs, according to the editor of their most recent reprinting, provide an extraordinary and unique introduction to the values of ordinary people at the end of the nineteenth century.[11]

To use Pitrè's proverbs as a source for the study of Sicilian values required a systematic approach; haphazard selection would have proved extremely misleading. The first task was to identify all social and occupational categories used in the proverbs. The second was to summarize the social lessons expressed about each category. A third task was to interpret Pitrè's proverbs against the background of changes in Sicily's economy and society during the late nineteenth century.[12] Appendix A compiles proverbs in several key categories. To simplify documentation of the proverbs, they will be cited here by volume and page number.

Pitrè's proverbs describe social values rather unlike those of Banfield's amoral familists. Sicilians had no name for the family group that Banfield and others call the "nuclear family" of father, mother and children. Although the nuclear family was not without significance in Sicilian social and economic behavior (as I will show), Sicilians also strongly desired social ties to people outside this group and they had clear rules defining moral social behavior outside the nuclear family. They wanted close and harmonious social ties to their *casa* of close relatives. Under special conditions, they also sought ties to their more distant kin, called the *parenti*. However, unlike the south Italian immigrants described by Yans-McLaughlin, Sicilians in the nineteenth century did not value involvement with their *parenti* over involvement with friends or neighbors. Sicilians in their proverbs also made few and relatively simple class distinctions; they offered generally negative but somewhat contradictory advice about relations between the classes. Often, in fact, the proverbs offered apparently contradictory advice, but when viewed against the reality of social mobility in Sicily in the nineteenth century, many of these apparent contradictions and ambiguities begin to make perfect social sense.

Family and Familism

Sicilian proverbs about close blood ties—those between parents and children and among siblings—form the most detailed and voluminous category in Pitrè's collection. Clearly, these were unlike any other kind of social relations, and they were always described positively. Proverbs gave a picture of "nuclear family" ideals only slightly different from that in Yans—McLaughlin's *Family and Community*. Pitrè accurately summarized

3

his research on Sicilian families when he noted that they encompassed simultaneously principles of both matriarchy and patriarchy.[13] The father headed the family and guided it in its economic endeavors. All family members were expected to work for the good of the family and to cooperate at all times. This was necessary because the nuclear family, as owner of property, had its own "interests" — *i fatti sui* — which inevitably brought it into competition with other families. Proverbs emphasized further that the father must control the potentially dangerous sexuality of wives and daughters (II, *"Donna e matrimonio"*). But proverbs praising women as mothers and housekeepers also balanced this large group of violently misogynous proverbs. Mothers ran the household and arranged children's marriages. Sicilians believed, in fact, that a family with no wife/mother rapidly became poor [II, 65.)[14]

Whatever importance they granted the nuclear family, Sicilians were not familistic in their social ideals. They desired and valued ties to people outside their nuclear families. A number of desired social ties to others originated in the family cycle: siblings remained siblings and parents parents, even as individual children married and formed nuclear families of their own. This meant that every family valued ties to an intergeneration bilateral group of close kin. For a young married couple it included the parents of both man and wife and all their brothers and sisters, whether single or married. Several proverbs suggested that cooperation with the wife's family would remain particularly close (II, 216). Sicilians' term for the family, the *casa*, did not correspond neatly to our term "nuclear" or "conjugal" family, but referred to this lineal group of closest relatives.[15]

Beyond the *casa*, Sicilians recognized another category of blood relatives called the *parenti*. Proverbs had little to say about specific relations to aunts, uncles, cousins, nieces, nephews, grandparents or grandchildren — less, for example, than they expressed about stepparents or in-laws. Instead, the proverbs evaluated all these more distant kin together. According to the proverbs' evaluation, the *parenti* differed but little from other social categories like friends (*amici*), neighbors (*vicini*) or godparents (*copare, parrini*). And proverbs about friendship, godparents and neighbors actually outnumbered those about the *parenti* (see Appendix A).

Sicilians evaluated all these social ties with great ambiguity. Most proverbs harshly criticized one or more, but a large minority offered praise in equally strong words. Apparently a friend, a neighbor, a godparent or a *parente* could be a very valuable person under some circumstances, while at other times he was not to be trusted. "Good friends, good *parenti*—pity the family with neither" (III, 253). "A man's fortune is another man" (II, 274). "Keeping to yourself makes for a good neighborhood" (IV, 378). "Do nothing for your *parenti*; treat your neighbors like thorns, and don't go near your godparents" (I, 314). "Lose your money, lose your friends" (II, 251). As this last proverb suggests, all these social categories were often associated with material gain, money and gold; they described what anthropologists call "instrumental relationships." "If you have money, you will find your *parenti*" (II, 258). Proverbs treating two categories simultaneously typically linked friends and *parenti* ("The peasant, grown rich, recognizes neither friend nor kin," II, 431). The neighbor may have been a slightly different social category, perhaps because the neighbor, as described in the proverbs, often was female ("No matter how big the chicken, she needs a *vicina*," I, 251). And when proverbs explicitly compared two of these categories, they usually deprecated kin, even close ones: "Your neighbor is your real *parente*," (II, 221); "A friend nearby is more than a *parente* far away," (II, 90); "A good friend is worth more than one hundred brothers" (IV, 215). Of all ties outside the *casa*, friendship then seemed most valuable to Sicilians.

Occupation and Social Class

Sicilians also recognized and created a social hierarchy based on occupation and property ownership. The person who owned something, even if it were a mule, could sometimes be called *padrone* (*patruni* in dialect). *Padrone* also meant a person who worked as he pleased, as did an independent artisan, professional or entrepreneur. These simple distinctions produced a socio-economic hierarchy in which the landowner ranked higher than the nonowner, the rentier higher than the manual worker, and, among workers, the independent artisan ranked higher than those doing dirty and dependent work.

On this basis, the Miloccans Chapman studied in the early twentieth century divided society into roughly three classes of people; class distinctions based on occupation and property seemed equally simple in the nineteenth-century proverbs.[16] Ordinary Sicilians had many names only for the landowning rentier class: *signuri, cavaleri, galuntuomi*, or *cappeddi* (hats). They distinguished the merchant (a clever man, to be approached with caution) from the artisan, always respected as a *mastru* (master). (In doing so the proverbs ignored the fact that artisans and merchants were often the same men.) The remaining Sicilians, peasants doing dirty and dependent work, were simply *viddani*. A very few proverbs acknowledged the existence of another kind of peasant, the landowning *burgisi*.

By contrast, government clerks in Sicilian town halls found Sicilian society far more complex. An 1896 electoral list from Sambuca di Sicilia categorized with loving detail both merchants (by the many products they sold) and artisans (by the many products they made).[17] Census takers and agricultural surveys distinguished among peasants by their complex contractual relations to the land—where the proverbs recognized only *viddani*, they saw *gabelloti, burgisi, enfiteuti, giornalieri*, and *annolori*, as well as other more specialized workers in particular types of agriculture (*pastori, fattori, massarioti, guardie campestre, giardinieri, ortolani*, etc.)[18] While local clerks and census takers recognized fine distinctions among peasants, they described the landowning rentier class as a unified group that they called *civile*, thus making a specific comparison between themselves and their peers and the "uncivilized" peasants.

Clerks and proverbs also described women's occupations—and again they described them differently. The civil records of Sambuca listed spinners, weavers, "workers," servants, tailoresses, needleworkers, peasants and midwives. Proverbs described only one female occupation—the disparaged servant woman, who appeared often as the producer of bastard children. And only communal records in the 1870's and 1880's listed many women as peasants, although we know from other sources that women did agricultural work, albeit in declining numbers by the end of the century.[19] Finally, the proverbs called housekeeping women by the term *massara*. This word had a male equivalent (*massaro*); it described not a particular kind of work but an attitude towards work—one of diligent application. Clerks and census-takers used instead the sex-specific term *casalinga* for the lower status woman while listing the wives and daughters of rentier men as *civile*.

No matter how it was described or divided into categories, the Sicilian class hierarchy was bottom heavy. Peasants—sharecroppers, day-laborers and shepherds (the *viddani* of Pitrè's proverbs)—constituted up to two-thirds of the population of many Sicilian towns. Proportions of landowning peasants varied considerably, from "very few" to "very many;" in 1901 they accounted for only 12 percent of Sicilian peasants.[20] Together with artisans and merchants (roughly 15 percent of the population of smaller towns), the families of landowning peasants formed a group intermediary between the *viddanu* majority and the *civile* minority (which rarely exceeded 10 percent of the population).

When they discussed the proper relationship between members of different classes, the proverbs collapsed all social distinctions into a simple one between "the rich" and "the poor." Clearly the *signuri/civili* were the rich, and the *viddani* majority were the poor. But where did the artisan or landowning peasant fit into this dichotomy? The proverbs gave no clear answer, although at least one proverb contrasted the financially cautious (and property-conscious) landowning peasant from the *viddanu*, who casually trusted in God to provide (IV, 233).

Once again, the proverbs about the proper relation of rich and poor offered somewhat contradictory lessons. They dwelt on the injustice of wealth: "The peasant sows and the owner reaps," (I, 264); "The poor feed the rich," (III, 268). Yet they also castigated the poor and admired the rich, "Don't bother having a peasant for your godparent" (I, 223). And they saw the rich and poor inevitably linked through mutual dependence, "Sooner or later even the rich need the poor," (I, 251).

The proverbs also discussed the patron-client tie that sometimes linked rich and poor.[21] The term *padrone* had yet a third meaning, for a patron was one who controlled the work of or "owned" the social loyalties of another person. (For this reason, English speakers usually translate *"padrone"* as "boss," although "boss" unlike *"padrone"* almost always implies employment.) Proverbs called the patron's client his *servu*, one who served. Use of the term *servu* pointed to the feudal origin of the patron-client tie.

Nevertheless, the patron-client tie was not clearly defined and positively valued, as it probably was under feudalism. According to the proverbs, a *padrone* or a *servu* could be a useful social asset, but more typically the relationship was fraught with perils. "The honest man is the patron to the *casa* of others" (II, 50). "The person who brings me something becomes my patron" (II, 336). "The *servu* needs patience, the patron prudence" (II, 381). "When the *servu* becomes patron, look out!" (II, 387). "Where the patron is greedy, the *servu* is a thief" (II, 388). In general, the proverbs implied that it was best to live without patronage for only "a good slave never lacked a patron" (II, 380).

Had Edward Banfield studied the proverbs of nineteenth-century Sicilians, he might have concluded that here, indeed, lived an exemplary group of "amoral familists." Did not their proverbs allow nuclear families to behave towards other precisely as they pleased? Not exactly. Contradictory social ideals actually shared a common social morality, one of social reciprocity. A moral social tie existed when it served the interests of all those involved, that is, when reciprocation was ongoing, with each partner giving and taking in roughly equal fashion. Reciprocity was important in maintaining ties between *parenti* and between non-kin. "Where there is give and take, there is friendship" (I, 93); "Give and take maintains the *parentela*" (I, 93). Both rich and poor Sicilians had good reasons for sharing contradictory social ideals. With an appeal to the benefits of friendship or kinship, the poor or the rich family could attempt to instigate reciprocation, by offering to give and expecting to get. The poor family unable to reciprocate or the rich family unwilling to do so could justify its refusal — a refusal that could extend to kin as easily as to non-kin — through reference to any of a large number of proverbial warnings. Both sets of social lessons assumed that usefulness and reciprocity defined a moral social tie. When viewed against a background of economic change and considerable social mobility in Sicily at the end of the nineteenth century, the competitive and cooperative social ideals expressed in the proverbs appear to complement rather than contradict one another.

The Social Origins of Conflicting Ideals

The social ideals of Sicilians at the end of the nineteenth century originated in agricultural development and the related dynamics of an increasingly complex hierarchy of social classes. Traditionally, Sicily produced wheat to export. At least since the Middle Ages, feudal owners of large estates (*latifondi*) and, later, their lessee-managers (*gabelloti*) supervised grain cultivation and pasturing by a peasant work force of sharecroppers and day laborers. In the 1830's and again in the 1860's, land reforms created a new class of landowners on the island.[22] *Civili* and growing numbers of peasant landowners continued to grow wheat, but they also extended the cultivation of grapes and fruit and nut trees. One writer estimated that between 1860 and 1880 alone, acreage cultivated in grapes tripled.[23]

The end of feudalism, the emergence of new landowning classes and the extension of new forms of cultivation led to a century of intense competition for land, for material goods and for social status in Sicily.[24] *Civili*, who had initially succeeded in purchasing church and feudal lands, attempted throughout the century to consolidate their tenuous social position. They simultaneously differentiated themselves from their former peers, the mass of poorer peasants, and sought acceptance by the old impoverished aristocracy. To do so they imitated the aristocratic practice of *amore della robba* — ostentatious display and conspicuous consumption.[25]

Like their feudal predecessors, *civili* abandoned practical agricultural pursuits to become rentiers; in doing so, they leased out their lands, continually tempting the peasant majority to compete with each other in the hopes of following the *civile* path to landownership and improved social status. This meant that *civili* represented both a new group of oppressors (whose common origins made them even more intolerable to their former peers) and galling proof that social mobility was possible. Landowning peasants, the *burgisi*, completed that proof. Peasants in the nineteenth century periodically joined together spontaneously to attack their *civile* oppressors; they also competed viciously with their peers in efforts to become *civili*. Little wonder, then, that proverbs reported conflicting evaluations of class relationships and often negative sentiments about cooperation.

However, with the desire to compete grew a related need to cooperate. A family literally could not survive economically without carefully limited cooperation with others. *Civile* employers needed employees; shepherds and peasants needed agricultural contracts or wages; artisans needed purchasers. No bureaucracy or formalized ties arranged employment and trade. To survive, every family — rich and poor — sought information from others about jobs, property, deaths and changes in fortune. In short, every family needed gossip. "Four eyes," a proverb reminded, "see more than two" (I, 299). Competition itself provided the justification for limited types of cooperation. Originating in a nuclear family's desire to improve economically, the management of social cooperation became the responsibility of the father as the head of the family.

In turn, Sicilians transformed cooperative efforts into the basis for a new form of competition, a competition for "honor" or "respect."[26] Honor first accrued to the *casa* of persons publically demonstrating proper fulfillment of their *casa* family roles, but also to families that succeeded in establishing moral (that is, useful and reciprocal) social ties to others. The bigger the network of friends, *parenti* or neighbors, the more respect the family enjoyed. Respect was a form of social judgment, and largely a product of gossip, so competition for respect itself then encouraged families to try to build social ties based on the exchange of information about the moral and social behavior of others. In this case too "four eyes saw more than two." In a very real sense respect became a resource, not terribly different from property. That, in fact, was how proverbs described it: "A man with credit, also has honor" (IV, 220). "Honor is worth more than money" (I,207). And, like any other possession, honor could also be lost (IV, 151).

In sum, nineteenth-century Sicilians were not amoral familists; Banfield was wrong in his historical reasoning. They did, however, face huge obstacles, some of them environmental, in achieving their social ideals. Many never succeeded in building a network reaching much beyond the *casa* — in that respect alone they resembled the amoral familists that Banfield described. Many Sicilians in the nineteenth century hoped to escape restraints imposed on them by emigrating. When they emigrated they set into motion a process that would transform not just their social relationships to others, but their social ideals as well.

Sicily itself did not remain static as the emigrants left. Competition through cooperation and the desire to be respected seem to have grown in importance since the nineteenth century, and to have been accompanied by an increasingly positive evaluation of kinship and friendship among Sicilians. Jane and Peter Schneider, reporting on fieldwork in present-day western Sicily, describe friendship as one of the area's most important cultural themes; Jeremy Boissevain also found close dedication to the *parenti*, including distant second cousins.[27] A century of emigration and gradual but real improvement in Sicilian living standards contributed to these changes by enabling almost all Sicilians to participate in social reciprocation, exchanging not just gossip but gifts and hospitality. Since the period of mass emigration, the usefulness of patronage also grew, as a means of access to the growing bureaucracies of the nation state — the school, the health or welfare system — and as a form of political organization.[28] Patronage probably became increasingly acceptable culturally during these years, too.

New York's Sicilians shared with nonemigrants a similar base in Sicilian social ideals and in the obstacles faced in achieving those ideals. Both groups of Sicilians responded to these restraints. Neither immigrants nor nonmigrating Sicilians maintained unchanged the social ideals of the past. For that reason the two groups should not be compared as if today's Sicilians were the brothers and sisters of yesterday's immigrants. Both immigrants and Sicilians departed from their shared roots, but they took somewhat different paths. The next chapters examine the shared roots and the divergent immigrant path.

CHAPTER TWO

Residential Choice in the Sicilian Agrotown

Just off a large street descending a western Sicilian hill in 1921, six houses clustered around the semi-enclosed space called the *cortile* Merlo. In one house lived Giuseppe M., a peasant, his wife and his youngest son. Giuseppe M. owned this small house. His brother's son Pietro — who had just returned from a long stay in Louisiana — lived with his wife and two young children in an adjoining house. (A landowning peasant, Pietro M. also owned another house on a nearby street; later in life he would give the *cortile* Merlo house to his own son, and move there.) Leonardo S., a peasant, probably rented rooms from Pietro M. He too had returned from many years in Louisiana; in 1921 he lived in the *cortile* Merlo with a wife and four children. Another peasant, Antonino V. owned his house, where he lived alone with his elderly wife. The much younger peasant day laborer, Giorgio S., lived next door with his wife and two children. (He too had lived for a time in the United States.) The aged Michele D. and his wife, both artisan tile-makers, formed the last family in the *cortile*.[1]

On the opposite side of the same hill, five families lived around the somewhat smaller *cortile* Cusenza. Michele R., an elderly man who herded goats and sold their milk, lived with his wife, his five children from a first marriage, and one stepson. A returned emigrant, born in a nearby town but married to a local woman, lived next door with his six American-born children. He worked as a day laborer. A sharecropper, Giuseppe M., lived with his wife and three daughters in a third house. Two young couples, soon to leave for the United States, rented space in the *cortile*. Pietro G., a day laborer born in a neighboring town, was just married to his considerably younger wife, and Calogero F. was also a recently married peasant.

Homeownership, nuclear family households and social diversity characterized these two neighborhoods. These, and other residential patterns in Sicilian agrotowns, were the product of hundreds of independent decisions, as the families of these towns sought residences. The purpose of this chapter is to examine residential choice in Sicilian agrotowns in the nineteenth century, and to describe the residential patterns that typically resulted.

The *cortile* Merlo and the *cortile* Cusenza still exist in the agrotown of Sambuca di Sicilia. In this chapter, Sambuca, in the southwestern province of Agrigento, provides data illustrating residential patterns typical of many agrotowns in the late nineteenth century. In many ways Sambuca was and is a representative agrotown.[2] It is located in an area of western Sicily that sent many residents to New York's Elizabeth Street in the years 1890-1910.[3] I chose to study Sambuca in some detail mainly because its archive was accessible and, for Sicily, quite well organized. In addition, Sambuca claims a local writer, Emmanuele Navarro della Miraglia, whose novels, and short stories, published in the 1870's and 1880's, left rich and thinly disguised descriptions of the houses, neighborhoods, streets and lives he observed about him.

Agrotown residential patterns are themselves interesting, shaped by both the existing physical environment and by the goals and resources of agrotown residents in the nineteenth century. The purpose of this chapter, however, is not merely descriptive. The chapter focuses on residential patterns with obvious social implications — on land use, social clustering and segregation, on Sicilian definitions of co-residence and on actual household composition and on residential mobility. Each of these residential patterns could influence which Sicilians shared space with others and thus each could restrict or facilitate social interaction. Each of the residential patterns described points in turn to the considerable obstacles that faced large numbers of Sicilians in pursuing their social ideals. The match of agrotown and Sicilian social ideals was, in many respects, a very poor one.

When Sicilians chose a home, they were not so much guided by their social ideals as by their notions of desirable housing and by their own limited resources. Sicilians had simple housing standards: They wanted above all else to own a house. "As little as it is, so long as it's mine" (I, 215).[4] They preferred a house on the second floor (a *casa di susu*) and called the second floor the *piano nobile* (I, 214, 217). On the second floor, the potentially curious eyes of neighbors were far away, while with a ground floor house (*casa di jusu*) "One never knows what will come raining down on one's head from above" (I, 216, 217). They also valued houses with plenty of light, since "dark houses bring the doctor" (III, 15, IV, 6). The large house with many rooms was their ideal (I, 217). But they also believed that the house should be appropriate to its occupants, and counselled "A little nest for a little bird" (I, 216).

Social ideals, did, however, influence housing choices. Parents wanted their children to continue to live close by after they married. And all Sicilians wanted a father's workplace to be near his home. But other than these locational preferences, Sicilians cared little where their house stood, or who was their immediate neighbor, so long as the house was not too near, "a mill, a river, a gentleman or a priest" (II, 414; I, 223).

The residents of Sicily in the nineteenth century could realistically hope to achieve only some of their housing ideals as they chose among the thousands of stone houses that, jammed closely together, formed the Sicilian agrotown. In this way too, the Sicilian agrotown matched the ideals of its residents rather poorly.

The Physical Setting

The *paese*—the large dense settlement of peasants, typical of the Mediterranean, which geographers have termed the agrotown—sits among agricultural lands, the workplace of its peasant occupants.[5] Two kinds of agricultural workplaces surrounded the *paese* in the nineteenth century, the *campagna* and the *corona*.[6] Large estates and extensive grain growing and pasturing characterized the more-distant *campagna*. The *campagna* was rugged, treeless and uninhabited land, usually at high elevations. Only the scattered headquarter buildings of *gabelloti* and the temporary straw huts built by shepherds filled its emptiness. Sicilians agreed with agricultural expert Sidney Sonnino in seeing the *campagna* as a menacing place, a dangerous place when contrasted to the civilized, safe and green *corona* that encircled the *paese*.[7] The *corona* oasis of greenery was relatively new, the product of peasant and rentier investment in intensive cultivation in the nineteenth century. Peasants and *civili* built little huts and more substantial buildings on their plots of land, so that the *corona* stood in very sharp contrast to the uninhabited *campagna*, especially in the months following the wheat harvest when distant fields were brown and burnt-over.

The agrotown *paese* was a large settlement, with one to fifty thousand residents, mainly peasants raising a variety of crops.[8] Except for local variation in crops raised, agrotowns varied but little in their economic functions.[9] Each town had its own local market and often a yearly fair as well. Each was linked independently to international markets for its agricultural products. Thus, within any region, there was very little functional specialization, and one agrotown resembled most others economically.

Historians and geographers offer several explanations for the existence of the agrotown settlement pattern. Some cite the Mediterranean's urban tradition, its scarcity of water and its malarial swamps in low-lying regions as possible causes for the growth of agrotowns. Others emphasize peasants' desire to protect themselves from coastal raiders or nearby enemies during the Middle Ages. Still others note that feudal barons, hoping to expand grain production in the fifteenth and sixteenth centuries, deliberately planned large towns to attract a sufficient labor force to Sicily's underpopulated mountain regions. These factors explain both the absence of Sicilian villages and the vast emptiness of the Sicilian countryside.[10]

In their urban forms, agrotowns varied considerably more than in their economic functions. The oldest towns developed from Greek or Roman settlements, and many others had medieval centers. The towns founded and planned by feudal barons centered around a clear grid of streets, and many older towns copied this plan as they expanded geographically.[11] In towns of all types, streets were interrupted by squares and often by smaller, courtyardlike *cortili*. Local building materials contributed to considerable variety, as did local aesthetic notions. Stone ranged from gray to white to golden brown; coastal residents liked to plaster and paint buildings white or some bright color, while mountain dwellers left their buildings unplastered and unpainted — in a word, drabber. Beyond these externals, however, house form varied but little throughout western Sicily.[12]

Sambuca di Sicilia, home of novelist Emmanuele Navarro della Miraglia, was a small city overlooking a characteristically empty countryside. (See Map 2-1.) To the south and east lay a large river valley; its tributaries helped make Sambuca's *corona* (*contrada* Adragna, *contrada* Balata) larger than average. A large well just north of town provided water before the town built a system of fountains. Beyond the trees and vines, especially to the west and north of town, elevations rose rapidly into the empty wheat-growing *campagna*.

Sambuca's present residents claim that their town grew from an Arab fort located at the northeast end of town. A medieval town nucleus — the "Saracean alleyways" — adjoins this supposed Arab fort. (See Map 2-2.) Sambuca then grew down the ridge on which it is located, toward the south and west. As it grew, long straight streets, built after 1500, adjoined the winding alleyways of the oldest quarter. A main street, the *corso*, interrupted by several large piazzas, divided the town into unequal

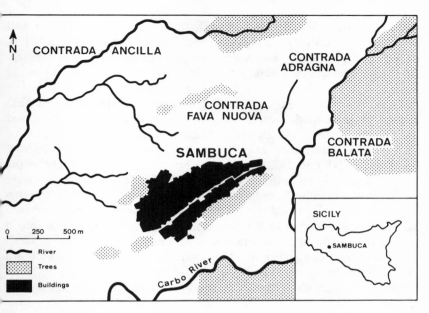

Map 2-1. Sambuca di Sicilia in Western Sicily

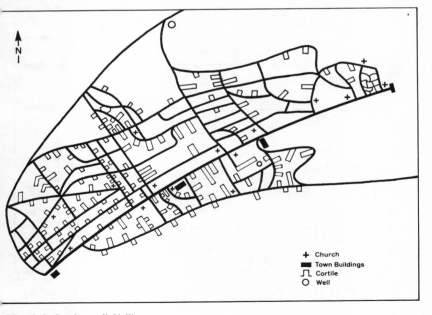

Map 2-2. Sambuca di Sicilia

halves. Navarro della Miraglia noted that this and other streets were well paved by the 1870's.[13] The region's yellowish grey stone and locally produced red tiles still give the town a pleasantly homogeneous appearance. Plastering and whitewashing is far commoner today than it was in the past.

As in many towns in western Sicily, Sambuca's streets opened onto several hundred small *cortili*.[14] These semi-enclosed courtyards played an important role in Navarro della Miraglia's stories and novels. Six or eight houses—sometimes more, rarely fewer—surrounded each *cortile*. See Figures 2-1 and 2-2. The *cortili* appeared most frequently in the newer parts of town, adjoining the long straight streets, but they were not unknown even in the oldest neighborhoods. Like the streets, the *cortile* theoretically belonged to the town, but homeowners who purchased all the houses surrounding a *cortile* not infrequently turned it into a private central courtyard by erecting a door across its entrance. No *cortile* was exactly like any other. Most were square or rectangular, but a few resembled long narrow alleys.

Like other agrotowns, Sambuca was and is a dense settlement serving

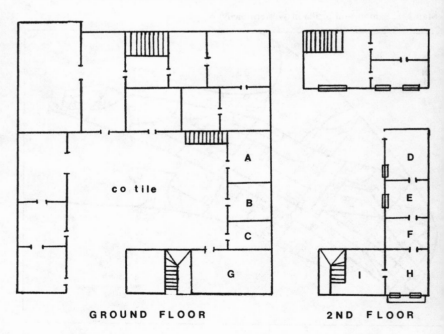

Figure 2-1. A *Cortile*

Figure 2-2. A *Cortile*

the needs of its agricultural residents. Its buildings reflected these needs. Besides over 2000 houses, a cadaster of buildings from 1877 noted a variety of other structures.[15] The ten thousand residents of this town were well supplied with fifteen churches; to the west of the town proper was a settlement of Capuchin monks; also on the western edge of town a "college" of nuns dominated a large piazza, while another religious order ran an orphanage and charity hospital on the main street. The city hall faced this street too, not far from the palace of a local baron. At the foot of the ridge a theatre built in the 1860's adjoined the *corso*, just across from a public garden, also built at that time. About a quarter of the buildings designated by the cadaster as shops and workshops bordered the main street, but the majority were distributed throughout the town. Also dispersed were half a dozen oil presses and scores of small buildings used for agricultural storage or stalls. In the late nineteenth century, a tile manufactury operated on the northern edge of town. Three mills for grinding grain, dependent on water power, worked seasonally in the countryside. By the 1890's an extensive system of small public fountains served all sections of the town with piped water. Residents of other agrotowns were not so lucky, for many towns first installed water in the twentieth century.[16]

Sambuca's housing, like that of other agrotowns, can be quickly described, for while variation in detail was considerable, only three types of houses existed. The first was the very small house with one or two rooms. Emmanuele Navarro della Miraglia described one such house in his novel *La Nana*. The house, property of the peasant Passalacqua family, was decorated with flowers and located at the rear of a *cortile*. It had only two rooms; the rear served as the son's bedroom and also as kitchen, storage space, and stall. The front room was both dining room and bedroom for the widowed mother and daughter, and only this front room received light, from the open doorway.[17]

Most simple agrotown houses were of stone and quite small, measuring upwards from ten or twelve feet square. See Figures 2-3 and 2-4. Each had a dirt or, at best, a brick floor, whitewashed interior walls unbroken by windows, and a cane ceiling beneath a tiled roof. The hearth was a large flat stone or a simple stone stove called a *focularu*. A loft in the rear of the room created an alcove.[18] Sambuca's cadaster showed that over half of the town's houses were of this simple type.

The second and third agrotown house types were far more diverse in form. Both were characterized by a second floor, with tile floors, windows and plastered ceiling and walls. (See Figures 2-5 and 2-6.) Typically these houses also had a more elaborate hearth in the form of a tiled

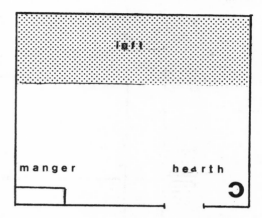

Figure 2-3. A Simple Sicilian House

Figure 2-4. A Simple House

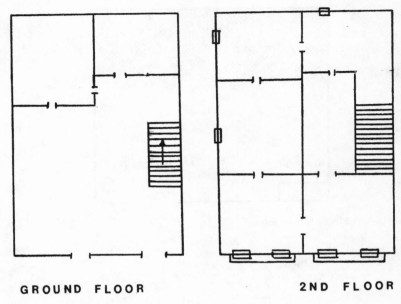

GROUND FLOOR   **2ND FLOOR**

Figure 2-5. A Larger Sicilian House

Figure 2-6. A Larger House

Sicilian stove and oven.[19] Sambuca's clerks found that about half of these two-story houses contained five to nine rooms. Together with three-room and four-room two-story houses, they proved a third of the town's housing. The *casa civile*, the third house type, clearly received its name from its usual occupant. This house type was far larger and grander than type two houses. It had as few as ten and as many as thirty rooms. A *casa civile* included additional comforts: a pit toilet and a private well, balconies and terraces, and its own private courtyard closed to the street by a big door.[20]

Except as "little nests for little birds," Sicilian housing fell far below Sicilian housing ideals. Most houses were neither light nor spacious nor located on the *piano nobile*. Agrotown houses did vary as much in size, shape, orientation, and facilities as did Sicilians in their occupations. In fact the types of Sicilian houses and their distribution roughly resembled the Sicilian class hierarchy described in the last chapter.

But why was it that houses built by Sicilians for Sicilians should have matched so poorly Sicilian housing ideals? Probably because housing ideals had changed and expanded with the growing socioeconomic differentiation of the nineteenth century. The housing ideal, the *casa civile*, was everywhere visible in a town like Sambuca. (With 2300 families in 1881, Sambuca had more than 100 such houses.) Unlike the culturally, geographically, and socially distant aristocracy of the previous century, the local rentier class could and did inflate the housing ideals of all Sicilians, as even ordinary peasants could entertain at least some hope of eventually achieving them. In the nineteenth century, changing ideals rapidly outstripped the rate of local building and local resources. The houses of the past remained — and seemed unsatisfactory. When possible, Sicilians bent old housing to their new ideals; when not, they lived in it just the same.

Choosing a House

Families rather than individuals chose housing in Sicilian agrotowns. Whether the father as head of the family economic unit or the mother as household head made housing decisions, we do not know. But we do know that a major goal of every agrotown family was to provide property, especially houses, for its children. Parents did not usually wait until they died to distribute this property; they gave houses, land and household goods to children as parts of contracts arranged at the time of their marriages. Exact customs for marriage contracts and the provision of housing varied from town to town.[21] In some towns parents hoped to give houses to daughters, while sons received land. Elsewhere, parents gave houses to sons and household furnishings to daughters. In Sambuca, however, families seemed not to share a common custom. For example, Sambuca's cadaster noted that in 1885 Castrenze A. gave a two-story house with three rooms to his son Giuseppe, while several years later, he gave a one-story two-room house to his daughter. About equal numbers of parents in Sambuca gave houses only to sons or only to daughters.

Providing housing for sons' or daughters' marriages required considerable planning and cooperative effort, but it was also a custom well suited to family incomes that expanded and contracted with the family cycle. In most peasant and artisan families, children's earnings alone made substantial savings possible. Mothers began to accumulate property (*spìnciri lu stigghiu*) at this time, and to collect family earnings in a tiny slit-mouthed bank, a *salvedenajo*.[22] In a very real sense, child workers paid their housing costs before they married by contributing to the family economy. Once married and living in their house, they had very low housing costs—a yearly property tax was the main expenditure.[23] Thus while children were young and could not work family housing costs were low; they increased only as children began to work and the cycle of accumulation again began.

It was no simple task to purchase houses; children's earnings were necessary because houses were relatively expensive. An English visitor insisted to the contrary that building was extraordinarily cheap—stones were abundant, he noted, and people did most of the construction work themselves.[24] The considerable numbers of Sicilians working in the building trades forces us, however, to question this accuracy. So do other scattered references to building costs. Leonard Covello estimated that a house, including the land on which it was built, might cost 1500 lire.[2] That price was seven times the yearly income of a day laborer. Another visitor guessed that a peasant sold his house for sixty to eighty dollars.[2]

By transferring property at the time of children's marriages, families distributed homeownership as widely as was possible. Homeownership was very common in Sicily; far more common than landownership, for example. In the 1901 census, the ratio of building owners (mainly although not exclusively, homeowners) to households ranged from one third in the province of Trapani to a high of three-quarters in mountainous Caltanissetta. These figures seriously underestimated actual rates of homeownership because local housing counts always overestimated the numbers of houses. (See page 27.) Smaller provincial towns like Sambuca had higher ratios of homeowners than provincial capitals like Palermo or Agrigento, and it was in the smaller agrotowns that the majority of

Sicilians lived in the nineteenth century. After eliminating jointly owned houses, the number of homeowners listed in Sambuca's 1877 building cadaster was only 13 percent lower than the number of households in the town in 1881. Eighty percent is a conservative estimate of the proportion of Sambuca families living in their own home in the 1880's. If this conservative estimate is accurate, it means that all artisans and petty merchants, all landowning peasants, and the vast majority of sharecropper families owned their own housing. (By contrast, only 12 percent of peasant families in 1901 owned land.)

Sicilian census data suggest that the number of homeowners declined between 1881 and 1901.[27] Obviously, more families failed to acquire houses for their children during these years. This encouraged the migration of children hoping to marry, or those beginning their marriages without the prerequisite property. Family composition was critical in determining which families failed in their efforts to provide houses for marrying children. In towns where houses were given to daughters, a sharecropper family with few (or considerably younger) sons faced difficulties, especially since by 1901 daughters could earn almost nothing. In Sambuca the town government responded by loaning money to destitute day laborers; the purpose was to enable them to dower their daughters during the 1890's.[28]

When families could not acquire new property for their children during the economically troubled years of the late nineteenth century, they divided parental property, often literally dividing the parental house. An example from Sambuca's cadaster shows how carefully Sicilians handled their property in these cases. In 1877 Audenzio A. and his wife Francesca owned a one-story seven-room house, numbered 13–17 *cortile* Marrotta. When their daughter married in 1880, the parents gave her two rooms (numbers 13 and 14) and they shared with her ownership of a third room (number 16). Sometime later, Audenzio A. sold two more rooms (at number 16) plus part of a room at number 17 to the owner of the house adjoining his to the rear. When Audenzio A. died, his will further divided the rooms he owned at 16 and 17 between his wife and his daughter. His widow was to use five eighths of this space, while his daughter's right was limited to three-eighths. In practice this probably meant that the widow occupied the larger of the remaining rooms until her death, at which time both rooms became part of the daughter's house.

Audenzio A. actually had few problems; he owned several rooms and apparently had only one daughter to dower. Others in the 1880's and 1890's had more children and less property. Some parents built new walls, creating two houses out of even one-room or two-room originals.[29] Others left their small houses undivided to all their children collectively in their wills. Only 2 percent of Sambuca's houses in 1877 were jointly owned in this fashion. The proportion probably increased thereafter, but the cadaster does not clearly reveal that process.

Homeownership remained the norm into the twentieth century, but the number of renters increased in Sicily at the end of the nineteenth century. Day laborers, the poorest shepherds, and some sharecropper families sought houses among the excess rooms and buildings owned by wealthier families. Landlords let houses to renters for one year at a time. Contracts began on September 1, like agricultural contracts. The two were otherwise unrelated. A sharecropper could rent from anyone; he was not obliged to rent from the owner of the land he worked. Renters also payed a yearly rent for their houses, in a lump sum.[30]

Agrotown rents varied but often were quite low. Sidney Sonnino reported Sicilian rents ranging from twenty-five lire to sixty lire a year in the 1870's.[31] Twenty years later a visitor described a family in Corleone paying forty lire a year for two small rooms. That represented 15 percent of the day laborer father's cash income of 270 lire. Since his son also earned 180 lire as a goatherd, the family gave out only 9 percent of its cash income for rent.[32]

Most Sicilians succeeded in reaching at least one of their housing ideals, that of homeownership. Renters remained a minority, albeit a growing one. Parental house purchases influenced where most families lived and what kinds of houses and households they occupied. Rental and property transfer also largely determined which agrotown families would move about in subsequent years. In these indirect ways, the choice of a house influenced the later social lives of both homeowners and renters.

Occupation, Class and Kin

Every agrotown had a social geography that reflected local customs for choosing a house. In the town as a whole, in street and *cortile*, and in the house and household itself, Sicilians occupied space in distinctive and distinctly flexible ways. Evidence from Sambuca illustrates each of these common agrotown residential patterns.

Locating families in specific space is not an easy assignment in town lacking manuscript census listings or city directories. Sambuca and most other southern Italian towns preserve few such sources from the nineteenth century. Beginning in 1921, however, many towns began keeping household files called *fogli di famiglia*. These schedules resemble family reconstitutions; more importantly, they list addresses, allowing some linkage to the nineteenth-century cadaster, and occupation.[33] The *fogli* provide considerable data about social clustering in Sambuca, albeit in the years just after the mass migrations. I compared *fogli* patterns to the observations of Pitrè, nineteenth-century visitors and Sicilian writers like Navarro della Miraglia. I found occasional discrepancies, but no large or overall differences.

By agrotown standards, a desirable location was one near workplace, parents or siblings, rather than any particular location within the town. This housing ideal limited occupational and class segregation considerably, as the example of the *cortile* Merlo and the *cortile* Cusenza made clear. Most Sicilians lived in occupationally and socially mixed neighborhoods.

In Sambuca, for example, the main street separated two distinctive sections of town. While these sections varied somewhat in occupational composition, both housed a mix of occupational groups. West and north of the main street, in the larger part of town, lived *civili*, artisans, and peasants. The *cortile* Merlo was in this section of Sambuca. The main street itself housed considerable numbers of artisan and *civile* families. South and east of the main street, a narrow and newer section stretched along the steep side of the ridge. Socially, this was the "wrong side of the *corso*." Not a single *civile* family lived there; no more than a handful of artisans lived outside of one large *cortile* that also opened off the main street. The *cortile* Cusenza was typical of this second section of Sambuca. Day-laborers formed a larger than average proportion of this overwhelmingly peasant district. Sidney Sonnino confirmed that similar areas developed on the outskirts of most agrotowns in the 1870's and 1880's.[34] But even these sections were socially mixed, with younger and older families, homeowners and renters, more and less prosperous peasants living in close proximity.

Parental desire to keep children close by after their marriages encouraged *casa* clustering in agrotowns, but the availability of housing at any particular time apparently placed severe limits on parents' ability to realize their goal. Sambuca's *fogli* suggest that in the early twentieth century, most of any family's *casa* lived in the same section of town, but not in the same *cortile*.[35] (See Table 2-1.) In her study of Milocca in the 1920's, Chapman reported roughly similar findings.[36] She discovered that the average family was related to three of the other nine households in a ten-household *robba* (a geographical unit much like a *cortile*). Two

Table 2-1. *Casa* Clusters

KIN TIE	% LIVING IN SAME		N
	Street/ Cortile	Section	
Parents/Married Daughter	28	34	203
Parents/Married Son	28	36	139
Married Sisters	24	29	72
Married Brothers	24	35	92
Brother/Sister (Married)	11	46	83

were households of *casa* kinsmen; one was the household of a more-distant *parente*. The degree of kin clustering in Sambuca in 1921 would have produced similar *cortile* groupings.

By giving nearby houses to either daughters or sons, agrotown parents could also have created distinctive neighborhood kin clusters. But again this was not always the case. In Milocca (where sons received houses), Chapman found patrilateral kinship clusters in each *robba*.[37] A man. one of his sons and his paternal uncle, or a man, his brother and his brother's son formed typical clusters. Sambuca's *casa* clusters, however, were mixed, with both patrilateral and matrilateral clusters in evidence. Perhaps this was because families in this town followed diverse customs in transmitting houses (see page 22) or because town custom had changed slowly over the preceding decades.[38]

Rich and poor, peasant and artisan, kin and nonkin lived in close physical proximity in Sicilian agrotowns. They could easily observe one another; they could mingle easily if they chose to do so. The plot of Emmanuele Navarro della Miraglia's *La Nana* turned on the social tensions typical of a mixed Sambuca *cortile*: as the young Rosaria Passalacqua sat in her doorway making stockings, she was watched by Pietro Gigelli, the only son of a rich rentier. The rear of the grand Gigelli mansion formed one high wall of the *cortile*; as Pietro observed the *cortile* below he found the peasant girl very beautiful.[39] Navarro della Miraglia understood very well at least one of the social implications of agrotown residential patterns. But the *cortile* was more than a source of illicit love matches — potential friends, patrons, *servi*, and both some *casa* and some more-distant kin were always nearby.

House and Household

Relatively well-off families like those of Michele D. and Pietro M. lived close to poor peasants in the *cortile* Merlo and other neighborhoods in Sambuca, but they occupied houses that identified their superior status.

Civili, of course, occupied a *casa civile*. Landowning peasants, artisans and petty merchants owned smaller two-story houses. The average peasant family and all renters occupied the simplest one-room and two-room stone buildings, like the home of the Passalacqua family. This meant that artisans, peasant landowners, and small merchants, like the rentier *civili*, and unlike the peasant majority, succeeded in providing their children with an ideal Sicilian house—that is, one with large light rooms on the second floor.

Still, no naive observer could determine where one agrotown house ended and where its neighboring house began. Agrotown houses, after all, were not free-standing buildings, but parts of larger spatial agglomerations, as Figure 2-1 shows. The room labelled "A" might have been a house or a stall. "A," "B" and "C" might have together constituted one house, three houses, or three rooms in a larger noncontiguous house "ADGHI." To complicate matters further, rooms were often owned separately from the ground or from the rooms beneath them.

Government efforts to apply strictly physical definitions to agglomerated south Italian housing led to comical and confusing results in housing surveys.[40] Sambuca's clerks followed national directives to define a house as any room or group of rooms with a doorway to the outside and a street number attached. Their 1877 cadaster therefore counted 3900 "houses" in a town with only 2300 households! (To correct for this bias, I used rooms per homeowner to estimate the distribution of house types above.) Published housing statistics, including the census, shared this bias.

Social and economic relationships resembling those within the nuclear family defined simultaneously a household and its house in Sicilian agrotowns. In other words, Sambuca's clerks had to know *cortile* relationships before they could "see" the houses of Michele D. and his many neighbors. A residence always corresponded to a co-residential group.

Sicilian households behaved like, and usually were, nuclear families. Any outsider became a member of the household by assuming the status of a child or that of a servant—there was little difference between the two. The household ate together and, in a one-room house, slept together. People from other households were rigorously excluded from the common table or the sleeping quarters.[41] Charlotte Chapman found this an early difficulty in her field work in Milocca. She located a family reluctantly willing to rent her a room. (Reluctantly, because no family wanted to assume responsibility for the conduct of a stranger, an unattached woman, by making her part of the household.) But Chapman rapidly discovered that Miloccans had no concept of "boarding." As one

who remained outside the nuclear family circle of economic cooperation, she could not join the family at table, except as an invited guest on
grand occasions. She received her cooked meal separately, eating alone
in her rented room.[42]
Few agrotown families departed from the nuclear family household
norm, at least in the 1920's. Sambuca's *fogli* showed that only about 5
percent of the families formed before 1900 ever expanded their
households after 1921. Even stem family households were rare. Of
course, immigration may have reduced the numbers of outsiders seeking
housing (orphans, widows or widowers, bastards) by 1921. More telling
evidence were the nineteenth-century proverbs that described residential
practices: Sicilians firmly believed that anyone from outside the *casa*,
even if properly deferent or submissive, represented a probable source of
strife. Warned one, "Woe on the house with cousins, godparents or
priests" (I, 229); another, equally threatening, insisted, "Never live two
families to a house!" (II, 232). While Sicilians valued social ties to others,
they did not therefore open their households to all.

Persons accustomed to submission—young orphaned children,
bastards and elderly widows—did sometimes enter the households of
others in twentieth-century Sambuca. Still, it is worth noting that a
substantial minority of orphaned siblings in Sambuca continued to live
independently in a household headed by the oldest brother after their
parents' deaths. And, among widows, it was only the lower-status peasant woman who went to live with a married child, usually a daughter;
most widows maintained a separate household until their deaths, much
as did the wife of Audenzio A. who tenaciously maintained control over
her five-eighths of a room.

Adult men could not so easily assume the childlike role assigned them
in a nuclear family household. In Sambuca, most men without families
of their own chose to live alone, probably much as did Charlotte Chapman in Milocca, in a rented room. Small numbers lived with other unmarried or otherwise unattached men. Town clerks clearly distinguished
such groups from "real" households: they listed no household head and
gave no relationship among the men except that of *covivenza* (literally,
"living together," or sharing a room for sleeping).[43]

Two examples show how the household defined the dimensions and
boundaries of the house in Sicilian agrotowns. Domenico F. in 1931 lived
at Sambuca's Via Graffeo 21 with his six-person family. A separate
foglio listed his brother Baldassare also livng at that address. By 1936
Baldassare F. and family lived at Via Graffeo 11, while Domenico F. and
family had moved to nearby Via Delfino. Despite a shared address, these

two peasant families did not consider themselves to be "living together" in a single house in 1931. They lived as separate households, each with its own *foglio*. One brother was not deferent to the other; they did not cooperate economically; their families ate and slept separately. Thus each family had its own "house" at Via Graffeo 21, even if each "house" had only one room. If Via Graffeo had had more than two rooms, the families could have shared space in many ways without forming a single household.

Quite different was the stem-family household of Giuseppe C. and his daughter Caterina. In 1921 Caterina brought her husband Felice R. to live in her father's household. By 1931 the daughter and her husband had three children, but they continued to be listed as part of Giuseppe C.'s household, appearing on a single *foglio*. Five years later there were two more grandchildren. Only in 1939 did Giuseppe C. die and Felice R. become head of the household. In this example, a stem-family household occupied a single large house. They could have shared or divided space as they pleased, but it remained a single house, because economic and social ties linked the two families. Giuseppe C., a peasant landowner, had probably retired from active farming by the time his daughter married, so his son-in-law's income as a shoemaker helped support the family. Caterina C. inherited her father's land and the house he owned in 1939. Undoubtedly the two families regularly ate together, as do stem-family households in Sicily today. Such households remain rare.[44]

These examples show that in Sicily any space occupied or owned by a household became, by definition, a house. And, just as eating together or sleeping together formed the functional boundaries around the household, the room or rooms used for these purposes divided the private center of the house from other, more public, spaces. In the *casa civile*, wealthy Sicilians made second-floor rooms their private quarters, separate from ground-floor storage rooms and animal stalls, and separate as well from second-floor rooms where servants worked or where outsiders—guests—could be entertained.[45] The decoration of private quarters and the more public receiving room (*salotto*) further emphasized the boundary. The *salotto* became a room for secular display. Navarro della Miraglia described imported pianos and heavy wooden furniture there. Unremodelled rooms today have stuccoed walls with elaborate stencilled or hand-painted ceiling borders and chandelier mounts.[46] Also popular were wooden cabinets with glass doors, holding "the usual display of cheap gaudy coffee pots and cups," as an English woman described them.[47] Ceramics and glass items, clocks and travel mementoes completed such a display. Private rooms, by contrast, held simple furnishings. Religious prints and embroidered bedding excepted, they also remained quite unadorned.[48]

Differentiation of function within the house was not limited to the richest Sicilians. Artisans, merchants, and landowning peasants duplicated the segregation of private eating and sleeping rooms in their smaller houses. Artisan workshops, merchants' sales rooms, or peasant storage rooms occupied the ground floor; the family lived upstairs on the *piano nobile.*[49] A typical artisan erected a *salotto* there, one containing a display in a chiffonier. Less prosperous than the *civili,* such families filled the *salotto* with as many straight-backed, locally made chairs as they could afford.[50] In some houses, the only other second-floor room was the private one, which served all other family functions. Depending on the number of rooms available, families might divide private quarters into sleeping rooms, living/eating room (*soggiorno*), and kitchen. (See Figure 2–7).

A common sharecropper family had only private space, yet within a single room or two families also carved out certain functional areas. Sicilians did not lack a sense of spatial and functional differentiation, as critics sometimes assumed.[51] The loft formed an alcove in the rear of a typical one-room house; families put the parental bed there. Older sons slept above, in the loft, while daughters occupied the main part of the room at night. In some houses, like that of the Passalacqua family, kitchen, storage, and stall were located in a rear second room, and the front room combined sleeping and eating quarters. Furnishings of the simple dwelling also resembled those in the Passalacqua's home: a high bed, sometimes with a small bed or storage chests beneath it, a table and several chairs. If poverty was extreme, the high bed, with its mattresses rolled back, doubled as a dining table or work surface. Both sleeping and eating areas were decorated when possible with religiously significant mementoes—calendars, saints' images, blessed palm branches, and the like.[52] In the Passalacqua house, described by Emmanuele Navarro della Miraglia, "a dry olive branch and a palm branch decorated with little blue ribbons" hung at the head of the bed. Around this hung pictures of saints "half of paradise and half of the calendar . . . confused . . . patron saints of every town and of every sort."[53]

The definition of a private space, accessible only to members of the nuclear family household, tells us that Sicilians in the nineteenth century viewed the physical proximity of others as a mixed blessing. However often members of a family moved among larger agrotown, *cortile* and house, they recognized the physical separation of the world into distinctive spheres, each with its own rules for human behavior.

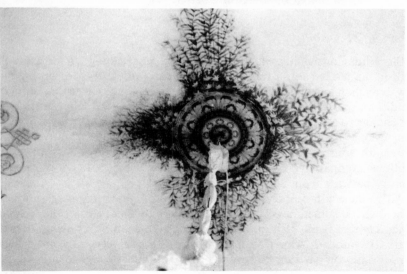

Figure 2-7. *Salotto* Wall and Ceiling Decorations

Thus, despite its limited size and comfort, the agrotown house was the focus of considerable family identification, as the word *casa*—referring both to the closest kin and to the building itself—demonstrates. Wrote one folklorist, "the *casa*, for the Sicilian, *is* the family, his own family."[54] Only renter families failed to attain the unity of social and physical worlds implied in the term *casa*. The house, inseparable linguistically or conceptually from the family, physically served the family's idealized withdrawal into itself from the competitive world outside, somewhat as it did in Victorian America or in working-class America more recently.[55] The family under its own roof was united, just as family members were united under the family head, the *capo di casa*, usually the father. All observers agreed that families loved their houses, no matter how humble: within the house, the *focularu*, the hearth, was singled out as the focus of the strongest home sentiments (I, 117). The bed and the table also symbolized family solidarity within its private space (IV, 82).[56]

Did loving their house mean that Sicilians were satisfied with it? Here evidence is scanty. Perhaps homeownership—the most important and most frequently achieved of Sicilian housing ideals—compensated families for their failure to achieve most other housing ideals. If Sicilians nevertheless did suffer from residential dissatisfaction, they did not respond as do many twentieth-century urban dwellers: They did not move about much in search of something better.

Residential Mobility

Since homeownership was widespread and since family identification with its imperfect house was strong, residential mobility was probably low in Sicilian agrotowns. Pitrè noted that "the people believe that family conditions will worsen after changing to a new house—and they attribute the change to the improvident act of leaving a lucky house."[57] However, conclusions about residential mobility must remain tentative, for systematic sources for the study of agrotown patterns are few. I offer a cautious comparison of Pitrè's comments to some early twentieth-century patterns from Sambuca's *fogli*.

All nineteenth-century observers agreed that renters, unlike homeowners, sometimes changed residence.[58] In twentieth-century Sambuca, a typical family that moved at all moved three to four times in thirty years. (By modern American standards, this is not very frequently; the appropriate comparison, however, is to the nonmobile homeowning majority of the agrotown.) The motives for changing residences varied:

changes in family fortune, disagreements with neighbors or landlords, or the landlord's desire to use his rooms for other purposes or for other families of renters.[59] Changes in family size and income probably also influenced patterns of residential mobility among renters, as they do in most societies.

Just as Sicilian parents preferred to find nearby housing for their marrying children, agrotown renters undoubtedly preferred to find new houses nearby when they wanted to or were forced to move. Unfortunately, in a town of nonmobile homeowners, renters, like parents, could not always find a nearby house. In Sambuca in the twentieth century, a typical move was relatively short, but longer moves were not at all unusual. In two-thirds of the moves described in Sambuca's *fogli*, families formed before 1900 found new housing in the same section of town. But a sizeable minority of moves were long indeed; the most common change of address was from Sambuca's old medieval center at the northeast end of town to the relatively new quarter at the southeast end of the ridge. Lengthy moves from the medieval center to the "wrong side of the *corso*" were also common. Since a typical renter family moved from three to four times, the vast majority of renter families moved at least once to a different section of Sambuca.

Theoretically, homeowning families moved only when family fortunes improved. In practice, even in this not uncommon case, a move could often be avoided. Proverbs especially warned against moving into a fine new house (IV, 220). Giovanni Verga described one way for the upwardly mobile to improve their housing without moving. In *Maestro Don Gesualdo*, a peasant family created a *casa civile*, rather than building or buying one. "The house of the Baroness," wrote Verga, "was vast, added together by bits and pieces according as her parents [the peasants] ousted one by one the various proprietors until they installed themselves at last with their daughter in the mansion of the Rubieras, and joined everything in common: roofs high and low, windows of every size here and there, as it happened, the great door of the nobles set in the middle of a lot of hovel fronts. The building occupied almost the whole length of the street."[60] This anecdote serves as a reminder that Sicilians put spaces together to form a house with the same ease and flexibility shown by Audenzio A. or the brothers F. in taking houses apart.

Despite limited sources, it does seem safe to conclude that most families in a single *cortile* or street—and even in a larger section of town—lived close to the same group of people for long periods of time in the nineteenth century. At first only renter families disturbed this continuity with their comings and goings. Between 1880 and 1920, immigrants, too, would help make the *cortile* a socially more dynamic place. But that, too, was a new departure from the older agrotown norm.

Summary

As they chose their houses, agrotown residents created a unique social environment, one that in part reflected environmental opportunities and restraints. While residential patterns themselves had no necessary or inevitable social consequences, one can find in agrotown patterns a number of likely implications for Sicilian social behavior. Residential patterns could open or close possibilities for social interaction, depending on how people in their everyday work and leisure activities shared space. That is the subject of the next chapter.

The dense settlement called the *paese* could not but influence work and leisure activities for the peasant majority in negative ways, since, contrary to Sicilian ideals, peasant workplaces lay far from peasant houses. As the next chapter shows, this restraint influenced the division of labor within the peasant family and made fulfillment of some nuclear family roles very difficult for agricultural workers of all kinds. At the same time, peasants' small ground-floor houses confronted families with the practically impossible task of simultaneously maintaining privacy while seeking to build social ties to other families.

More positively, the absence of social segregation in agrotowns offered agrotown occupants the opportunity to mingle easily with *casa*, some *parenti* and nonkin, and with persons of a variety of social and occupational backgrounds. Furthermore, low rates of residential mobility should have allowed intermingling among a relatively stable group over significant lengths of time, at least among the homeowning majority. These patterns seemed to offer relatively good opportunities for social flexibility in building a useful and large social network of kin, friends, neighbors and *padrone*. For some agrotown residents—artisan men and peasant women—this was the case. But for peasant men it was not, and the consequences of this discrepancy for agrotown social life were enormous.

CHAPTER THREE

Everyday Life and Sicilian Society

By restraining everyday work and leisure activities, housing is believed to influence human social behavior. Sociologists describe housing's effect on residents' "lifestyles," while German folklorists refer to its effect on *Wohnweisen*.[1] (English speakers have not made "houselife" — Lewis Morgan's translation of the German term — part of their vocabulary.[2]) Since "lifestyle" need not refer specifically to ecological patterns, I will instead call the ways people use their physical surroundings for work and leisure "everyday life." "Everyday life" has the advantage of familiarity, but there is no widely accepted definition of the term.[3] This chapter describes how agrotown housing restrained everyday life, influencing social interaction and attainment of Sicilian social ideals in the nineteenth century.

By "everyday life" I mean the daily, seasonal and yearly cycles of work and leisure activities and their ecology. Describing everyday life is usually the first task of ethnographic description.[4] It is the basis for social analysis because everyday life provides people with opportunity for social interaction and, thus, for the creation and maintenance of social ties to others.

Ethnographic description of past everyday life is a challenge for the historian, who, unlike the anthropologist, must depend on the observational skills of others. No matter how high the hopes, the historian does not always uncover the equivalent of the deposition that LeRoy Ladurie used as his main source in writing *Montaillou*.[5] This chapter depends not on one excellent but rather on many limited sources to describe everyday life and its social consequences. A sizeable number of middle-class Sicilians left fictional accounts of their observations of nineteenth-century agrotown life. Of these "insiders," Emmanuele Navarro della Miraglia surpassed even the much-cited Verga. No small detail escaped his careful attention; when he wrote of eating, for example, he distinguished nutritional ideals from real meals, peasant from *civile* diet, everyday repast from feast, and summer from winter staples.[6] Accounts by three kinds of "outsiders" also proved helpful: British and German visitors tended to focus on the curious and quaint, while writers of Italian government surveys and folklorists or anthropologists working in the early twentieth century provided more systematic observations. Casual talks with present-day residents of Sambuca revealed some interesting details. So did physical artifacts—mainly tools and household goods—and old photos.[7] By using a variety of sources, I was able to cross-check which people performed particular activities in varying places through time. With that information I interpreted the social relationships typical of agrotowns in the years immediately preceding the mass migrations to the United States.

As a nonparticipant, the historian faces particularly great difficulties in offering an insider's interpretation of the social behavior described. Normally we historians cannot gradually learn the meaning and significance of everyday social behavior by living among the people we study—a process at the very heart of the anthropologist's or ethnographer's method of participant-observation.[8] I accepted that limitation, and I turned when I could to the interpretations of Sicilians living in the nineteenth century, especially to Giuseppe Pitrè. Nevertheless, I also did what I could to participate as well as observe. I spent three months—two in summer and one during late winter—living in several ("type two") agrotown houses. However, let me not exaggerate, my life in Sambuca in no way resembled that of an ordinary peasant in the nineteenth century. If nothing else, though, I learned about noise and quiet, and about how wind and rain or a brilliant sun affected where and when one works and plays in an agrotown, and I heard for myself how very close by were the voices of my neighbors. In the summer I learned to keep one ear turned to those noises from the outside, so that one evening when I heard the unmistakable sounds of a Brooklyn accent, I too could race to my balcony to learn that an American relative had arrived for his annual summer visit. At the end of my stays in Sambuca, I was always surprised by how terribly far away the end of our quite short street seemed to me. I think I did learn something about how Sicilians perceived the environment around them. Each of my experiences subtly colored my interpretations of social life in nineteenth-century agrotowns, and made me aware of just how much the lives of ordinary Sicilians changed during the past century.

A Typical Day

It is difficult to identify a single pattern of work or leisure for agrotowns so sharply divided—as they were—by class and gender distinctions. A comparison of two ordinary families and their activities demonstrates easily the considerable variation in Sicilian experience in the nineteenth century. The agricultural Mangiaracina and the artisan Mulè families (see Table 3-1) are fictionalized versions of real families living in Sambuca at the turn of the century.

Table 3-1. Two Agrotown Families 1900

MANGIARACINA,	Giuseppe	Head	35	Day laborer
	Cristina	Wife	24	housework
	Maria	Daughter	3	-
	Calogera	Daughter	1	-
MULÈ,	Calogero	Head	40	Shoemaker
	Caterina	Wife	Dead	-
	Audenzio	Son	15	Shoemaker
	Teresa	Daughter	11	Student
	Antonina	2nd. Wife	25	seamstress
	Maria Stella	Daughter	3	-
	Anna	Daughter	1	-

In the Sicilian nuclear family, the father's role was to guide family economic efforts to improve its position in the agrotown hierarchy of classes. For a lower-status agricultural worker like Giuseppe Mangiaracina, this meant rising before dawn on a September morning to begin a fifteen-kilometer walk to a distant large estate.[9] There for a week or more at a time Giuseppe M. would live as did the men described by Navarro della Miraglia in "Una Masseria." To feed himself during that time, he carried with him, in a sack, half of a large loaf of bread made by his wife; as part of his wages he would also receive at the *masseria* (headquarters building of a large wheat-growing estate) an evening bowl of farm soup.[10] In September, day laborers like Giuseppe M. found work as plowmen, preparing fields for fallow under the direction of a *gabelloto*.[11] (Sharecroppers worked nearby preparing their individual plots for planting.) And, if Giuseppe M. was like many other common laborers in western Sicily, he might pass by the headquarters of another large estate on his way back to his agrotown home the following weekend—with luck he might find employment for another week in that way.[12]

37

With responsibility for caring for children and for the house, the ac
tivities of a woman like Cristina Mangiaracina seem far more varied tha
those of her husband. Household work began before dawn: Wives ros
even before their husbands to get water for their families.[13] In towns lik
Sambuca, water-gathering meant only a short trip to a nearby publi
fountain fed with piped water. There, in the morning and again in th
late afternoon, women from several adjoining streets or *cortili* clustered
awaiting their turn to fill their earthenware jugs.[14] In more isolated o
smaller mountain towns, the only sources of water remained outside o
town in nearby valleys.[15] Wealthier families purchased water from mal
water vendors, but poorer women saved money by transporting water in
dividually over the paths between water supplies and hilltop homes.[16]

Throughout the day, women like Cristina Mangiaracina mixe
housework and childcare. In the early morning hours they dressed an
nursed smaller children, set out coops of chickens, rabbits, or other sma
animals, made the bed and swept straw and feces from one corner of th
house into the street.[17] In some towns, to which present-day residents o
Sambuca referred with great amusement, women carried "night pots" t
a preferred dumping spot outside of town.[18] Women lucky enough t
have brick or tiled floors often washed them daily, throwing the water int
the street when they finished.[19] Others sat outside their doorways, mak
ing brooms or other small articles, knitting or spinning.[20] Younge
children played close by; mothers did not allow them to wander ver
far.[21] On almost any day, one woman in the *cortile* had laundry to dc
Since not all women owned a *pila* (washtub), borrowing occurred.[22]
woman like Cristina M. not uncommonly went into the home of a well
off neighbor in order to help with the heavier household chores.[23] Sh
received money or food for her efforts, or she might receive nothin
more than permission to use the oven of the better-off woman on Satu
day, allowing her to bake her family's bread.[24] Women also took egg
from their cooped hens to sell to more prosperous neighbors.[25]

By late afternoon most heavy household chores were completed. A
this time of day male vendors wandered through the streets, seeking t
sell or barter their food products to the women sitting outside their doo
ways.[26] Later still began preparation of the evening meal, requiring ye
another trip to the fountain.[27] During the day, a poor woman and he
children ate little or nothing except bits of bread from the large loaf.[2]
And, as Navarro della Miraglia indicated, some poorer families mad
this bread their evening meal as well. When a woman instead prepared
cooked meal, she often coarsely ground a small amount of grain, whic
she cooked with beans, greens or herbs into a thick porridgelike soup.[2]

She made only a small straw fire in a portable stove. Cooking in the doorway (houses rarely had chimneys), she watched workers from the nearby fields returning to their families.[30] As the sun went down, women closed their doors to eat with their families and eventually to sleep.[31]

Artisans' lives, like those of peasants, also centered around productive work. A shoemaker like Calogero Mulè began his day later than did day laborer Mangiaracina, for his workplace *bottega* was downstairs from his private living quarters. Day began with the arrival of a jug of water for the family's use, transported to Antonina M. by a poor widowed neighbor woman.[32] (Such a woman might be allowed to live in one of the Mulè family's small ground-floor rooms in exchange for labors like this.[33]) If the family was a prosperous one, the wife cooked coffee before family members hurried to their other tasks.[34] The shoemaker went with his son Audenzio to the *bottega*, while his wife attended to a variety of household chores. She nursed her younger child, cleaned the rooms in which the family lived, washed their tiled floors, and selected ingredients for the family noontime meal.[35]

Although the oldest son of the Mulè family was too old to still attend school, his younger sister Teresa probably attended one of Sambuca's two schools.[36] Taking a break from work with his father, Audenzio accompanied Teresa to the school and on his way back from this errand, he had ample time to wander about the town, looking at girls his own age as they worked in neighboring *cortili* with their mothers.[37] He could also stop at the central piazza, talk there with the men gathered about, carry a message from an artisan or *civile* man to his father, or watch for the arrival of the post coach, with its newspapers from Palermo.[38]

An artisan family like the Mulès usually met in their upstairs rooms to eat an early afternoon meal together. On a September day, they might dine on eggs and bread and vegetables (stored, following the harvest on their small plot of land, in a cool ground-floor room behind the *bottega*.)[39] After this meal, the shoemaker and his son returned to their work, while Antonina Mulè continued her chores with the help of her stepdaughter. They washed dishes from the meal and began to sew together, either on dowry items for Teresa or on a simple dress that the seamstress was preparing for a peasant neighbor's wedding.[40]

Occasionally the Mulè family again came together to make a brief visit to a friend or kinsman in the early evening. The birth of a baby might be the motivation for such a visit, perhaps to the home of the peasant that sharecropped the Mulè family's small plot of land.[41] Visitors brought the mother small gifts for her child.[42] The peasant host offered his guests wine and sweets while they admired the baby and its white garments.[43]

39

Guests exchanged compliments and gossip during the short visit. After wards the Mulè family walked together with another artisan family bac towards their houses. The men paused near the piazza and remained there but sent their sons back to the workshops to finish some simple chores le undone. In the piazza, shoemaker Mulè and friend discussed a local elec tion with other artisans; later they listened to a *civile* man read alou from a newspaper that had arrived with the post coach.[44] Meanwhile Ar tonina M. and her younger children returned to their house, where th older women continued sewing. The family again came together for light evening meal, just after sundown. Because she was behind in he sewing, Antonina M. lit an oil lamp and continued to work long after th rest of her family went to bed.

Activity, Time and Location

The comparison of the Mulè and Mangiaracina families shows tha any assessment of the match of social ideals and agrotown physical er vironment must take into account class and gender differences. While th incomes of the Mulè and Mangiaracina families might not have differe much — both agrotown peasants and artisans seemed terribly poor t visitors from northern Europe and America — their lives could scarcel have differed more.[45] Work responsibilities made variation especiall clear in the lives of Calogero Mulè and Giuseppe Mangiaracina, but eve housework — the shared responsibility of their two wives — varied wit class. The wife of an artisan or peasant landowner had a more varie supply of food and fuel, and her family ate together far more frequentl The artisan's wife had a larger house, more furniture, clothes, linen pots and dishes. At the same time, she enjoyed more household help. Fc poorer women trying to maintain similar standards of cleanliness (Pitrè, a trifle defensively, insisted they did), the absence of possessio created other housework burdens.[46] Cristina M. had to clean up anim and human messes and try to maintain order in the storage of foo straw, fuel, furnishings, and family possessions in the single small roo that served as the family shelter.

Even the division between male and female tasks within the famil varied by class. It was especially strong and clear in the artisan famil While artisans like Calogero Mulè could always depend on female fami members to cook and clean for them, agricultural workers left home work. They sometimes performed chores normally described as women responsibilities while in the countryside. Men working in the fields cou and did cook for themselves, although they might never do this in the presence of their wives.[47] (See Figure 3-1.)

Seasonal changes affected agricultural families far more than artisans' families. Several hundred proverbs in Pitrè's collection detailed the importance of the repetitive agricultural cycle; Sicilians linked this agricultural cycle to the church's equally cyclical system of religious celebrations.[48] The first important harvest of the year was beans, in June. Peasants harvested grain from June to September, depending on altitude. The wheat harvest demanded many laborers during a relatively short period; wages rose to their yearly peak at that time. Whole families travelled to these harvests, where men harvested and women and children gleaned.[49] Grapes, cactus fruits, fruits, and nuts ripened during September and October, thus overlapping with plowing for the next wheat crop. Olive harvesting and wheat sowing overlapped in November.[50]

By late November the rainy season began, and with it a period of diminished agricultural activity. This was the time for weddings and rest,

Figure 3-1. Men Cooking in the Countryside (*Presepe.* Museo Pitrè)

41

extending through Christmas. It was also the time when a newly watered countryside produced a variety of wild vegetables, greens and snails. Water holes and streams filled. From Christmas until June, fully six months, little agricultural work was required: pruning of vineyards, planting beans and vegetables, cultivating wheat all took far fewer hours than the harvests.[51] Landowning peasants and sharecroppers slowed the pace of their work during the winter. Most day laborers and sharecroppers, finding only irregular employment, suffered severely, and could scarcely be said to enjoy their "leisure." Such men gathered daily in a piazza labor market, sometimes staying the entire day, ever hopeful of finding someone needing their labor. When truly pressed for food, they and their families scavenged wild foods in the countryside.[52] Winter was also the time for weaving, a chore done exclusively by women in towns where the domestic production of cloth still maintained some importance.[53]

Although the artisan's business increased during the months preceding Christmas weddings, most artisans controlled the pace of their work. And they chose to work throughout the year. Stone masons might stop work during the heaviest rains of winter, but they also regarded winter as the best time for constructing a sturdy wall.[54] The seasons had a far smaller significance for artisans than for peasants.

When the ancestors of Calogero Mulè and Giuseppe Mangiaracina centuries before built the dense settlements called agrotowns, they made it difficult for their descendants to make homes anywhere else. The countryside, uninhabited, remained uninhabitable, with no roads, no water supplies, no churches. As a consequence, agricultural workers had no choice but to leave their homes and families for long periods of time. Another consequence was that women's participation in wheat cultivation remained limited.

The lowest-status agricultural workers — day laborers, shepherds and agricultural guards — spent proportionately more time working in the distant *campagna* and proportionately less time in and around their urban homes.[55] Sharecroppers and landowning peasants also wasted hours travelling to their work places, but two factors lessened their burden. First, these peasants alone owned animals — they could ride to the fields. Secondly, they were more likely to cultivate at least one or two plots of land in the *corona* just outside town. From there, they could return nightly to their homes.

There was one exception to this general rule, however. The *gabelloto* the man who leased large wheat estates from absentee landlords and managed them for a profit, spent much time in the countryside. Most owned land, also; all were aspiring *civili*. (And, in fact, many *civili* of the late nineteenth century had a *gabelloto* father or grandfather.) The time spent at the headquarters of the wheat estate proved a social hindrance to the ambitious *gabelloto*, for it made him "rough," the very opposite of "civile."[56]

By contrast, the artisans and petty merchants of a town like Sambuca—shoemakers, butchers, tile-makers, carpenters, stone masons, iron workers, barbers, grocers and operators of taverns or cafes—chose to work close to their homes. Most worked in shops directly below their living quarters. Winter rains might force them into their shops, and in better weather they rarely worked further away than the street outside their shop doors. Only carters and millers had occupational motives for travelling into the distant *campagna*, and they, like the *gabelloti*, gained a reputation as tough and uncivilized men as a result. Artisans and merchants worked and relaxed as they saw fit. In their leisure, they might meet with others in their own shops or visit a large central piazza where other men gathered. In the 1890's Sambuca had at least six sellers of wines and spirits; their taverns also served as leisure-time gathering places, especially in winter.

Similarly, an agrotown's rentiers, taking little active interest in the land they owned, rarely ventured into the countryside. Whether their "work" consisted of speculation, useful profession or conspicuous idleness, they chose (and thereby defined) a central gathering place in the agrotown as the best place for their "work".[57] Navarro della Miraglia poked fun at the *civili* sitting on the stone wall that surrounded a square in the simple country town of "Gibelmoro." Elsewhere, rentier men met in pharmacy or cafe. In Sambuca by the end of the century, they owned relatively luxurious club rooms on the main street.[58]

Women could combine childrearing, household and agricultural work only with some difficulty in Sicily. That is why they travelled to the distant wheat-raising *campagna* only once in the year. However, the harvesting of the intensively cultivated crops raised in the nearby *corona* fell to women, while plowing and planting of wheat (which coincided with these harvests) became men's work. Women could harvest and process nuts, fruits, or vegetables and still return nightly to their homes. They could also bring young children with them to the nearby fields where these crops were raised.[59] The agrotown settlement pattern certainly encouraged agricultural families to divide labor in this way, guaranteeing employment of as many family members as possible while harvests raised demand for labor to yearly peaks.

During most of the year, women remained within the agrotown.[60] But

43

staying there did not mean working within one's own four walls, at least not for peasant wives and daughters. It was absolutely impossible for a poorer woman to accomplish many of her household chores while remaining in her home. She had to haul water, either from fountain or distant spring. Since it was easier to transport dry clothes than to carry water, women usually preferred open streams for laundering during the rainy winter season. (A favored washing spot outside of Sambuca served the entire female population of the town; it was about a mile away from the southern edge of housing.) A peasant woman's efforts to earn money could also require her to leave her home, either to exchange eggs or to do housework in other women's houses. Even for smaller tasks, small one room houses made poor work places — they had no chimneys, no windows and little room. In winter women might weave there by oil light, but all evidence shows that women worked outside their houses in the street or *cortile* whenever weather allowed.[61] This is why Navarro della Miraglia called the *cortile* "a kind of shared living room."[62]

Artisans' wives, living in lighter and larger houses, had more choice over where they worked. Nothing in the structure of their homes prevented them from going into the *cortile* or street to work, so they must have preferred to work where they did — inside. Artisans' wives often chose the "best room," the one most likely to have windows, as their work place. The women who helped their husbands run small shops also easily combined housework, sewing and selling. A tailoress or seamstress left her home to fit the clothes, of course; but only the skilled midwife always worked outside her own house.[63]

For most of the year, then, higher-status men, women, girls, and young children permanently occupied the Sicilian agrotown. Higher status men gathered in scattered ground-floor *botteghe* and shops or in centrally located squares, shops and clubs. Higher-status women worked upstairs in their own houses; lower-status women toiled below in *cortile* or street, at the fountain or water hole, or in the house of a higher-status woman. Their husbands, sons, and brothers were far away, during the day in the best of cases, for weeks at a time in the worst. Harvest altered this pattern temporarily; lower-status women travelled briefly to the *latifondo* and more often to nearby harvests, while men worked for long periods on distant estates. Even a *civile* family spent several weeks during the harvest, living in a *corona*-area "country house."[64] Wintertime drew almost all Sicilians into town. While higher-status men retreated into protected work and leisure places and lower-status women spent more time in their damp small houses, unemployed men sought work about town, wherever the better-off gathered, in piazza, artisans' shops or tavern.

As the last chapter predicted, the agrotown imposed severe restraints on agricultural families in their everyday lives. The settlement pattern required men to travel large distances to work and limited mothers' participation in wheat raising. Furthermore, the house itself practically forced women and children in agricultural families to find work and play places outside their homes. Unlike men—who created male gathering places in central locations—peasant wives chose to do much of their work just outside their doors, in street or *cortile*. Thus the majority of Sicilians had very limited choice over where or when or with whom they performed their everyday work and leisure activities.

Agrotown Social Patterns

Obviously, some agrotown dwellers had far better opportunities than others to interact with members of their own families and to form social ties to others. But physical proximity and the opportunity to interact do not alone ensure that real social relationships will result. Two people can pass on the street without talking. And, even if they do talk, people alone decide what type of relationship they will begin. The social ideals described in chapter 1 guided Sicilians in forming, structuring and maintaining their social ties to others. Environmental restraints could only limit everyday opportunities to achieve those goals by making certain kinds of interaction difficult if not impossible.

Peasant families in agrotowns faced the nearly impossible task of defending the privacy of family life—an important symbol of their solidarity in competition with others—in a one-room house. A passerby, the women in the *cortile*, or a caller could easily check the condition of the bed linen, the amount of grain stored in the corner, the absence of household goods, or the dirt floor.[65] Little wonder that Sicilians preferred homes on the second floor, where they could better control access to their private dwelling rooms. Proverbs expressed considerable anxiety about threats to this private family space, especially through doors and windows.[66] "Every house has its door [its weakness]" (III, 92); "When happiness is in the house, disgrace is just behind the door" (II, 92); "The back door is often the ruination of the house" (I, 221); "All the world's ills come in through the door" (II, 153); "When you eat, shut the door, and when you talk, look behind you" (III, 295); "The door is open to him who contributes—otherwise, you stay outside" (IV, 229); "The

neighborhood is a snake, if it doesn't see you it hears you" (I, 219). Th
need to defend nuclear family privacy, originating in competition, mad
cooperation difficult for the majority of agrotown residents. Peasant
could not easily receive visitors or offer hospitality in their house
without exposing their private space.

Peasant men in particular found their ideals in conflict. With fields fa
away, they could not simultaneously direct the family's economic tasks
control the sexuality of the women in the family, and form the social tie
necessary both to survive economically and to accumulate respect. Yet a
these were part of their ideal role as fathers. An artisan man clearl
directed the family economic endeavors: He trained his sons in his oc
cupation, and together they formed a family enterprise, even whil
the son attended school.[67] The sons of landowning peasants, som
sharecroppers and independent shepherds also worked under thei
fathers' guidance. But sons in many poor families sought work outsid
the family unit. As herders they wandered the countryside with othe
young boys; as domestic servants they followed the directions of a *civi*
or his wife. And, as they grew older, most sought work as day laborer:
They might even compete for work with their own fathers. Few peasal
fathers, then, actually directed their family's collective economi
endeavors.

Away from home for much of the year, the peasant man slept i
regularly with his wife; he could not control her sexuality. This, I believ
was the material basis for much of the anxiety expressed in the provert
about faithless wives. (Pitrè himself noted that the proverbs he collecte
painted an unrealistically negative picture of women's behavior, I, cc
iii–iv.) Illegitimacy, while not unknown, was lower than in other parts c
Italy where settlement patterns demanded no family separation:
Government surveys reported that even the supercilious *civili* judged pe
sant morality favorably.[68] All the same, the possibility of fema
adultery fascinated and appalled Sicilians of all classes. Several c
Navarro della Miraglia's short-story plots involve the peasant wife's i
fidelity. Seduction of the peasant daughter was another popular them
as in *La Nana* and several of Verga's short works.

By contrast, most women in either peasant or artisan families coul
devote themselves to their housework, children and household, as ide
demanded. They could remain with their children in and around the
agrotown homes. The symbolic association of the physical house an
mother's love was, in fact, a strong one: "My *casa*, my mother!" (I, 217
Unlike their husbands, peasant wives also continued to supervise the
older daughters, training them for their later lives as housewives an

mothers, working together with them until the daughters married. In this way, too, women could usually live up to idealized notions of motherly responsibilities.

Peasant women went to some lengths to prove their faithfulness and submission to their often-absent husbands. They waited on them at table, addressed them with the respectful form of address and — sometimes — were beaten.[69] What they did not do was seclude themselves in their houses as final proof of their fidelity. Given their household responsibilities, it would have been difficult for them to do so. Still, they even refused to signal a fictional seclusion (as Sicilian women in smaller towns do today) by symbolically turning their backs to the street or *cortile* from the doorway where they sat. (See Figure 3-2.) Only unmarried daughters remained relatively secluded.[70]

This was so because a peasant family literally could not afford either the real or fictional seclusion of the mother as proof of the father's control over her sexuality. The family, too, desperately needed to form instrumental ties to others. A story by Navarro della Miraglia suggests that most families chose to reap whatever cooperative benefits they could from the wife's active social efforts outside the household: The author pokes fun at the foolishness of an overly jealous man who locked up his

Figure 3-2. "The Street is Their Drawing Room" (William Seymour Monroe, *Sicily, The Garden of the Mediterranean* (Boston: L.C. Page, 1909)).

47

wife while he was away. In accepting the nonsecluded wife, most familie tacitly recognized the father's limitations as organizer of famil cooperative efforts. A man's work companions were an ever-changin group of competitors with few resources beyond their own labor (whicl they sought to sell). A man's visits to male gathering places were few an seasonal.[71] Both factors made it difficult for peasant men to forn reciprocal instrumental relations to others.

Women faced fewer difficulties socially. Pitrè wrote that "th women . . . cannot stand being unable to see each other, to talk, to worl together."[72] And a proverb encouraged women to "Capitalize on you neighborhood" (I, 220). A woman's *cortile* neighbors and, to a lesser ex tent, those she met daily at the fountain, were a stable group, changin only slowly with residential mobility. In addition women share household responsibilities; these labors were less commonly sold for wage Instead, they could be exchanged, at little cost to resourceless families. Ove long periods of time even the poorest woman could occasionally offer neighbor her help in heavy housework, in childrearing or at a time o family crisis — a death, for example.[73] If she did this for an artisan's wife she gained a *padrona*, and she could expect a returned favor — use of loom or sewing machine.[74] She could also expect others to recognize th existence of this social tie and respect her family because of its existence Women gossiped constantly in their neighborhoods. This exchange of in formation was both the basis for social relationships and the means o evaluating them. "Vermicelli for dinner tonight, eh?" a gossiping grou asked a pompous and outraged priest in one Verga story,[75] whil Navarro della Miraglia traced the spread of gossip after a local *civil* returned from a visit in Palermo.[76] Trivial gossip like this was a form o social evaluation. It also allowed a woman to arrange marriages and t help find work for herself, her husband, or other family members. Fou eyes, as the proverb said, were certainly better than two, especially whe a man's two eyes only infrequently looked round the agrotown.

Nevertheless, the peasant family also suffered for depending so heavil on women to form its social network. Since this network arose from sim ple household and childrearing exchanges, a family's network of in strumental ties rarely extended much beyond the entrance to the *cortile* Both men and women found all their friends there. According to Chap man even the highly-valued close relatives of the *casa* rarely played muc of a role in the family's social exchanges if they lived outside this sma area.[77] And even the patron who helped a sharecropper with loans o grain during the lean preharvest months was likely to be the artisan o *civile* whose house overlooked the *cortile* below.

A woman's efforts to build a social network around her family also provided yet another justification for virulent Sicilian misogyny. The higher-status men who wrote stories and novels about agrotown life admitted that their peers, artisans and *civile* men, used their prestige to prey upon the peasant woman, offering help in exchange for sexual favors. A common theme in the proverbs was the absent peasant man, assumed to be a cuckold (II, 75). Most lower-status women, however, seemed to have successfully avoided the higher-status men who resided continuously in the agrotown with them.[78]

The wife's social ties to others served as yet another reminder that the peasant father failed properly to fulfill his family role. Anthropologist Susan Carol Rogers traced the emergence of a powerful "myth of male domination" to male peasants' resentment of women's social powers.[79] Certainly Sicilians of both sexes had reason to use such a compensatory myth. No matter how respectful the peasant wife, no matter how carefully she served her husband at table, she could not resolve the conflicts among idealized family roles and the social ideal of a useful network of instrumental ties to others. As long as environmental obstacles remained high, "The husband is like the government at Rome, all pomp; the wife is like the Mafia, all power."[80] Idealization of male domination helped compensate for its absence.

Peasants, we saw in chapter 1, were not culturally familist. Neither were they familist in practice, although their small and female-dominated social networks rarely met Sicilians' ideals. One or two close *casa* kin, a single more-distant kinsman, three or four unrelated families, and a nearby patron formed a family's *cortile* social world. To the extent that local controversy touched this world, neighborhood women might act collectively. Verga, for example, described women engaging husbands in their quarrel with a local gentleman when the men returned from work at the end of the day.[81] Women did not, however, form voluntary associations like friendly societies, political clubs or labor unions. Neither did peasant men, at least before the 1880's. It seems likely, then, that peasant localism rather than peasant familism limited peasant experimentation with voluntary association until the late nineteenth century.[82]

Artisan and *civile* families faced none of the obstacles that frustrated peasant families in their pursuit of Sicilian social ideals. Both groups easily maintained family privacy in the dwelling rooms that they separated from a space to entertain guests and offer hospitality. Their large-doored and many-windowed houses symbolized not a threat to family privacy but the achievement of housing ideals.[83] Artisans regularly slept with their wives and trained their own children, fulfilling the role of the ideal father and thereby acquiring respect. They met with other men regularly and played a much larger role in forming family social networks than did their housebound wives. These social networks were not geographically limited, as was the peasant's neighborhood group, and were not the source of anxiety about the social power or infidelity of women. Jane and Peter Schneider argue that *civile* families placed less emphasis on female submission as a consequence.[84] Navarro della Miraglia supported that contention: He described *civile* women participating, conversing and even flirting during the constant round of visits in which these families engaged.[85] Chapman also observed that artisan families in the early twentieth century shared the social practices of the rentier families.[86] More patriarchal in their social relations, such families had less reason to idealize patriarchy.

Artisan, *civile* and aspiring *civile* men usually succeeded in building the large and complex social networks idealized in the late nineteenth century, but they achieved this ideal in a variety of ways. Artisans enjoyed a long history of occupational cooperation in their guilds. Abolished in the 1830's, the guilds reappeared in new forms—as the fraternity that honored a patron saint with a yearly *festa* and, especially in the 1880's, as the mutual benefit society limited in membership to "honest workers."[87] By contrast, *civile* men competed desperately in changing and loosely organized factions for control of both local wheat trade and local government. In Sambuca they formed two quite stable competing political cliques that warred bitterly over spoils in the late nineteenth century. (Residents cynically called these two groups the "ups" and the "downs.") Together, *civile* men also organized their club; its main function was to maintain, in its limited way, *civile* class solidarity, usually by excluding the rough but eager and increasingly prosperous *gabelloti*.[88] *Gabelloti*, controlling employment on the large estates, in turn formed extensive networks of peasant and shepherd clients (*servi*). Centered in the forbidding *campagna*, the *gabelloto's* social network often assumed the form and function of a mafia band.[89]

Thus, the agrotown remained socially fragmented. Rarely a single community, at best it can be characterized as a series of overlapping networks. Peasants' many small networks were geographically based and small, while artisans' and *civili's* were larger and class based. In addition, each agrotown had a few large cross-class networks with powerful *gabelloti* at their centers. For two brief but important decades, *civile* and some artisan men experimented with the consolidation of large cross-class political factions that could have considerably simplified the com-

ɔlex social structure of Sicilian agrotowns. Literate artisans attained suf-
·rage in 1883; during the years that followed, Sambuca's artisans formed
wo mutual benefit societies (the *Unione Elettorale* and the *Società
·Franklin*). No documentation survives to tell us about the functions of
hese organizations. But elsewhere in Sicily such mutual benefit societies
lid function as vote-gathering mechanisms for existing *civile* political
·actions. In Sambuca, *civile* efforts to unite politically with artisans
ultimately failed; perhaps independent artisans did not relish abandoning
heir group identity to beome *servi* of the town's rentiers. Besides, ar-
isans had other social options. In Sambuca a group of shoemakers,
·abinet-makers, and tailors began during the 1880's to build a very dif-
·erent cross-class network, one that forged alliances to the peasant ma-
ority. By the end of the century, Sambuca's artisans, in cooperation with
ι small number of peasants, formed a workers' club and opened a
vorkers' school to teach peasants to read and write. Drawing on
iicilians' tendency to define rich and poor as vastly different groups,
hese artisans announced their loyalty to the poor, even though we have
·een that their lives in many ways more closely resembled those of the
entier "rich." By 1900 Sambuca's artisans called themselves Socialists.[90]
n general, however, these cross-class social alliances had little impor-
ance until the twentieth century.

Summary

Environmental restraints overwhelmed the poor Sicilian hoping to
.chieve his social ideals; the agrotown was a very poor match. Peasant
iicilians had every reason to be dissatisfied with their social lives. Nor
.id they hesitate to express dissatisfaction with their plight, which in its
arger aspects came to be called *la miseria*. Both peasant men and peasant
vomen faced huge obstacles in their efforts to behave properly as family
nembers and to behave "civilly" as members of a larger social group.
·easant women could find consolation in mothering their children in the
lealized fashion, but they suffered under the assumption that they were
nfaithful sexually. The peasant man failed, as supervisor of his wife's
exuality and as the idealized father who guided the family economically
nd socially.

Most of the Sicilians who migrated to the United States left their
grotown homes in search of work, as the next chapter shows. Never-
heless, it is important to remember that social dissatisfaction played a
ɔle, influencing how people perceived their economic troubles. It was
ot the case that migrants sacrificed a satisfying social life in order to

pursue economic goals elsewhere. The dissatisfaction of ordinary peasant men and women with their Sicilian social relationships is the background against which migration and life in the United States must be interpreted. Migrants left Sicily not to establish familiar social ties elsewhere but to build lives both economically and socially more satisfying than the ones they left behind.

CHAPTER FOUR

Sicilian Migrants

Leonardo A., one of six children born to a Sambuca day laborer and his wife in the 1880's and 1890's, migrated to Chicago sometime around 910. (This and subsequent examples are drawn from the draft records and household registration files of Sambuca.) Many other Sambuca residents lived in Chicago in the early years of the twentieth century, but Leonardo A. was the only member of his *casa* to leave Sicily. Twenty years later, in 1931, he continued to reside in America, while his elderly parents and grown siblings remained in Sambuca.

Unlike Leonardo A., the children of Sambuca barber Antonio C. enjoyed the company of many of their brothers and sisters in the United States. Castrenze C. first applied for a passport in 1897, when he was twenty-six years old. His brothers Marianno, Antonino and Giuseppe all moved to Brooklyn before reaching their twentieth birthdays. By 1931 nine of the C. siblings—three women and six men—lived in that city. Two sisters remained in Sambuca: One still lived with her aged mother, and the other had married a local man.

Giuseppe O. and Caterina M. married in Sambuca in 1891, and their first child was born there a year later. Shortly thereafter, Giuseppe O. probably left Sicily, for his wife bore no more children until, years later, she joined her husband in Louisiana. Between 1898 and 1910 the couple bore seven children, most in Patterson, Louisiana, a small town in the state's sugar-growing region. By 1912 at least part of the family returned to Sambuca, where a last child was born in that year. Of Giuseppe O. and Caterina M.'s eight children, four married and died in Sambuca. The other four lived in the United States in 1931. Both Giuseppe O. and Caterina M. died in Sambuca.

Compared to other southern Italians, Sicilians began to migrate quite late: Before 1880, fewer than one thousand left their agrotown homes annually to emigrate abroad.[1] During the 1880's, when Italians from the Abruzzi, from Calabria, Basilicata and Naples established Little Italies

53

all over the United States, only several thousand people yearly left Sicily.[2] By 1898, however, 26,000 departed — and the numbers increased rapidly after 1900. Thirty-seven thousand emigrated in 1901; 59,000 in 1903; 127,600 in 1906. Ultimately, every fourth migrant to the United States in the years 1880–1920 was a Sicilian. After the turn of the century, most Sicilian emigrants headed for the growing cities of the United States. A large but not calculable number contributed to New York's growing Italian-born population, which reached 340,770 in 1910.[3]

By the time of the New York State Census in 1905, approximately 8200 Italian immigrants and their children crowded into the tenements of Elizabeth Street. Although we have no way of knowing for sure, most probably were Sicilians. The Immigration Commission's survey of homeworkers found that "all the people who live on the west side of Elizabeth Street between E. Houston and Prince Street are Sicilians," while its survey of southern Italians in several New York neighborhoods (including Elizabeth Street) counted almost 50 percent from Sicilian provinces.[4] Together the residents of Elizabeth Street formed a population about the size of a typical agrotown like Sambuca.

As the examples from Sambuca suggest, emigrants from Sicilian agrotowns represented a variety of social backgrounds. Some migrated alone; others migrated as complete or incomplete family groups. One consequence was that the immigrant residents of Elizabeth Street — despite their Sicilian origins and culture — differed socially from an agrotown population. Selective migration meant an unbalanced sex ratio in immigrant populations. Historians have also emphasized the youthfulness of immigrant groups in the United States. Both characteristics could influence immigrant social behavior in the Little Italies of the New World.

While important, unbalanced sex ratios and youthful majorities do not tell us all that we need to know about how an immigrant group differed from an agrotown population socially. Social ties among Sicilians also began to change during migration, as migrants left agrotown restraints behind. Migrating, Sicilians often succeeded in expanding their social networks, especially ties to their own kin. While the population of Elizabeth Street was socially fragmented, selective migration and New World job opportunities also considerably simplified the complex class hierarchy typical of an agrotown. Immigrant social relationships on Elizabeth Street would necessarily reflect these changes. In order to avoid attributing every distinctive social pattern on Elizabeth Street to the influence of a changing physical environment, the social consequences of migration must first be described.

Familism and Migration

Poor peasants responded in several ways to economic changes sweeping the European countryside in the nineteenth century. Migration was one response. Compared to a peasant revolution or strike, it seems a peculiarly individualistic or familistic solution to those changes. Economist J. S. MacDonald offered an explanation for Italian peasants' varying responses to economic change: In areas of household agriculture peasants migrated in large numbers, while elsewhere equally poor proletarianized cultivators instead organized militant unions and supported the Socialist party.[5]

Historians' interpretations of immigrant social patterns have depended heavily on MacDonald's findings. Noting the institutional weakness of Italian-American communities, Virginia Yans-McLaughlin traced its origin to those areas of southern Italy (the "Deep South") where household agriculture and familist social values produced high rates of migration.[6]

Sicilians engaged in household agriculture, combined with work as day laborers; culturally they were not familist. They did not resemble the typical emigrants of the "Deep South." Artisans formed voluntary associations and—in Sambuca, at least—peasants were beginning to join them in class-conscious organizations. Even peasants' lack of a large social network reflected only their failure to achieve their social ideals. Nevertheless both peasants and artisans migrated in great numbers, especially after the turn of the century.

J. S. MacDonald recognized that the origins of Sicilian migration were complex.[7] He explained the lateness of Sicilian emigration by pointing to peasants' failed attempts to solve their problems collectively in the nineteenth century. Only when the Italian state crushed peasant organizations—the well-studied and fascinating *Fasci Siciliani* of the 1890's—did Sicilians turn instead to the "familist" solution—migration.[8]

Western Sicilian evidence does not support MacDonald's explanation. Migration was not a particularly familist response to poverty. MacDonald himself popularized the concept of migration chains, which characterized migration as a carefully organized social movement.[9] Migration, like voluntary association, was a socially organized process. And, in Sicily, people chose not one form or the other, but tended to experiment simultaneously with both responses when faced with economic difficulties. The lateness of Sicily's migration and its volume originated not in some peculiar Sicilian social or cultural trait, but in the industrial and agricultural development of the island—which differed considerably from that of other parts of southern Italy.[10]

55

Sicily's earliest migrants were artisans; their migration coincided with a decade of vigorous artisanal organization.[11] A survey of Sicilian towns in 1889 listed artisans, shoemakers, "workers," and some peasants living as immigrants in New York, Chicago, Louisiana and South America.[12] Thereafter, artisans and workers continued to migrate in disproportionate numbers according to data collected from persons applying for the *nulla osta*, a procedure preceding the granting of a passport.[13] During the 1890's artisans everywhere built ties to peasants; they provided much of the leadership for the *Fasci Siciliani*, for peasant strikes and for tax protests 1892–93.[14] Early immigrants and those active in early workers' organizations shared similiar social and economic backgrounds. In Sambuca, for example, over half the men listed in draft records of the 1880's as migrants to the United States were shoemakers — precisely those artisans most active in local politics and responsible for forming the early Socialist Party.[15] Immigrants and Socialists may have, in fact, been brothers and cousins.

Artisans' simultaneous efforts to organize and to emigrate reflected mainly their declining economic opportunities. While artisans in the 1860's and 1870's found a good market for their services as local *civili* built and furnished grand houses and financed the construction of theatres, public gardens and town halls, the era of expanding expectations was a short one.[16] Competition from imported products destroyed Sicily's native manufacturies after 1870.[17] The threat of downward social mobility encouraged both emigration and political response during the 1880's and 1890's.

A roughly similar pattern of response characterized Sicily's peasants as prices for crops fell. First affected were wheat growers, in the 1880's.[18] Not surprisingly, both emigration and the organization of *Fasci* began in wheat-growing towns of western Sicily, as Table 4–1 shows. Migration from wheat towns increased and remained higher than average even after government repression of the *Fasci* in 1894; continued migration, however, did not prevent further outbursts of peasant agitation in the twentieth century.

Until 1900, the majority of Sicilian towns exporting other crops — grapes, fruits and nuts — lost fewer residents to migration and experienced relatively fewer peasant strikes during the 1890's. These peasants enjoyed a good and expanding market for their crops until late in the century, long after crisis rocked the worldwide grain market.[19] The cultivators of these crops emigrated late, first depressing, then raising overall rates of emigration from the island. And these peasants alone seemed to reject political organization as a response to falling agricultural prices. These peasants were not culturally "more familist" than wheat-growers. (They organized mutual benefit societies as often as wheat cultivators, for example.) Instead, they, unlike wheat growers, worked under agricultural contracts that allowed them to raise their own food — to subsist — during periods of low prices.[20] This option may have undercut collective action, but it also undercut emigration: even after 1900 migration rates from these towns lagged slightly behind the wheat-growing towns.

Neither migration nor political organization threatened the social and economic centrality of the Sicilian nuclear family; both represented efforts to solve family poverty through cooperation. The long-run implications of emigration or political organization may have in fact been very different, but only hindsight makes the extent of these differences so very clear to us. It seems pointless, then, to portray emigration as a typically familist response to economic change, contrasting it to more collective solutions. In both cases, Sicilians tried as best they could to build and use social networks to their advantage. In both cases they acted according to agrotown social ideals. Migration in particular offered new and practically costless opportunities for cooperation. Sicilians responded enthusiastically: Migration to the United States was, as most historians now agree, an intricately organized social movement.

Table 4-1. Crops, Migration and Working-Class Organization

N	CROP EXPORTED	AVERAGE ANNUAL ADJUSTED INTERCENSAL POPULATION BALANCE PER 1000 RESIDENTS		PEASANT MILITANCE: % WITH	
		1881–1900	1901–1910	*Fascio* 1893-94	Peasant Strike 1900–10
		(a)		(b)	(c)
76	Wheat	−8.8	−14.0	80%	40%
33	Other Crops	−3.6	−12.4	42%	6%

a) Provincial Capitals and sulfur exporting towns omitted. S. Somogyi, *Bilanci Demografici dei Comuni Siciliana dal 1861 al 1961* (Palermo: Universita di Palermo, Istituto di Scienze Demografiche, 1971).

b) Renda, *I Fasci*, App. 1.

c) Ministero di Agricoltura, Industria e Commercio, *Statistica delle Scioperi avvenuti in Italia* (Rome: 1884–1903).

The Social Organization of Migration

About the organization of migration, historians still know relatively little. The fact that family and communal ties facilitated migration, the theme of recent studies, is an important starting place.[21] But since family and other social ties assumed several forms and functions even in one agrotown, this observation alone does not tell much about the social structure of an immigrant population. Writing with his wife Leatrice, J.S. MacDonald demonstrated that village-based chains provided the foundation for community building in urban immigrant neighborhoods.[22] Analysis of migration chains can reveal much about the origins of immigrant social structure. Here the focus is on the relative importance of nuclear family migration, the usefulness of kinship in forming chain links, and the size and origin of migration chains.

South Italians went to considerable trouble to keep the nuclear family together during migration, but they did not always migrate as a family unit. Like their Buffalo counterparts, about half of Elizabeth Street families in 1905 had experienced separations while migrating.[23] Typically, the young migrated, so that Elizabeth Street contained a disproportionate number of families with no or only young children.[24] These families with young children numbered among the financially most hard pressed in the immigrant population.[25] Finally, although family migrants were the majority, Elizabeth Street contained many more persons without families (8 percent of the population) than did a typical agrotown (about 3 percent). In agrotowns, the housing of individuals without families posed an occasional problem; migration could only increase that problem.

The decision to migrate represented a nuclear family's desire to compete, improving its position in the agrotown class hierarchy. To emigrate, however, was not simply a competitive matter. The typical emigrant needed and sought help. Early migrants willingly offered help, money or information. Much help and all information—like agrotown gossip—cost nothing, and allowed the immigrant family to expand its social network. The family expected, in turn, to benefit from future reciprocation, for the emigrant was a better social risk than the Sicilian peasant had been. The family also expected to enjoy the social respect that accompanied expansion of its social network. The point is clear: migration did not depend on existing social relationships but provided resources for the creation of new ones.

The importance of kinship in organizing migration is usually assumed.[26] Evidence for its importance comes mainly from small numbers of oral histories of immigrants arriving in the United States in the twentieth century, that is, after chains were well established.[27] The social ties linking migrants into a chain have never received systematic study, so firm conclusions are premature.

Some evidence does point to the likelihood that immigrant kinship patterns originated not in southern Italy—Sicilians neither idealized nor practiced close ties to *parenti*—but in the migration process itself.[28] Initially, kin may have played only a limited role in organizing migration chains. Of 765 families recently arrived in the United States in 1905 and living on Elizabeth Street, about half had no kin whatsoever living nearby. (See Appendix B for an explanation of how kinship outside the household was estimated from census data.) Better evidence comes from the group of immigrants without families who in 1905 sought housing on Elizabeth Street; 150 became boarders with nonkin while only ninety found a place with a relative. The boarders—whether new friends or former neighbors—had become *paesani*, a social category completely unknown in Sicilian agrotowns.

Kinship grew in importance, and it probably did so at the expense of friendship and neighborhood ties in the organization of migration. The ratio of households including nonkin boarders to those with kin declined on Elizabeth Street through time: from .58 in 1905, to .54 in 1915, to only .25 in 1925. And, by 1931, almost every resident of Sambuca listed in town *fogli* as living in the United States had at least one relative in the immigrant population.

Members of the *casa* cooperated most frequently in emigrating, as Sicilian social ideals would predict. Because migrants were young, it was siblings who formed most links in *casa* chains. On Elizabeth Street in 1905, brothers and sisters of household heads (or their wives) represented half of the kin included in the household. Similarly, about half of the 765 Elizabeth Street families analyzed for kin outside the household had the sibling of one spouse living nearby. Over 80 percent of the migrant children listed in Sambuca's *fogli* as residents of the United States in 1931 had at least one migrant sibling.

Cooperation among more distant kin, the *parenti*, increased most noticeably during migration. *Parenti* represented 15 percent of the kin invited into Elizabeth Street households in 1905. Twenty years later that proportion increased to over one-third. One-quarter of the 765 families analyzed had at least one more distant relative living nearby in 1905 — an estimate that certainly underestimates the real proportions. A higher estimate (but still one that is probably low) comes from the Sicilian data, which reflects the ties established among *parenti* through time. Since Sambuca's *fogli* listed the full names of parents and grandparents of immigrant children, cousins, aunts, uncles, nieces, nephews, grandparents and grandchildren could be identified among the immigrants living in the

United States in 1931. More than a third of the immigrant children in this group had at least one immigrant *parente*. Most of these had several.

Why did migrating Sicilians come to prefer *parenti*, over neighbors or friends in building migration chains? One explanation is that young migrants left behind most of their *casa* kin, who in Sicily formed the core of their social networks. Only 5 percent of Sambuca's migrant children in 1931 could count on the company of all their siblings in the United States, and the average Elizabeth Street family analyzed had in 1905 only two close relatives of the *casa* living close by. Young emigrants may have looked more favorably on *parenti* as replacements for parents and siblings. The limited size of the *cortile* neighborhood/friendship group may also have limited its usefulness in peasants' migration. However hazy and dangerous kinship sometimes seemed to agrotown residents, it was the only nongeographical social category available to most peasants. As such, kinship may have "travelled great distances" better than the claim of *paesano*/friendship or neighborliness.

The consequences of migration for immigrant social relationships should be obvious. Immigrants could rarely recreate the multigenerational *casa* in their early years in the United States. They could eventually depend instead on siblings or *parenti* for exchange, respect and emotional support. Life in New York's tenements and in other American Little Italies would reinforce further the usefulness of intra-generational ties, eventually eliminating the Sicilian social and cultural distinction between *casa* and *parenti* to produce the distinctively immigrant kin group *la famiglia*.

Migration chains of kin and nonkin became the foundation on which immigrants could build a larger social network — their size could determine whether immigrants needed to turn to non*paesani* in their efforts. John Briggs' research showed that in Utica, Rochester and Kansas City members of a few large migration chains "lived side by side with large numbers of individuals who could count relatively few fellow townsmen or *paesani* in the colony."[29] He concluded that historians exaggerate the importance of *campanilismo* (village-based loyalties) and the cause of immigrant solidarity or the foundation for immigrant community.

Like the cities studied by Briggs, Elizabeth Street was socially fragmented by village chains. Observers at the time distinguished two large subgroups, one from the Sciacca region and one from the area around Palermo. While broadly correct, these observers underestimated the diversity of Elizabeth Street residents' origins and overestimated the size and importance of some communal subgroups.

Briggs used parish records — unavailable for Elizabeth Street — to identify and analyze the communal origins of Italian immigrants; as an alternative I experimented with tracing distinctive patron saint names in census listings. In every agrotown, persons named after the local patron or patroness abounded.Sambuca residents favored Audenzio and Audenzia. In a given year, Sambuca's parents named as many as 10 percent of their children after the town patron. Almost a quarter of Sambuca families had at least one child so named. Pitrè's work identified the patrons of many Sicilian towns, providing a guide to town origins.[30] (See Appendix B.)

In 1905, persons named after Palermo's patroness, Rosalia, numbered 51, while those with the name of Sciacca's San Calogero numbered 91. If we estimate one family in four named a child after the patron, then the chain from Palermo itself contained 200 families. A larger chain originated in Marineo. This was the largest chain on Elizabeth Street. Far more typical was the small chain with only about 20 or 30 families. (Only two families from Sambuca were identified on Elizabeth Street; in both, Sambucari had married residents of Santa Margarita Belice, a nearby town with many residents on the street. Immigrants from Sambuca bound for New York normally chose a variety of Brooklyn locations as their new homes.)

None of these figures give a secure estimate of chain size. But they do suggest that the numbers of persons in migration chains varied considerably. As in the smaller cities that Briggs studied, Elizabeth Street immigrants in large chains lived alongside people with relatively few *paesani* nearby. Only a minority of Elizabeth Street residents could count on a large chain to provide them with a ready-made large social network useful to their future American life. If they wanted to build such a network, they would have to turn to non*paesani*.

Class and Immigrant Occupations

Immigrants came from diverse occupational backgrounds. Not limited to agricultural labor, considerable numbers of immigrants from Sicily had worked as fishermen, artisans or petty merchants.[31] In Sambuca, the children of both agricultural day laborers and artisans migrated in above-average proportions. Immigrants from the town represented almost every possible occupation from the group that Sicilian proverbs loosely characterized "the poor" as well as from the middling group of artisans. Only "the rich"—the *civili*—failed to migrate in significant numbers.

In Sicily occupation largely determined social patterns: artisans achieved Sicilian social ideals while most peasants did not. Yet historians have almost completely ignored the class dynamics of immigrant groups, choosing to emphasize the typical experiences of the "working-class" majority (which is sometimes described as resembling peasants, sometimes as resembling artisans), with occasional contrasts to the *prominenti* or middle-class immigrant elite.[32] It is true that migration truncated the class hierarchy of an agrotowth by almost completely eliminating the *civili*. Nevertheless it left intact the very important distinction between artisan/petty merchant and peasant.

This distinction could easily flourish in the New York job market. New York offered varied occupational opportunities, and most American jobs could easily fit into the Sicilian dichotomy of dirty/dependent and clean/independent manual occupations. New York at the turn of the century was a rapidly expanding city: In parts of Manhattan and the outlying boroughs, the building of houses and offices and the construction of the roads, bridges and public transportation necessary to keep increasingly far-flung parts of the city in communication created thousands of unskilled and skilled jobs. New York was also a center of much light industry, including its famous garment industry, and of commerce, trade and banking. Finally, the city's growing population, including its expanding population of Italian speakers, created demand for some commercial, skilled, and professional service workers.[33]

Both John Briggs and Josef Barton have emphasized that immigrants' European occupational experiences influenced the kind of jobs they took in the United States.[34] In New York, too, immigrants did not randomly fill jobs. Table 4–2 summarizes the occupations of Elizabeth Street residents in 1905, comparing them to the occupations of New Yorkers as a whole. It shows that Elizabeth Street's immigrants concentrated in unskilled work, the garment industry and petty enterprise.

Opportunities for middle-class immigrants were poor in New York City. Elizabeth Street's *prominenti* served the immigrant population as physicians and pharmacists, teachers, white collar workers, agents, bankers and importers. Bankers and importers were few in number in 1905, suggesting that the banker-, agent- or importer-*padrone* may have played a less important role here than in other newer or smaller immigrant colonies.[35] The *prominenti* provided little employment for the mass of ordinary immigrants; instead they were dependent for their success on the support of laborers and artisans. In short, they could never assume the social role of the *civili* in an agrotown.

Table 4-2. Immigrant Occupations

Occupation	All New Yorkers 1900		Elizabeth Street Italians, 1905	
	Male	Female	Male	Female
Unskilled	31%	43%	49%	4%
Clothing Industry	8	27	16	94
Skilled, Building	10	-	5	-
Skilled, Other	12	7	11	1
Petty Enterprise	9	1	16	-
Other	30	21	3	1
	100%	99%	100%	100%
	N = 1,102,471	N = 243,874	N = 2,368	N = 1,018

SOURCES: U.S. Bureau of the Census, *Twelfth Census, 1900, Special Reports, Occupations* (Washington: Government Printing Office, 1904), table 43.

By contrast New York offered expanding opportunities to work at desirable independent or skilled occupations. In fact, immigrants of artisanal or petty-merchant background came to New York in above-average numbers. Only 31 percent of the south Italian New Yorkers surveyed by the Immigration Commission admitted an agricultural background.[36] (In Cleveland, 50 percent did so; in Chicago, 63 percent; in Buffalo, over three-quarters said they had worked in agriculture before migrating.) Thus, while artisans or petty merchants were only a sixth of the family heads in a town like Sambuca, their representation increased to a quarter of Sambuca's male immigrants and to a third of the male workers on Elizabeth Street in 1905.

Unfortunately, census takers failed to describe carefully the work of these immigrant workers; for example, it is impossible to distinguish the independent artisan from the skilled employee. It is clear, however, that in both cases, bakers, butchers, painters, carpenters, masons, plasterers and plumbers performed work easily distinguished by Sicilian standards from dirty/dependent labor. Since Elizabeth Street was a pushcart market area, petty entrepreneurs were especially numerous among its occupants. As elsewhere in the United States, Sicilian immigrants dominated peddling and commerce in fruits and vegetables.[37] On Elizabeth Street, Sicilians also peddled fish. Cafe and saloon operators, restrauteurs and grocers, and dealers in coal, ice and wood completed this occupational group.

Although there were many small factories in the area immediately surrounding Elizabeth Street, large numbers of its Italian residents found work only in the clothing industry. Here again, census takers failed to make careful distinctions among workers: It is not possible to distinguish less skilled and more dependent garment "operators" from the skilled and independent tailor. Other sources indicated that many women became factory operatives, while men performed skilled work as cutters, pressers or independent tailors.[38] Home finishing (mainly basting and finishing garments) attracted huge numbers of Elizabeth Street's female occupants; the street was known as a center of this work.[39]

Alone among New York's occupations, factory work did not neatly fit Sicilian occupational categories, for it was clean but nevertheless dependent work. For women, however, garment making, whether at home or in the factory, represented a kind of work clearly more desirable than the harvesting and domestic work of Sicilian agrotowns. Thus women migrants, too, enjoyed good opportunities for doing desirable work in New York.

In New York, common unskilled labor shared much with European agricultural labor—it was dirty, insecure, dependent and back-breaking work. Almost three quarters of unskilled Elizabeth Street men worked as laborers, digging tunnels and excavating subway passages, or carrying and digging at building construction sites. Other men performed a variety of only slightly more specialized tasks: dockwork, bootblacking, carrying hods, driving wagons, cleaning streets, picking rags, and portering.

Both selective occupational migration and New York's job market had somewhat contradictory social consequences for immigrants. As novels and autobiographies show, not all the immigrants who transformed themselves into small shopkeepers or skilled workers received training in Italy, while not every artisan immigrant succeeded in escaping the dirty and dependent unskilled work he usually performed as a recent arrival.[40] The clear Sicilian distinction between artisans and peasants guided immigrants in understanding and ranking most New York jobs, but the distinction itself blurred in the process. In general, however, the proportion of persons, male and female, doing artisanlike work increased with migration to Elizabeth Street.

With this change could grow the expectation of achieving Sicilian social ideals. The extent to which immigrants succeeded in achieving either their old or their newly developing ideals depended on more than expectation, hope, or will, however. In New York, immigrants faced an entirely new physical environment. Would it frustrate their social efforts as had the homes they left behind?

CHAPTER FIVE

Tenement Residential Patterns

New Yorkers noticed the growing Sicilian settlement on Elizabeth Street with alarm. Their dismay reflected their concern with the curious ways Sicilians occupied their tenement homes: residential patterns that to New Yorkers meant social chaos and that seemed socially and biologically dangerous. Jacob Riis in *Ten Years War* described one particularly troubling Sicilian habit:

> Only the other night I went with the sanitary police on their midnight inspection through a row of Elizabeth Street tenements which I had known since they were built fifteen or sixteen years ago. That is the neighborhood in which the recent Italian immigrants crowd. In the house which we selected for inspection, in all respects the type of the rest, we found forty-three families where there should have been sixteen. Upon each floor were four flats, and in each flat three rooms that measured respectively fourteen by eleven, seven by eleven, and seven by eleven and one half feet. In only one flat did we find a single family. In three there were two to each. In the other twelve, each room had its own family living and sleeping there. They cooked, I suppose, at the one stove in the kitchen, which was the largest room.[1]

Riis sensibly noted that not all the "tenement house evils" they uncovered could be blamed on the Sicilian occupants. One building he described had not had water for a month, because after cold weather had frozen the pipes the building manager, an Italian undertaker, "had not taken the trouble to make many or recent repairs." When Riis asked the man why the houses had been left to decay, the *padrone* replied, "with such tenants nothing could be done." But Riis found this unconvincing and argued with the man: Italians, he had found, were "most manageable and . . . with all surface indications to the contrary, they are inclined to cleanliness." The undertaker, Riis reported, "changed the subject

65

diplomatically," because, "no doubt with him [it was] simply a question of rent."

Riis, a material determinist like many early reformers, may have exaggerated the overcrowding he found on Elizabeth Street in order to demonstrate better the destruction of "the home ideal" by the "tenement house evil."[2] But he was correct in seeing rent as an important housing question—not just for the tenement landlord, but also for the Sicilians wishing to make new homes on Elizabeth Street. From the moment immigrants left Ellis Island, their decisions about where and how they lived were shaped by the hard realities of housing supply and demand in this growing American city. Those realities were indeed hard—tenements fell far below Sicilian housing ideals. But then, so had most Sicilian housing. The match of tenement and Sicilian ideals was certainly no worse than that of the Sicilian agrotown, and in many ways it was actually better.

Tenements

Elizabeth Street was part of only one of several large and growing Italian neighborhoods in the expanding city of New York. In New York's best-known Little Italy, the Fourteenth Ward, Elizabeth is two blocks east of Mulberry Street. Map 5-1 shows the location of the Fourteenth Ward and other Italian settlements in Manhattan—the Sixth Ward, Greenwich Village, and East Harlem. In New York's other boroughs, Italians concentrated at the Brooklyn end of bridges to Manhattan and along several major avenues and public transportation routes in the Bronx. In 1905 most of these neighborhoods were predominantly areas of first settlement; Greenwich Village, East Harlem and Brooklyn also absorbed small groups of immigrants abandoning their initial homes in southern Manhattan.

Elizabeth Street and the Fourteenth Ward could claim a long history as an important residential area in lower Manhattan.[3] In the late eighteenth century, the eastern boundary of the Fourteenth Ward (the Bowery) was a country lane leading to Manhattan's farmlands; and the northern part of the ward, while already cut by today's streets, still contained pastures and gardens. It was between 1800 and 1850 that the ward filled rapidly with private dwelling houses. At this time the Fourteenth Ward provided housing for shipyard workers and mechanics as well as for some more prosperous families.[4] It was a native bastion—but to its south (in the Sixth Ward) grew the city's first immigrant slums.

By 1850, when New York's population reached 515,647, Irish immigrants began moving northward from the Sixth into the Fourteenth

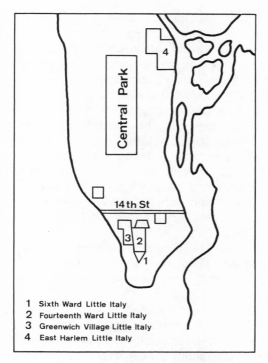

1 Sixth Ward Little Italy
2 Fourteenth Ward Little Italy
3 Greenwich Village Little Italy
4 East Harlem Little Italy

Map 5-1. Manhattan Little Italies (New York City Tenement House Department, *First Report.* New York: Martin B. Brown, 1904)).

Ward. In response, native-born residents almost completely abandoned the ward in the years after the Civil War. Rather than selling their lands and homes there, they leased them to speculative builders and lessees.

The population of the 104-acre Fourteenth Ward continued to grow rapidly in the years following the Civil War. The home of 25,196 in 1850, the ward housed 30,171 by 1880, and 35,420 by 1900 — an average of 339 persons per acre. The Irish dominated what had become an entirely immigrant residential area. After 1860 Italians in small numbers sought homes in the ward; their numbers increased rapidly during the 1880's. By 1890 two-thirds of its occupants were Italians and only one-third were Irish. Ten years later Italians had completely taken over the ward.[5] Only a scattering of elderly Irish immigrants remained.

As the population of the Fourteenth Ward changed, so did its housing. Between 1865 and 1900, speculators built over 150 tenements in the area, mainly uniform barracks specifically intended for low-cost rental to poor immigrants. Builders erected tenements in front of older houses, produc-

67

ing "front" and "rear" buildings on a single lot. Other owners divided older dwelling houses into several apartments. This burst of housing speculation during the last half of the nineteenth century guaranteed a mixture of housing types on every block of the area. (Sources for the study of Elizabeth Street housing are discussed in Appendix B.)

Over one hundred tenements bordered Elizabeth Street in 1905. Housing reformers distinguished four types: the "rear" tenement, the "barracks" type of old law tenement, the "dumbbell" old law tenement, and the "new law" tenement. (By definition, all tenements contained three or more apartments.) A very small number of dwellings with fewer than three apartments, and an even smaller number of single-family houses formed a negligible part of Elizabeth Street housing. Eight percent of Elizabeth Street apartments were in "rear" tenements. Almost half were in "barracks." A third were in "dumbbells" and about seven percent were in "new law" tenements.

Figures 5-1 through 5-4 show the floorplans of each of these apartment types. In design, apartment size, and facilities Elizabeth Street buildings varied somewhat, but less so than did agrotown housing. Reformers characterized rear tenements—accessible only through an alley or the tenement built on the front of the lot—as the least desirable tenement type. Toilets for these buildings were always in the yard separating them from the front tenements, and in general the rooms were smaller than in other buildings. They were also dark, because of their location.

"Railroad flats" with rooms strung in a straight line like railroad cars on a track characterized buildings erected specifically for rental at low cost. The oldest such buildings, the "barracks" built between 1850 and 1880, were of brick, four or five stories tall. Basements and first floors often contained rooms for stores. Narrow, steep and unlighted staircases in central hallways led to upstairs apartments. Sinks and, in the newer barracks, toilets found their place off the narrow corridor on each floor landing. Barracks apartments typically contained two and three rooms. Only rooms facing the street or back yard had windows, so these apartments, too, were quite dark. The room entered from the hallway possessed vents for attaching a heating or cooking stove; in the newer barracks, this room also boasted a tiny sink. Otherwise, water supply and toilets were in the hallways or outside.

Architects attempting to correct some of the worst aspects of the barracks tenements created dumbbell apartments in 1879, but like their predecessors, these flats, too, followed the railroad plan. The central stairway remained tiny and steep, and the central hallway on each floor

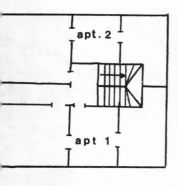

A REAR TENEMENT

REAR TENEMENT [A CONVERTED SINGLE FAMILY HOUSE]

Figure 5-1. Rear Tenements

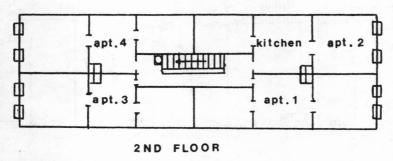

2ND FLOOR

Figure 5-2. A Barracks Tenement

69

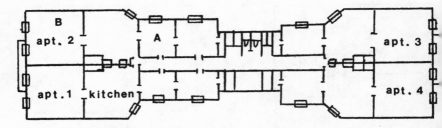

Figure 5-3. A Dumbbell Tenement

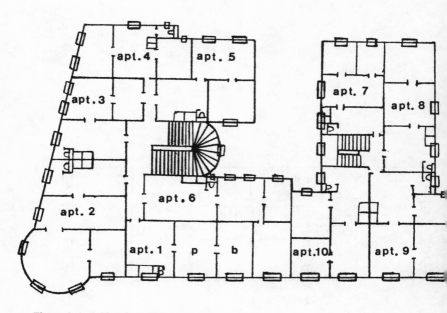

Figure 5-4. A New Law Tenement

remained narrow—as did the four apartments that opened off it. From the hallway, one entered a room equipped with sink and laundry tubs. With its own tiny window onto a central airshaft, this room inevitably became the kitchen. A "front" room faced street or rear yard, while one or two small "back" rooms obtained light from the airshaft. Back rooms often possessed independent doorways to the corridors, an addition that architects specifically called a concession to the fact that many New York residents kept boarders. Flush toilets were located outside, in the hallway. Critics found dumbbells only a small improvement over the barracks; they complained that it was impossible to construct "healthy" rental dwellings on the typical narrow New York lot.[6]

After heroic efforts by New York reformers, New York State passed new tenement building regulations in 1901: New York builders responded with the "new law" tenement. By 1905, there were nineteen new law tenements in the Fourteenth Ward. Italian builders had constructed a number of them. New law tenements extended over several narrow lots, so their plans could depart from the railroad flat design. The new law demanded larger and better fireproof hallways with lighting. Most Elizabeth Street new law apartments had three or four rooms; these rooms were a little larger than dumbbell rooms and each boasted a window. Residents continued to enter the kitchen (now equipped with toilet as well as with sink, vents and laundry tubs), but interior rooms were often accessible only through other rooms, as in apartment 1, Figure 5-4. Not a single apartment on Elizabeth Street, even in the new law apartments, provided a bath.

New York's new housing laws also required landlords to improve older tenements by constructing vents and inserting internal windows in barracks apartments, by replacing yard pit toilets ("school sinks," unattached to the city sewer) with sanitary toilet facilities and by providing fire escapes. However reluctantly, many Elizabeth Street landlords filed plans for making these alterations between 1901 and 1910. Usually they installed windows and built toilets or water supplies (in hallways or apartments).

The fact that they did so may have reflected their desire to keep their tenants more than a wish to comply with city law, which was poorly enforced. For landlords were not alone in their interest in the Fourteenth Ward: Commercial and industrial enterprises had long competed with them for area land. Already in the nineteenth century, the ward became what urban sociologists call a "zone of transition." Transition was well underway when Sicilians began arriving on Elizabeth Street. Buildings on streets parallel to Broadway were converted to loft and warehouse useage in the 1880's and 1890's, when factories appeared all over this part of southern Manhattan. By 1900, almost every block in the ward housed some kind of manufacturing enterprise. The change in the ward was significant. Authors of *The Tenement House Problem* found it necessary in 1903 to correct a common public belief that business had succeeded in "driving out the tenement houses in the quarter."[7]

Elizabeth Street shared with the rest of the ward this transitional character, as Map 5-2 shows. Tenement buildings covered about half of its lots, mixed with commercial and light manufacturing buildings. The Bowery and the other large streets surrounding the ward provided stores, hotels and banks, as well as major public transportation routes. Western and southern blocks of the area had the highest proportions of industrial and warehouse buildings, and garment shops, small candy and box factories, printing establishments, furniture, carriage and shoe factories, and one large "provisions" house offered workplaces among the residences. Schools, churches, and fire stations were also scattered haphazardly through the ward. Every block contained stores and shops in the tenements, and Elizabeth Street alone contained two distinct street pushcart markets.

Competition between residential and other interests continued in the twentieth century, but the transition on Elizabeth Street slowed. By tearing down and replacing barracks, builders and landlords succeeded for almost fifteen years in increasing available housing—the last new law tenement erected in the Fourteenth Ward began renting in 1913. City planning played a larger role in threatening local housing supply during these years than did industrial competition. In 1907, the City cut a new street—Kenmare—through the heart of the Fourteenth Ward. Its goal was to improve traffic access to the Williamsburgh Bridge. New housing replaced every apartment destroyed. School building became a kind of unintentional form of urban renewal, for new schools always replaced the oldest housing in the Fourteenth Ward. Thus, by 1915, the number of apartments available on Elizabeth Street had increased, but only slightly, to nineteen hundred. The housing supply also improved, for more than twice as many of these apartments were now in new law buildings. After 1915, area housing supply changed little. Industries, too, lost interest in the Fourteenth Ward as factories sought locations better served by transportation.

Unfortunately, no Sicilian immigrant arriving to make a new home on Elizabeth Street recorded his or her impression of this new urban environment. Many of the street's physical features, if compared to a Sicilian agrotown, would have seemed new and unfamiliar—the height

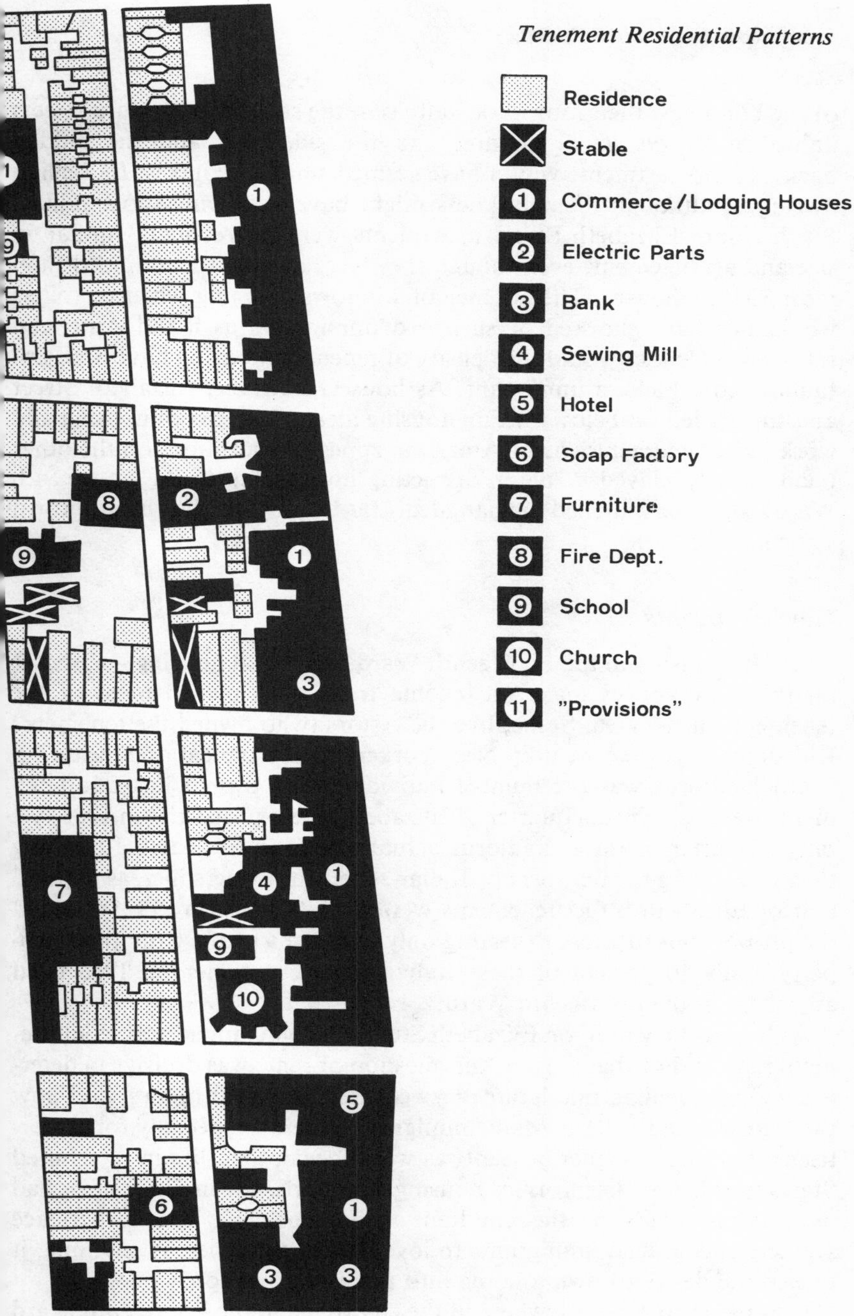

Tenement Residential Patterns

- Residence
- Stable
- ① Commerce / Lodging Houses
- ② Electric Parts
- ③ Bank
- ④ Sewing Mill
- ⑤ Hotel
- ⑥ Soap Factory
- ⑦ Furniture
- ⑧ Fire Dept.
- ⑨ School
- ⑩ Church
- ⑪ "Provisions"

Map 5-2. Elizabeth Street Land Use, 1905

of the buildings, their long dark staircases, the straight New York streets unbroken by *cortile* or square, and the sidewalks and the hidden backyards. Apartments would have seemed small in contrast to Sicilian dwellings, although their darkness might have been only too familiar. Furthermore Elizabeth Street apartments were depressingly similar in size and arrangement, even though they were also better equipped than most Sicilian houses. The absence of windows, running water or toilets would not have shocked or surprised immigrants as it did American reformers. Neither would the density of tenement housing have been unfamiliar to a Sicilian immigrant. As houses, however, Elizabeth Street apartments fell far below Sicilian housing ideals. The mix of housing and work places characteristic of American zones of transition, on the other hand, clearly played a role in attracting immigrants to the Fourteenth Ward. This mix matched Sicilian ideals far better than did the agrotown settlement pattern.

New Restraints

All the housing in the Fourteenth Ward was rental housing — absentee landlords hoping to make an income from rents owned most of the tenements in the area. Some, like the Astors (who owned the tenements Riis described) were wealthy New Yorkers. More typical of Fourteenth Ward landlords was the humble individual who owned just one tenement. Italians owned a quarter of Elizabeth Street properties in 1905, yet only a quarter of these landlords actually lived in or near the building they owned. As the numbers of Italian tenement owners increased (until half of Elizabeth Street tenements were in their hands by 1925), so did the proportions of those expecting only to make a profit from their property. Only 10 percent of these Italian tenement owners in 1925 lived anywhere in the Fourteenth Ward.

As long as they lived on Elizabeth Street, Sicilian immigrants would remain renters. For that reason "the question of rent" was decisive in determining how Sicilian immigrants viewed their tenement homes, and how they chose a home there. Many immigrant renters — especially former artisans, but many former peasants as well — began their life in the United States well below their former housing standards, for in Sicily most had been homeowners or the children of homeowners. This experience scarcely encouraged immigrants to love their new homes; if anything, it turned the desire to own a home into a burning passion.

Compared to rents elsewhere in the city, rents in the Fourteenth Ward were quite low. A quarter of the apartments on Elizabeth Street had two rooms, with rents ranging from about $6.40 monthly for a rear tenement to $9.50 monthly for a dumbbell tenement. Slightly over half of Elizabeth Street apartments had three rooms, renting from $8.00 to $15.00 a month. About a fifth of the street's apartments had four rooms, renting for from $9.00 a month in rear tenements to almost $20.00 a month in some new law tenements.[8]

However, area rents appear much higher when expressed as a proportion of an unskilled laborer's income. A common laborer earned about $475 yearly during the first decade of the century.[9] The rental of a two-room barracks apartment required only 20 percent of that income, while a new law four-room apartment could consume over 50 percent of a laborer's income. The average rental of an Elizabeth Street apartment in the first decade of the century was about $12.50, or almost a third of a laborer's monthly income.[10]

Rents appear still higher when compared to Sicilian housing costs. Most Sicilians lived cost-free during the years following their marriages, for they had paid their housing costs by contributing to their parents, who bought houses for them. Even Sicilian renters customarily spent less than a fifth of family income on rent. Were Sicilian immigrants shocked by New York rentals? Lillian Betts (a social worker who lived for a time among Fourteenth Ward Italians) noted suggestively, "Rent is the outlay they resent."[11]

Sicilian habits of using space flexibly and defining the private dwelling as the nuclear family's eating and sleeping space proved useful tools in solving the problem posed by high rents. As Riis observed, Sicilians lived two and sometimes three families to an apartment. Census takers called these arrangements "partner households." Almost a fifth of Elizabeth Street apartments in 1905 contained a partner household.

Careful observers found that partner households functioned not as one but as several households. In three–and four-room apartments, immigrant families used space in much the same ways the brothers Domenico and Baldassare F. had in Sambuca. The families remained economically independent, one family subletting a room from the other.[12] The families did not eat together; they did not own (but might use) household goods in common. Annie Daniel, a reformer familiar with Elizabeth Street's sweated garment workers, reached the same conclusion as Lillian Betts: The families sharing an apartment "lived entirely separately."[13] They divided the space of the apartment between them so that each family had its own "private dwelling" for eating and sleeping, while sharing the kitchen and its cooking stove and sink.

By forming a partner household, families reduced their rent to less than ten dollars a month, or one-quarter of a laborer's wages. Riis correctly analyzed the origin of overcrowding in "high rent, slack work and low wages," and Lillian Betts concurred, noting "It is the rents that compel the combination of families . . . ."[14]

Despite strong economic incentives, families formed partner households only under particular spatial conditions. Not all apartments could be divided easily in ways that Sicilians found appropriate. (See Table 5-1.) Three rooms seemed necessary, and their arrangement also played a significant role. Most new law tenements, for example, contained some apartments like "1" in Figure 5-4. In that apartment, entrance to room "b" was through room "p," so a family occupying "b" could only enter it by walking through the "private dwelling" of its partner family. In the dumbbell apartments, by contrast, entrance to every room in all apartments was through the shared kitchen or through the common hallways: A family occupying room "A" in Figure 5-3 entered without violating the privacy of the family in room "B." Partner households occupied a third of the apartments in buildings like these, while only 23 percent of the apartments in buildings with some apartments of the first design contained partner households.

Table 5-1. Family, House and Partner Household

Family Size	% Partner Household	N
2	45%	37
3	39	44
4	35	39
5	31	28
6	18	22
7	12	23
Family Type[a]		
Young Couple	46%	25
Young Family[b]	34	97
Transitional Family[c]	18	45
Old Family[d]	35	20
Old Couple	35	5
Tenement Apartment Size		
2 Rooms	7%	23
2 and 3 Rooms	17	38
3 Rooms	18	52
3 and 4 Rooms	25	39

[a]Avery M. Guest, "Patterns of Family Location," *Demography* 9 (1972): 161.
[b]No working-age children
[c]Some working-age children
[d]All children working age

Usually, only families willing to sleep together in one room could occupy a partner household: Young couples, old couples and those with few or only very young children did so in above-average proportions. Families with growing sons and daughters, however, sought space to divide sleeping quarters by gender. Three children seemed to form the dividing line; the proportion of families living in nuclear households increased once family size reached six. Families with six members rented an average of 2.8 rooms, while smaller families (regardless of size) rented only 2.4 rooms. By 1915, when the numbers of recently arrived small and young families had declined, the partner household had almost disappeared from Elizabeth Street.

Elizabeth Street apartments placed real limits on an immigrant family's desire for living space; here there were only "little nests." Middle-class, skilled and unskilled families alike rented an average of 2.4 rooms. This means that large numbers of artisan families and some former peasants began their life in the United States by occupying quarters considerably smaller than their Sicilian homes. Even in the early years of the century, as the population of the Fourteenth Ward increased rapidly, immigrants looking for homes there refused to rent the smallest apartments. Some rear tenements in 1905 were abandoned, and in occupied rear tenements vacancy rates were also high. By 1915 vacancy rates in other older buildings also increased, to 25 percent in barracks, for example; by 1925, with area population declining, only the new law tenements with their larger apartments enjoyed full occupancy.

In their efforts to keep rents low or to purchase more space as family size increased, immigrant families, like dissatisfied renters everywhere, moved often. "One never," wrote a puzzled Lillian Betts from her tenement home, "becomes accustomed to the kaleidoscopic changes of one's neighbors." Families could move in, "be as settled at the end of two hours as at the end of two months," or "move out in half an hour."[15] Four-fifths of 765 Elizabeth Street families traced in subsequent census listings disappeared from the Fourteenth Ward before the 1915 count. Not all these moves, of course, were motivated by the search for better housing: As an area of first settlement, Elizabeth Street housed considerable numbers of families and individuals with no committment to residence in the United States or to their jobs in New York. But the desire for better housing did motivate the immigrant families who had not left the ward by 1915. All occupied a new apartment, mainly on Elizabeth Street within one or two blocks of their homes in 1905. All improved their housing by moving.

New Opportunities

Dissatisfaction with existing housing encouraged immigrants to move frequently as incomes and family needs for space changed. High rates of residential mobility on Elizabeth Street had a number of desirable social consequences. It gave immigrants considerable choice over the exact location of their homes, a choice denied agrotown residents. Unlike Sicilian peasants, immigrants could choose to live near their changing workplaces. Unlike agrotown homeowners, they could also usually live near whichever other families they chose. Social clusters on Elizabeth Street could reflect immigrant ideals, and suggest that new expectations developing during migration guided immigrant residential choices. The expectation of closer relations to the *parenti* and, to a lesser extent, to the *paesani* would be further reinforced by urban life in the United States.

In choosing a house, middle class, skilled and unskilled immigrants made no effort to segregate themselves spatially; they were, after all, accustomed to living physically close to families of varied occupations and status, and they sometimes found cross-class social ties useful. The proportion of middle-class immigrants varied randomly from 2 to 6 percent of the occupants of any Elizabeth Street block. The proportion of unskilled workers was high on every block and in almost every tenement. As in Sicily, both more and less prosperous immigrants lived relatively close to each other, as did older and younger families. This pattern persisted through time.

The desire to keep home and workplace close together did, however, encourage considerable clustering among workers in several occupations. Male clothing workers lived in disproportionate numbers close to a garment factory located between Broome and Spring Streets. About half of the married women living on the blocks adjacent to this sewing mill did some variety of garment work; on streets to the west fewer married women worked sewing garments. (This difference was not a product of underenumeration of women workers by particular census takers.) Peddlers, too, lived close to their markets or, more accurately, created market areas near their homes. Fish and cheese peddlers clustered on the southern blocks of the street, while fruit and vegetable peddlers concentrated between Prince and E. Houston Streets. Fish peddlers formed especially dense clusters, almost completely filling the tenements at 11 and 125 Elizabeth Street. In fact, three-quarters of the fish peddlers on Elizabeth Street lived in only five tenements.

Other occupational clusters could not have reflected work locations. Dockworkers, fishermen and longshoremen lived near the fish peddlers and garment workers on the southern blocks of Elizabeth Street, while unskilled day laborers and skilled workers in the building trades clustered further north among the fruit and vegetable peddlers. Occupational clusters like these undoubtedly reflected the fact that *paesani* and kin aided each other in finding work as well as housing. The occupational clusters did, in fact, neatly overlap with the two large migration chains from the regions surrounding Palermo and Sciacca. Households with a member named Rosalia (Palermo) concentrated on Elizabeth Street between Prince and E. Houston and around the corner between Mott and Elizabeth. Households with members named Calogera/a (Sciacca) spread through several blocks further south. Smaller chains followed a similar pattern, forming recognizeable clusters that nevertheless always encompassed several tenements and usually stretched for two or more blocks. Tenement houses were almost never Sicilian villages replanted on the Lower East Side.

Immigrants lived closer to their *casa* kin than had agrotown residents, as Table 5-2 shows. A slight matriarchal bias in Sicilian kinship ideals — emotional preference for the relatives of the wife/mother — may have influenced immigrants' choice of neighbors, for married daughters lived closer to their married sisters and their parents than did married sons. Immigrants, who had become increasingly involved with their *parenti* during migration, strengthened these ties also by choosing to live close together on Elizabeth Street. The size of the kin network affected residential choice as well. A family with only one kinsman of any type living on Elizabeth Street offered a place in the apartment in 80 percent of the cases. Fully three-quarters of the relatives of families with kin ties to seven or more other families or individuals lived outside the tenement building. When the size of the kin network reached ten families or more, only about two-thirds lived on the same block or directly across the street. Thus, a sizeable minority of kin in these unusually large networks lived rather far away by Sicilian standards.

Table 5-2. Kin Clusters

KIN TIE	% Living in Same		N
	Tenement	Block	
Parents/Married Daughter	92	8	142
Parents/Married Son	77	8	95
Two Married Sisters	70	23	131
Two Married Brothers	34	37	111
Married Sister/			
Married Brother	70	19	212
Two *Parenti*	45	23	223

A tenement provided apartments for at least twice as many families a a Sicilian *cortile*; it, rather than the still-larger block, street corner, o street, was the geographical equivalent of the Sicilian immediat neighborhood in the *cortile*. The social diversity of the tenement in Nev York often surpassed that of the *cortile*. Take, for example, 25! Elizabeth Street, a dumbbell tenement. In 1905 it housed 109 people (2 families) in 20 two room and three room apartments: Living there were 2 laborers, 12 home garment finishers, 9 garment workers, 3 fruit peddlers, masons, 2 barbers, a gilder, an ironworker, a bricklayer, a laundress, a ho carrier, and a flower-maker. Young families predominated at 259 Elizabeth but 8 of the tenement's families already had children of working age. Recen arrivals were a majority, but 9 families had been in the United State more than five years. And, while half of the families at 259 Elizabeth ha a kinsman living in the tenement (and 6 had other relatives livin elsewhere on Elizabeth Street), no single kin or *paesani* chain linked eve a small group of the inhabitants.

Immigrants on Elizabeth Street re-created a familiar social setting an actually improved on the socially mixed agrotown *cortile*. Better-off an less well-off, younger and older families lived physically close. Relative of the *casa* lived in the same tenement, often within calling or shoutin distance. Immigrants could also continue to explore the rewards of socia involvement with their *parenti*, building on their experiences in chai migration. *Paesani*—a potential pool of friends—were a significan minority among immigrants' immediate neighbors. Most important, thi social diversity coexisted with a short trip to work, a fact that woul liberate many immigrant men from their undesirably limited family an social roles in Sicilian agrotowns. The outlook for achieving Sicilia social ideals on Elizabeth Street seemed good; the tenements matche Sicilians' ideals far better than had their original agrotown homes.

New Restraint or New Ideal? The Malleable Household and the Kitchen Salotto

Like immigrants everywhere in the United States, Sicilians o Elizabeth Street formed "malleable households," inviting kin and nonki to board in their households. About a fifth of Elizabeth Street families i 1905 had relatives or boarders, mostly male, living with them in thei apartment homes. Boarding was unknown in Sicily; an outsider becam part of the household there only by assuming the role of a child or se vant in the family. Immigrant boarders did not assume that role, yet the ate and slept with their host family, after paying a flat weekly fee in exchange for food and sleeping space.[16] The very term used for these paying guests — *bordanti*, a word with no Sicilian or Italian equivalent — suggests the newness of a social relationship, which, in Sicilian ideals, threatened nuclear family privacy and solidarity, and exposed wives and daughters to the temptations of other men.[17]

Although boarders contributed to the family income, boarding was not primarily a temporary response to the restraint of high rents by low-income families. Partner households, just such a response, quickly disappeared on Elizabeth Street, but households with boarders or boarding relatives appeared almost as frequently in 1915 and 1925 as in 1905. A typical Elizabeth Street family kept fewer than two boarders, who thus contributed about 10 percent of family income. Even partner households kept boarders, although the economic incentive for doing so was low in such families. The families of unskilled laborers or recent arrivals were no more likely to keep boarders than were other families. Boarders did not usually replace the financial contributions of departed children in elderly families, for the vast majority of boarders and boarding relatives in 1905 lived with a peer, not a person of their parents' generation. Furthermore, people lacking complete families of their own could have chosen to live as did such men in Sambuca, in nonfamily households of two or three, at only slightly higher cost than a boarding fee. Yet only 3 percent of Elizabeth Street apartments in 1905 contained such a nonfamily group, and by 1915 this type of household had completely disappeared.[18] Both immigrant families and immigrants without families may have had incentives to create boarding; but they did not do so only in response to financial or environmental restraints. Their decision to create a system of family boarding suggests that changes in their social ideals had occurred during migration.

Tenement families treated boarders who were kinsmen slightly differently from unrelated boarders — but only slightly. For example, families brought relatives into their homes regardless of the size of the apartments they occupied, while families taking in boarders rented slightly larger than average apartments. Significantly, a family renting a two-room apartment was as likely to invite a relative into its home as was the family living in a larger apartment, but families in two-room apartments included nonkin in below-average proportions. Whether kin or nonkin, however, boarders ate with the family, and usually slept in the kitchen, sharing that sleeping space with the family's older sons.[19] Immigrants sometimes called boarders "boys" (since they lived without wives) a term that suggests that not all vestiges of the childlike status of the outsider in the household disappeared immediately with the creation of boarding. [20]

A closer look at partner households also indicated that at least some were also malleable households; not all "lived as Sicilian neighbors" in their shared apartments. The two families in a partner household had to cooperate in providing gas for lighting all parts of the new law apartments — individual gas accounts were impossible. In practice, this mean that families had to agree on when and how to feed the coin-operated gas meter — a simple but very real form of joint financial planning. Some families shared not only the partner-household kitchen, the kitchen stove, and household equipment, but also food, some meals, and child care. [21] Thus, like families keeping boarders, a number of partner household families seemed surprisingly unconcerned about the private space and private functions so vigorously defended in Sicilian agrotowns.

Elizabeth Street immigrants chose to allow outsiders to eat and sleep together with nuclear family members. Their choice signals a significant and conscious departure from Sicilian ideals about nuclear family solidarity in its competition with others. Immigrants accepted new kinds of cooperation at the very center of family life. Just as the ideal of family solidarity had defined the division of private from public space within the Sicilian house, departures from that ideal produced a new division of space in Elizabeth Street apartments.

In the temporary partner households, the kitchen often became a kind of shared *cortile*. Nuclear households, however, made the kitchen the center of family life. [22] Always heated by the stove, the room became the *soggiorno* (dining and living area); in most two-room and three-room apartments it served nights as the boy's bedroom. In other words, the tenement kitchen became the equivalent of a Sicilian family's private dwelling area, much like the simple peasant house in agrotowns. In New York, however, it is clear that immigrants expected to use the kitchen as a *salotto* too. This was a surprising departure from Sicilian practice.

The kitchen in a two-room apartment was decorated, and sometime furnished, with elements from both Sicilian bedrooms and Sicilian good rooms. The arrangement of saints' pictures, holy items, palms and ribbons that, in Sicily, hung at the head of the marital bed, often graced the kitchen wall in New York. [23] Similarly, the *turnialettu*, a deep flounce of cloth that encircled the Sicilian bed, hiding the storage space beneath it appeared in New York draped around sinks and laundry tubs or under the shelves of kitchen dish cupboards. New York kitchens also frequently displayed worldly goods arranged in a large china cupboard or on a dresser with a lace or lace-edged cloth: the familiar coffee cups, clocks, pictures, certificates, mirrors, and mementoes.[24] Immigrants obviously expected to entertain guests in the very room that served them as private space, as the center of family life.

Still, the ideal of the good room remained strong among immigrants, and many families eventually erected one in a three-room or four-room apartment. Children's earnings allowed families to purchase furnishings, generally overstuffed, for a separate *salotto*.[25] This good room served as a sleeping room for older daughters; during the day women often chose to work there because it was usually the room facing street or yard and consequently better lit.[26] But it seems to have served only rarely as a *salotto*; the kitchen remained the favored place for visiting and entertaining.

The formation of malleable households and the decoration of the kitchen *salotto* provide further evidence that Sicilian immigrants developed increasingly positive expectations of social ties to people outside the *casa* during and after migration. They no longer seemed to fear the competitive dangers of allowing them to enter freely the very center of family life. The concluding chapter returns to this and other aspects of immigrant social life, offering an interpretation of society and culture among Italian immigrants living in the United States.

Environmental Change and Residential Patterns in New York

New York tenement houses could not and did not alone produce distinctive tenement residential patterns. In fact, Elizabeth Street's residential patterns differed somewhat from those on the other — the Jewish — side of the Bowery, even though housing on both sides was roughly similar. Jews, for example, never lived in partner households, but took in larger numbers of boarders than did Sicilians. The experiences of Elizabeth Street's immigrants provided no evidence to support material determinism.

New residential patterns emerged on Elizabeth Street as Sicilian immigrants responded creatively to some new environmental restraints and enjoyed their new-found freedom from the old environmental restraints imposed by the agrotown. Amos Rapoport was certainly correct in stressing the importance of what an environment made impossible. High rents, for example, made it difficult for immigrants to live as nuclear families during their early years in the United States; and high rents made it even more difficult for immigrants to remain many years in a single

83

apartment, even if they lived long in the Fourteenth Ward. In Sicily low residential mobility encouraged close ties among female neighbors; in New York that precondition would not exist. On the other hand, mobile renters in New York's tenements could create residential patterns that should have been conducive to achieving their social ideals — whether old ones or newly emerging ones.

My discussion of the mixed match of tenement and immigrants' needs and desires points to the problem that faced Elizabeth Street residents: The tenements matched Sicilian social ideals far better than they matched Sicilian housing ideals. The major consequence of moving from agrotown to tenement was that immigrants found their housing and social ideals in conflict.

The young immigrant family, newly arrived in the United States, did not necessarily perceive that conflict immediately and clearly. Young families, after all, had low incomes; they could, when necessary, live in small quarters without offending their own notions of propriety. Furthermore, they moved about more frequently than immigrant families as a whole (only 12 percent remained in the Fourteenth Ward from 1905 to 1915) and could not enjoy the social benefits of the tenement neighborhood as fully as less mobile families. Concerned with jobs, with whether or not to return to Italy, and with making ends meet, these families had few motives for worrying about their unachieved housing ideals.

The conflict between housing and social ideals grew in families that stopped moving frequently as their eldest children began earning wages (Almost half of such Elizabeth Street families remained in the Fourteenth Ward from 1905 to 1915.) Child wage earners allowed the family to consider its housing ideals quite seriously; older families occupied many of the largest apartments on Elizabeth Street — the new law tenements.[27] Moving less often, the older family could enjoy to the fullest the social opportunities of the tenement neighborhood. But better housing was in limited supply on Elizabeth Street. Houses for purchase scarcely existed. Most families could never hope to purchase a multifamily tenement, for the down payment alone represented seven to eight times the income of a family with several wage-earning children.[28] The number of new law apartments — the architect's answer to better housing in immigrant neighborhods — increased with time, but older families in 1905 competed for their use with the partner households of younger recently arrived families. And, in any case, new law apartments could not become family property.

Immigrants longer resident in one tenement neighborhood felt sorely this conflict between housing and social ideals. There would be no easy solution to their predicament; they themselves knew they could rarely achieve both simultaneously. Every survey of immigrants' attitudes toward their tenement homes expressed this conflict. Tenement dwellers enjoyed the social life of their neighborhood, and they appreciated that rents there remained lower than elsewhere in the city. But they disliked their dark, small, and rented upstairs apartments.[29] The strength of the conflict between housing and social ideals — and the difficult choices it posed — becomes even clearer when we see how closely immigrants could actually approach their changing social ideals in their everyday life among the tenements.

CHAPTER SIX

Everyday Life in New York

Perhaps the best introduction to everyday life in the tenement neighborhoods of New York is not the written descriptions of a visitor like Betts or Riis, nor the account of an immigrant son like Mario Puzo, but the work of Ralph Fasanella. In his thirty-five years of painting Fasanella captured on canvas his memories of the neighborhoods of lower Manhattan, where he grew up and worked.[1]

In Fasanella's paintings, there are no gray buildings—even though a quick walk down Elizabeth Street on a rainy day provides a reminder that these buildings can, in fact, appear rather grim and foreboding. Instead, Fasanella's tenements are all intense colors. Their facades are completely filled with many windows, which allow brightly colored tenement interiors to break through to the outside street scene. There are curtains of various colors and differing styles at each window, and each window is unique, throwing its own light into the outside world, rather than the other way around. Occasionally, as in "Pie in the Sky," the artist cut away an entire wall, so the viewer gets a better look at life inside the tenement apartment. In other paintings, like "Family Supper," the interior of a tenement kitchen dominates the painting without excluding the world outside; below it, the street, while behind the kitchen loom the tenements, factories and water towers of New York City.

In Fasanella's city, the kitchens, windows, streets and tenements are full of people. "It is rare," writes a critic, "to encounter a Fasanella painting with much empty space in it. If there is a wall it will have a sign painted on it . . . ." Children leave chalk graffiti on sidewalks; laundry hangs on tenement rooftops; women lean out tenement windows; men gather on street corners. But, his critic continues, "there are few single individuals." Instead, there are masses of humanity.[2]

Fasanella's painted memories belong, of course, to only one man—man who obviously loved the city and the intense coming-together of people possible in urban immigrant neighborhoods. His humanity-filled

86

canvasses share much with the Italian immigrant neighborhoods described in immigrant novels and autobiographies and in the reports of social workers and city officials. However ugly the tenements themselves, tenement life, as Lillian Betts noted and Fasanella confirmed, was kaleidoscopic—densely-crowded, group-oriented, an ever-shifting world of changing social and physical boundaries. The tenements matched Sicilian social ideals quite well; many immigrants had the opportunity to live as they chose on Elizabeth Street. Although still financially poor, every peasant immigrant family improved its social resources by moving to New York.

A Typical Day

By comparing the lives of two immigrant households, we quickly grasp one reason that Fasanella painted his interiors so brightly. Although some occupation-related differences persisted on Elizabeth Street, almost every Sicilian immigrant family lived in the tenements much as had artisans in Sicilian agrotowns. The families compared below are based on real ones living in 1905 at 233–35 Elizabeth Street. See Table 6-1, which summarizes each household and its members. Their home, a new law tenement, is pictured in Figure 6-1.

Table 6-1. Two Immigrant Households, 1905

VITALE,	Vincenzo	Head	35	Grocer
	Giuseppa	Wife	33	Housework
	Angelina	Daughter	14	Candy Factory
	Gandolfo	Son	12	School
	Maria	Daughter	10	School
	Grazia	Daughter	7	School
	Pietro	Son	4	–
BENTAVIGNA,	Marianno	Head	26	Laborer
	Rosa	Wife	25	Home Finisher
	Giovanni	Son	7	School
	Maria	Daughter	4	–
	Giacomo	Son	1	–
MARIA,	Gandolfo	Partner	29	Laborer
	Antonina	Wife	28	Home Finisher
	Giuseppe	Son	4	–
	Giachino	Son	1	–
RE,	Michele	Partner	29	Hod Carrier
	Antonina	Wife	26	Housework
	Vincenzo	Son	6	School
	Giuseppe	Son	1	–

Figure 6-1. 233-35 Elizabeth Street

Vincenzo Vitale, the grocer, rose very early to enter his store from the apartment behind it. He received a shipment of rolls and bread from a nearby bakery; shortly thereafter, his son Gandolfo took a sack of breads to make deliveries to regular customers.[3] By 6 A.M. his wife Giuseppa and his little son Pietro joined him, helping during this time of day.[4] The grocer's daughter Angelina cooked coffee for the younger children, and, taking her bread with her, walked westward toward the candy factory on Mott Street where she worked.[5] Returning from his chores, son Gandolfo and his two younger sisters left for school, prob- ably P.S. 21, only a block away. During the morning hours, Vincenzo Vitale tended to the grocery business. He received his weekly payment from the fruit peddler who parked his pushcart in the space in front of his store. Later he met at a local cafe with an importer of Italian pro- ducts.[6] To do so, he left the store with his wife, who interrupted her cleaning chores to be there. Then she returned to her housework: making and folding beds, scrubbing the "oil cloth" kitchen floor and beginning to wash clothes in hot water drawn from a boiler above the big black stove.[7] The grocer's young son Pietro stayed with his mother as she moved from store to apartment and back again.

At noon, the children of the family returned from school, and Giuseppa cooked a lunch of eggs and leftover potatoes before returning again to the store to help her husband.[8] Staying there longer than usual, she had not finished her washing by the time her three children again returned from school in the midafternoon. Giuseppa therefore left the chore of hanging clothes out the back windows to her daughters Maria and Grazia. While son Gandolfo and Vincenzo Vitale sat in the grocery store, she went out into the street to purchase vegetables from the pushcarts there.[9] When she returned, her daughters had taken the youngest child, Pietro, with them to play in the street.[10] The mother began cooking an evening meal of meat and beans. Late in the afternoon, when her older daughter returned from work, she sat with her in their good room while Angelina received a music lesson at an old piano from a young *pro- fessore*.[11] The grocer came to drink coffee with this young man, leaving the store to his son.[12]

The family gathered for their evening meal quite late, after Vincenzo and Gandolfo had closed the store. The family sat in the kitchen under the gas light for most of the evening.[13] After dinner, the grocer's wife made buttonholes on men's jackets, while the grocer talked about business with his son; the two school-aged daughters did the dishes and then looked at their school work. Angelina wanted to iron the dress that she would wear the next day, but her father protested that the kitchen became too warm when the stove was lit so often.[14] At about ten o'clock the entire family went to sleep.

The day also started early for the Bentavigna family. Marianno Ben- tavigna and his partner Gandolfo Maria were laborers on the same digg- ing job. They, their wives, and the small children came into the kitchen from their sleeping rooms at the same time. His wife Antonina sent one child for bread, while making coffee.[15] The wife of Bentavigna's third partner, Michele Re, appeared slightly later, and cooked coffee in her pot. The seven small children of the three families played on the floor of the kitchen while their mothers made beds. Rosa Bentavigna walked to the entrance of a nearby sewing mill, arriving there just as streams of women were entering the building.[16] Rosa Bentavigna found the older woman who normally went and obtained for her bundles of basting work. She carried these back to her home, where she distributed them to the two other women in her apartment, and to several neighbors as well.[17] During the morning hours, the three women basted pants together in the kitchen, while their preschool children played in the tenement hallway.[18] At noon the older children returned from school, and were sent to purchase salt and sardines. The women ate as they worked;[19] the children, taking their food and their younger siblings with them, left the house.[20]

They returned again in the late afternoon, dragging with them a number of large crates they had found on the street.[21] The sister of one of the partner wives, a woman who lived on the floor below, came to visit and to drink coffee.[22] She said that her children, too, had been looking for wood in the streets, and had not been to school that day.[23] Rosa looked out the window to see if she saw her own children, who had returned again to the street below.[24] As evening approached, the women again sent their children to Vitale's store to purchase food for dinner. Rosa Bentavigna and Antonina Maria expected their husbands to return from their jobs together. They cooked a pot of soup for both families.[25] The third partner, Michele Re, returned later than the other men. He, his wife, and their two children retired to their room while the other families ate. Then Re s wife went to Vitale's store and herself purchased a bit of pickled fish.[26] When she returned, the other families had almost completed their evening meal. She chopped one of the wooden crates into small pieces for fuel, and then took bowls and forks from the kitchen cupboard to prepare dinner for her husband and children.

When the third family finished its evening meal, all the men in the household left to walk together in the street, stopping briefly at a cafe.[27] The three wives worked together washing dishes, and later they unfolded the kitchen bed where Giovanni, Marianno and Vincenzo Re would sleep.[28] They sewed together under a small gas flame until their husbands returned.[29] A neighbor joined them at their work, while her husband played cards with other men in her kitchen.[30] The neighbor left the other women when their husbands returned and soon the entire household was asleep.

Activity, Time and Location

Chapter 4 showed that considerable proportions of immigrant men and women, by migrating to New York, found work that resembled in some ways the work of Sicily's artisans. The comparison of two immigrant households demonstrates further that many aspects of everyday life in New York duplicated the patterns of the Mulè family in chapter 3. A clear division of labor characterized immigrant families, but also allowed some cooperation in a family enterprise, as was true of artisan families in Sicily. In a mixed settlement like Elizabeth Street, where work and home were close, all immigrant men could count on the daily services of a wife, mother or *padrona* (in the case of a boarder) — few would ever have to cook for themselves, as peasant men did. Immigrant children, at least while young, lived much as had Audenzio and Teresa Mulè. And, surprisingly, the tenements — although completely different in form from an artisan's house — helped make immigrant wives' housework much like that of the artisan wife Antonina Mulè.

Like artisans' children, immigrant children could combine work and school. Very young children worked with their mothers; boys and girls did roughly the same chores.[31] Reformers expressed shock when they found children of three years pulling basting threads from pants — but three-year-old workers were actually few.[32] An Italian mother explained why; her children of that age, she said, had to play, they could not work very well.[33] A weekday survey of two Elizabeth Street blocks in the 1890's found only 9 percent of the girls aged six to fourteen and 5 percent of the boys that age at home.[34] Continuing work requirements could, however, lead to higher truancy rates.[35] Children also worked gathering fuel as part of their family responsibilities — Robert Chapin estimated that half of all Italian families in 1909 burned wood scavenged in this way.[36] After the age of nine, boys moved outside the family to work as newsboys, delivery boys, and messengers; the sons of artisans and petty merchants helped their fathers parttime.[37] Daughters continued their earlier activities, helping their mothers and doing piecework production with them.[38]

At age fourteen, most Elizabeth Street children left school for work. Eight of ten sons and only slightly lower proportions of daughters in 1905 earned wages. At this point, the close parent-child work and training relationship typical of Sicilian artisans was abandoned. Daughters found work not with their own mothers, but in garment, box, candy, and flower factories. Boys rarely worked with their own fathers. Like their sisters they found factory jobs, and, while a third were skilled workers of some kind, only a very small number shared their fathers' trades. Few sons worked with their petty entrepreneur fathers; instead many became white collar clerical workers or professionals.

In New York, the household work of wives of skilled and unskilled workers varied but little. Like artisans' wives in Sicily, women on Elizabeth Street could easily combine wage-earning work with child care and household chores. Relatively more wage earning proved an incentive to keep other household chores minimal, and this was more easily accomplished in partner households than in others. Census data for 1905 show that the number of women earning wages both in the garment factory and as home finishers was higher in partner than in nuclear households. Women in such households could earn wages because they sometimes shared supervision of their children.[39]

Women on Elizabeth Street also resembled artisans' wives in Sicily in devoting considerably more time to cooking. Food in New York was cheap in relationship to the income of unskilled workers. Whereas Sicilian laborers purchased bread, beans, oil and greens with as much as 85 percent of their cash incomes, a poor immigrant family could eat like an artisan or *civile* family and spend only 50 percent of its income to do so.[40] American reformers found immigrant diets inadequate.[41] But immigrants knew that they ate well and frequently, and, apparently, with great enjoyment.[42] Chapin found only 10 percent of the very poorest families to be "underfed."[43] Italians in New York regularly ate breakfast, a meal almost completely ignored by all Sicilians (even today).[44] They consumed more pasta, more cheese, and more sugar than the typical Sicilian peasant. They ate meat and drank coffee at least as frequently as the humbler rentier families of an agrotown.[45] Reminisced one woman with pleasurable exaggeration: "Don't you remember how our *paesani* here in America ate to their heart's delight till they were belching like pigs and how they dumped mountains of uneaten food out the window?"[46]

The tenement had its effect on women's household work, however. To continue the Sicilian wife's habit of baking bread required new skills and solutions to new problems. The cheapest types of oil and coal stoves were totally unlike Sicilian stoves and ovens.[47] Most of these ovens could not produce a satisfactory Sicilian loaf—large, with a thick crust.[48] Lillian Betts described her neighbors taking dough to a nearby baker, whose brick oven produced a more familiar product.[49] Many more simply bought bread.

Like wives in Sicily, immigrant wives worked hard to keep their floors clean, but they remained oblivious to other chores that American social workers believed essential. The scrubbed wood or oil-clothed Italian tenement house floor might stand in odd contrast to unpainted and smoke-begrimed walls.[50] And women took no responsibility for garbage, the "mountains of uneaten food," once it was swept or thrown outside the house itself: Tenement house inspectors complained unceasingly of collections of garbage and junk in rear yards, air shafts, cellars and spaces between buildings.[51]

Few immigrant women could, like a typical artisan's wife, count on help with the housework once their families left the partner household to live alone or with boarders and relatives. Nevertheless, the tenement reduced some of the chores normally performed for the artisan family by the lower-status domestic helper. Even primitive "school sinks" and toilets eliminated the Sicilian housewife's attention to this fundamental human sanitary task. Because of limited space, fewer women kept small animals, except for a few caged rabbits, chickens, or birds. (Tenement house inspectors found sheep and goats in tenement cellars, but these larger animals were in the care of men and boys, not women.[52]) And, while housing reformers found the water supply on Elizabeth Street especially poor (it depended on wooden rooftop storage tanks), immigrant women judged water in New York accessible and readily available—which it certainly was, compared to Sicily.[53] Here was a real miracle of the tenements, completely invisible to Americans' eyes.

Finally, the wives of both skilled and unskilled immigrant workers had a new household responsibility on Elizabeth Street, one practically unknown in Sicilian agrotowns—cooking, laundering and cleaning for boarders. The wife in a household with boarders or boarding kin performed household work for an average 1.7 extra men. Only a few families had female boarders who, helping the wife with housework, had a different social role; as in Sicily, these few women became the equivalent of a servant.[54]

New York's industrial, seasonal and school cycles varied more than the inexorable Sicilian agricultural calendar, and these cycles affected virtually every family, again blurring the typical agrotown distinction between lower and higher status work. In New York, tailors, masons and unskilled laborers alike worked five to seven months yearly.[55] Skilled workers in the bulding trades and common laborers suffered unemployment from November to March, while those employed in garment production had little to do from June to September and again from December to April.[56] A few skilled cutters and pressers in garment factories worked ten or eleven months of the year, but only parttime during slack periods.[57] Some skilled workers (barbers, shoemakers or printers) and fewer unskilled workers (porters, drivers, bootblacks) worked more regularly through the year. Among petty entrepreneurs, the coal dealer flourished in winter, while the ice dealer or the peddler of fruits and fresh vegetables was without much work.[58] Only the grocer could depend on year-round demand.

Elizabeth Street women and children also worked seasonally. Women averaged 221 days a year, or about as many days as their husbands.[59] Busy seasons in the garment industry and other sweated industries fell within the school year, so many mothers had real incentives to keep children, especially daughters, home from school during peak seasons.[60] Boys, finding work in a variety of trades with differing cycles, might more easily combine parttime or summertime jobs with longer school attendance.[61]

When immigrant families chose to live in the Fourteenth Ward or close to the father's place of work, they removed the cause responsible for many differences in the everyday lives of Sicilian artisans and peasants. Like Sicilian artisans, all immigrant married men commuted daily from home to workplace. For some the workplace was the home: Professional tailors, temporarily unemployed, sick or disabled men all worked producing garments at home.[62] Petty entrepreneurs also made pasta or ice cream there, or they repaired shoes, watches, or other small items.[63] Like Vincenzo Vitale, Elizabeth Street grocers, barbers, cafe operators and some independent artisans rented or leased ground floor shops that adjoined their apartments.[64] Bakers rented nearby basements, and sometimes they moved their families into these cellar workrooms.[65]

More important, whether porter, handyman, mason or digger on a construction project, waiter in a cafe, agent for an absentee landlord, or factory operative — unskilled or skilled men living on Elizabeth Street could find work in the Fourteenth Ward or nearby in southern Manhattan. When Edward Pratt studied the industrial causes of congestion of population in New York in 1911, he found that 55 percent of the Italian men working below Fourteenth Street walked to work, and 70 percent required less than an hour to travel to their jobs.[66]

Women worked even closer to home. One Elizabeth Street census taker who, unlike some, very carefully enumerated a wide variety of women's work, found 15 percent of the married women on his blocks working for wages outside the home, two-thirds in a garment factory (probably the one only a block away).[67] Over 40 percent of the married women he enumerated worked in their homes or in their husbands' shops — of these 130 were garment finishers.[68] Pratt's survey of Italian women working in Lower Manhattan found that fully three-quarters

94

walked to work and that 85 percent travelled to work in less than one hour.[69]

Like the artisan wife in Sicily, the married woman working "at home" literally worked inside her apartment, usually in the kitchen, but sometimes in the bedroom or best room.[70] Occasionally women moved into tenement hallways to work in warm weather, or onto fire escapes or the tenement roof.[71] No observer described an Elizabeth Street woman doing garment work on the sidewalk or street, although women sometimes sat together evenings on sidewalks in other neighborhoods.[72] Peak garment seasons coincided with early spring and winter weather, limiting work outside a warm or lighted place.[73] The tenement roof, even in warm weather, was still a climb away from the tenement apartment, not just outside the door as was the Sicilian *cortile*. So was the street, which had the further disadvantage of being a busy market area, crowded with men and their pushcarts.[74] Thus the tenements freed men but placed real restraints on the immigrant woman's choice of a workplace.

Like their parents, children chose to work in or very close to their homes. Only 5 percent of Elizabeth Street sons in 1905 actually worked at home, but a fifth of daughters worked there, making garments. The majority of both sons and daughters worked outside the house. Of ten children working in the provisions house on Mott Street (see Map 5-2), nine lived around the block on Elizabeth Street. And of thirteen Fourteenth Ward immigrant children working in an Elizabeth Street metal parts shop, ten lived on Elizabeth Street between Prince and E. Houston. The street's large sewing mill also worked its attractions: More sons and daughters on Elizabeth Street found work in the garment trade than children living on the streets to the west.[75]

Elizabeth Street women, like artisans' wives in Sicily, also did most of their household work within their own four walls. The rear yard pump was fast disappearing in the early twentieth century.[76] By 1911, according to the Immigration Commission, no woman in the area had to leave her tenement in order to get water, although a considerable number of families on Elizabeth Street continued to share a sink with the occupants of six to sixteen other apartments.[77] Caroline Ware reported that "some old timers told of resisting" the installation of water "on the score that anyone who was too lazy to lug her water upstairs was no good."[78] It seems unlikely that these old timers were immigrant women. Cooking facilities, too, were found only in the kitchen, thus locating cooking and related chores there.[79] Although most families owned their own smaller stoves, newer tenements included heavy cast iron ones permanently installed in the same room with sinks and laundry tubs. And even the older tenements offered vents for portable cooking stoves in only one room. Women had a number of options for laundering. As long as the water supply had been a pump in the rear yard, women had gone there in good weather to do this work.[80] But when water was in a dark corridor or in the apartment, women usually did the washing inside their apartments.[81] Drying laundered clothes became a real challenge for tenement wives. In good weather, women carried wet clothes to the roof, but both soot from nearby chimneys and "laundry thieves" endangered the drying clothes.[82] In good weather, women also used clotheslines attached to their buildings, but those in lower apartments worried about a rain of red and blue drips from a colored wash above, or about a shower of refuse tossed from an upstairs window.[83] For many months of the year, laundry hung in the kitchen.[84]

In Sicily, artisan wives had food in their store rooms, and they could count on travelling vendors or poorer women to come to them selling other products. In New York no food peddlers wandered through tenement hallways, although a few did sell ice, notions or sewing machines.[85] The street market food vendors were not far away. In Italy today, women simply shout from upstairs apartments before lowering a basket to exchange coins for purchased food.[86] Lillian Betts—whose fine eye for curious details surely would have caught such a practice—did not report her neighbors shopping this way. Perhaps tenements were too tall or the street too noisy. Instead, Betts reported that women, anxious to avoid climbing the stairways, sent children to make the thrice-daily purchases for meals.[87] She insisted that women might not leave their apartments for months.[88] But here, Betts contradicted her own observations of women travelling with their bread dough to local bakers; other market scenes and descriptions prove that women did at least some of their own shopping.[89] (See, for example, Figure I-1.)

Unlike Sicilian women, however, Elizabeth Street mothers could not easily combine wage-earning or household work with continuous supervision of children's play. We need only recall that in the Bentavigna household three grown women and five children under school age would have had to share a fourteen by eleven foot kitchen if all remained together during the day. Even with minimal needs for personal space, such overcrowding was intolerable. The problem was not unique to Elizabeth Street's Sicilians. Wrote Robert Alston Stevenson in 1901, "What to do with the children in their playtime is a question that bothers mothers all over New York."[90] To provide nearby play places for young children, families erected barriers around fire escapes or sent them to play in the small corridor just outside of the apartment.[91] School children left their mothers far behind as they sought play space on the tenement roof (where they swam in rooftop water tanks during the summer), in rear yards and on the pushcart-jammed street curb.[92] School-aged children often took their younger siblings with them.[93]

Adolescent children continued to spend much free time outside the house. Boys, of course, joined their friends, forming the street-corner groups typical of immigrant sons in immigrant colonies everywhere.[94] Girls, like their mothers, however, enjoyed little or no leisure. In season, there was always sweated work. And even when house chores were finished in the off-season, mothers tried to restrict daughters to "going up and coming down" or to sitting on the stoop with other girls.[95]

Like Sicilian artisans, immigrant men frequently left their homes and families between evening meal and bedtime. In good weather, they, too, gathered with other men in small groups in the streets and rear yards.[96] Weather placed limits on outdoor recreations in New York; furthermore, there were no large open spaces in the Fourteenth Ward that could serve as a central piazza; but in compensation, the Fourteenth Ward in 1910 offered numerous commerical gathering places – 117 saloons, 40 cafes, and 4 five-cent vaudevilles, as well as billiard halls, puppet shows, barbershops and confectionaries.[97] Despite these opportunities, and unlike agrotown residents, immigrant men also casually invited other men to smoke and play cards in their kitchens. Even more ritualized visits, involving the exchange of gifts, might occur there.[98]

The pattern of everyday life on Elizabeth Street resembled that of an agrotown – but only if we can imagine an agrotown detached from its countryside and without its peasants. On a normal winter day a substantial number of unemployed men worked in their upstairs homes or gathered with other men and sought work on the street. Employed men worked nearby in street-level jobs. Working-age children also worked nearby. Married women sat upstairs in their kitchens, sewing pants and supervising the youngest children. Most boys and girls came and went, up and down the long staircases that linked house, school, and street play places. Summer altered the pattern. Unemployed women might join their children on the tenement roof; they spent much time at their apartment windows watching the street below. Men and older boys worked longer hours, but nevertheless usually returned each evening, first to their families for an evening meal and then, if they wished, to the street for casual recreation.

Environmental Change and Everyday Life

Environmental change accompanied the move from Sicilian agrotown to Elizabeth Street tenement, and it affected men, women and children differently. The mixed residential and industrial character of Elizabeth Street eliminated a major impediment to women's employment and a major limitation on the Sicilian father's opportunities to interact with his own family and with neighbor men. Like artisans in Sicily, immigrant men were in a good position to interact with others. School children and older boys enjoyed similar advantages. As a result, immigrant everyday lives resembled those of Sicily's artisans. Most immigrant families came within reach of achieving their social ideals. A family of former peasants had every reason to feel that it had rapidly improved its life by moving to Elizabeth Street — even if its income was still very, very low.[99] For an artisan family, life on Elizabeth Street would have seemed reassuringly familiar rather than pleasantly improved.

Nevertheless, the move from agrotown to tenement also left room for discontentment. Immigrant women in particular had good reasons to be displeased with Elizabeth Street tenements, for they imposed new restraints on many women. The small tenement apartment, which adjoined an equally small and dark hallway and which was stacked either above shareable open spaces on the street or below those on the roof, placed new restraints on children at play. They could not easily find play space under their mothers' direct supervision. That supervision had been important to Sicilians, and immigrant mothers went to considerable lengths to maintain it. "There is," one writer noted, "a continual shouting up from the children on the street to the mothers at the windows and vice versa."[100] Fasanella, too, often painted the immigrant woman at the window, surveying the world from above. Furthermore, the large numbers of immigrant daughters working in garment factories spent far less time under their own mothers' supervision than did a typical girl in a Sicilian agrotown. Mothers complained bitterly about the separation.[101] The tenement made it difficult for immigrant mothers to behave in ways social ideal demanded.

The absence of shareable space just outside the door posed new restraints for the immigrant woman, and this fact reminds us that the immigrant woman's duplication of the housebound life of the Sicilian artisan wife did not necessarily reflect her choice. In fact, women's efforts to use unlikely nearby but semicommunal workplaces — the crowded partner household kitchen, the cramped, cold and uncomfortable tenement hallway — seem to suggest that at least some immigrant women were

more interested in behaving in familiar ways than they were in living in
relative isolation like artisans' wives. Responding creatively, such women
used the central dumbbell airshaft as a communication tube and, of
course, they visited with their twenty or more neighbors on the roof, the
stairways, the front stoop, out their windows, and in their own apartments.[102]
They also complained about the tenements — far more, for example,
than did immigrant men and immigrant children. One commented

> In my country peoples cook out of doors, maka the wash out of doors, eat
> out of doors, tailor out of doors, make macaroni out of doors. And my
> people laugh, laugh all a time. And we use the house only in the night time
> to maka the sleep. America — it is *sopra, sopra* (up, up with a gesture of go-
> ing upstairs). Many people one house, worka worka, all a time. Good
> money but no good air.[103]

More than one Italian describing his life fictionally or in autobiography
portrayed his mother fading away from some mysterious but tenement-
related malaise. One died; another returned home, unable to adjust to tenement life; a third complained bitterly of her isolation; another missed
the air and sunshine of her native Calabria.[104] Even allowing for fictional license, it does seem likely that women viewed life in the tenements
differently than did men, for they did encounter there new restraints as
well as new freedoms.
Thus it is difficult to know how to interpret the immigrant woman
who, addressing a high status Italian male visitor, exclaimed "I hardly
ever go out of the house!"[105] Was she making a simple statement of fact?
Was she exaggerating a bit — quite consciously (for she herself admitted
that she went out to shop) — in order to impress the man with her high-
status behavior? Or was she, like another woman who concluded
begrudgingly "at least here we have water in the house,"[106] also com-
plaining a little? Certainly immigrant women had good reason to complain a little about their everyday lives in the tenements. Whereas the
move to Elizabeth Street freed men to pursue Sicilian ideals, it limited
immigrant women's opportunities to interact with others. Although immigrant women lived lives more like artisans' wives as a consequence,
they seemed unsatisfied. Immigrant women's dissatisfaction helped
reshape immigrant social relationships as much as their husbands' new-
found freedom.

CHAPTER SEVEN

Immigrant Society and Culture

In the past fifteen years, historians have significantly and provocatively re-interpreted immigrant society and culture. Most recent studies rightly emphasize the continuing importance of Old World values and show how these and New-World economic opportunities interacted to create distinctive immigrant families and communities.[1] By comparing the lives of Sicilians in Sicily and New York, this book contributes to that re-interpretation. It sheds new light on the Old-World values of one south Italian group. And it demonstrates that the housing environment – a largely neglected aspect of urban America – played a role in influencing immigrant adjustment to the New World.

The purpose of this final chapter is to examine immigrant society and culture, using the experiences of Elizabeth Street's Sicilians as illustrations. In many ways, the social lives of these Sicilians resembled those of Italian immigrants in other American cities, large and small. My purpose in describing Sicilian immigrant society is not to point to its uniqueness. Instead, by viewing immigrant society and culture against the background of Sicilian social ideals and of environmental possibilities, this chapter offers a modest reassessment of the process of social and cultural change in an immigrant colony. In particular it addresses several aspects of Italian family and community life central to studies by Virginia Yans McLaughlin, John Briggs and Judith Smith.

The Nuclear Family and American Individualism

Most immigrant families should have looked with some satisfaction at their closest family relationships. By moving to New York, a former peasant father or mother could behave in ways that Sicilians had defined as ideal. But many immigrant families expressed not satisfaction but considerable dissatisfaction with their family life. Some even claimed that America destroyed the family. As evidence, they pointed to their children's behavior, "the loss of respect on the part of the children."[2] Historians have tended to accept immigrant parents' complaints about the children, emphasizing intergenerational conflicts that resulted in large part from children's new and individualistic ideals.[3] From the public school and from American popular culture, immigrant children — it is argued — learned that they had a right, as children, to play and to recreation; more threateningly, they learned that they had a right, as individual wage-earners, to their own wages. Children's individualism, according to immigrant parents and family historians, undermined the economic solidarity of the nuclear family.

Of Sicilian family relationships, it is true that the parent-child tie alone seriously departed from Sicilian ideals. Mothers went to great efforts to do so, but they could not supervise young children as closely as the Sicilian mother in the agrotown *cortile*. The school took the child away until age fourteen; thereafter it was the factory that removed sons and daughters from the home. Sons sometimes learned to work, but they rarely earned wages under their fathers' guidance — a significant and undesirable change for the artisan minority, a significant but familiar form of failure for the former peasant majority. Most daughters, too, went out to earn wages, a significant and undesirable change for immigrant families of all backgrounds. Each of these changes, however, did not reflect children's choice; they were largely family responses to environmental restraints.

It is also true that, at least in some families, immigrant children struggled with their parents over control of their wages. According to studies of immigrant family budgets, Italian children in their early working years unquestioningly turned over all their wages to their parents. After age eighteen, many immigrant sons contributed only a fixed sum to the family: in effect, they became boarders. Daughters continued to turn in wages until they married, or if they did become boarders in their own families, they waited considerably longer before doing so.[4] This pattern raises two interesting questions: If children learned individualism in the public schools, why did they wait several years before demanding control of their own wages? And, was it really the case that immigrant boys assimilated American individualistic values more completely than did girls?

I do not feel that immigrant children "lost respect" and attempted to undermine family solidarity. Neither did they behave in new ways because they had assimilated in whole or in part "new" individualistic values. A quick review of the function of family solidarity in Sicily explains my conclusion. Sicilians believed that family solidarity was necessary if the family was to compete successfully. In practice the agrotown nuclear family competed with others for jobs and resources; of equal importance was competition on the local marriage market, since marriage contracts were the major mechanism for distributing family property. Furthermore, the typical goal of family economic solidarity was the provision of sizeable marriage settlements including land, houses and household goods, for the children. In a very real sense each Sicilian nuclear family used family solidarity to provide the material basis for the next generation of nuclear families: they invested in reproduction of the *casa* kinship group. As a consequence, a Sicilian child expected to benefit quickly, materially and "individually" from contributing to the family.

Not so in the United States. As immigrant families started the uphill struggle to property ownership, they hoped to use children's savings to buy a house, one that would serve the existing nuclear family (and, perhaps, the family of one married child). Saving for that house made sizable marriage settlements for all the children impossible. From the immigrant child's point of view, then, it was the parents who, lacking property, first abandoned family solidarity. More than one immigrant child wondered how he or she would marry under such new conditions. The struggle over the wage envelope required no particular training in American individualism. And immigrant daughters simply reached a different agreement with parents than did their brothers: After contributing their wages, they continued to receive some kind of movable marriage settlement — furniture, household equipment or a marriage celebration.[5]

Immigrant parents were right about one thing; immigrant children no longer behaved as did proper Sicilian children. Older siblings and cousins — "little fathers" and "little mothers" they were called — replaced mothers in supervising children's street and backyard play groups. Far more than in Sicily, immigrant children socialized each other, at play, at school, and at work.[6] By doing so, they became not more individualistic, but more closely identified and involved with a social group other than the *casa*, one which Herbert Gans would later term the kin dominated peer group.[7] The peer group was neither a nuclear family, a *casa*, nor a typically Sicilian network of instrumental ties to others. Parents did not live cheerfully with the conflict between peer group and Sicilian ideals. By focusing on their children as the source of the conflict, however, parents ignored the fact that the children actually followed in parental footsteps.

A Family Social Cycle

Relationships between individual, kin, and social network began to change in the immigrant first-generation. As chapter 4 showed, immigrants turned surprisingly often to their kin to form chains of migration. In their early years in the United States, immigrant families created malleable households and the kin-dominated peer group; both these forms of social experimentation were probably intended to replace neighbors in highly mobile tenement neighborhoods. In this first stage of the family social cycle, the pattern followed later by immigrant children — intense involvement with peers and a wider sense of solidarity with *parenti* — was already well established. In later years, when families moved less often, the lowered boundary between nuclear families and peer groups persisted. Still, many families late in life sacrificed the satisfactions of both peer and neighborhood friendship networks in order to seek better housing far from areas of first settlement like Elizabeth Street. An immigrant family's social network, in other words, developed dynamically through time; at almost any stage in this social cycle it differed from the social networks typical of Sicilian agrotowns or idealized by nineteenth-century Sicilians.

In Sicily, Sicilians both wanted and needed a network of useful social relationships to others, and neither immigration nor life in the United States changed their motives. For the majority of immigrants with small children, a social network was still an economic necessity. Most fathers earned too little to support a family, and even with a working mother, family income provided no margin of protection against sudden unemployment, sickness, or a return to Italy. Budget studies showed that young immigrant families survived because they received gifts of clothes and money, as well as other forms of small but critical material help.[8]

But from whom? In Sicily, peasants turned most often to their neighbors, a group which included a number of kin and people of higher status. In the United States they also turned to their neighbors. Mangano observed, "The Italian, inside of the week, will have spoken to all he has seen pass his door, and without a doubt will have found some one whom he has taken into his confidence . . . ."[9] Mangano wrote of "his" door, but no doubt female neighbors did the same, for he noted, "the coffee pot is constantly at hand, and if anyone should drop in between meals it is expected that he or she will accept a cup of coffee." Women recruited neighbors for garment work, after training them in the necessary simple skills of basting.[10] Their cooperative efforts were not completely without success. One neighborhood network of Elizabeth Street women—surprised by a visit of state inspectors controlling violations of homework licensing—"posted outlooks and began their sweated work again."[11]

Still, the younger family's efforts to build a neighborhood social network could scarcely produce more than temporarily satisfactory results. Middle-class neighbors were few, and young skilled workers were almost as hardpressed financially as young unskilled workers; they, too, were poor potential patrons. The tenement "kaleidoscope" moved ever onward, as did the majority of young families. In its constant comings and goings, a young family behaved as Mangano described—it began establishing ties to its neighbors. Nevertheless it could not always count on long-time neighbors for the help it continued to need badly.

Whereas Sicilians had viewed their neighbors as their real kin, Sicilian immigrants responded to high mobility by attempts—often successful—to make their kin into their real neighbors. The malleable household represented a first effort to ensure cooperation under new and kaleidoscopic conditions, by lowering the family's jealous boundary around itself. In increasing numbers, malleable households were formed with *casa* and *parenti* kin, as Chapter 5 showed. In the face of kaleidoscopic residential mobility, the clustering of kin became a further way to replace mobile neighbors with a more dependable and slowly changing group. So did, as well, the kin invited to eat, drink or play cards in the tenement kitchen. Given the youthful composition of the immigrant population, this was almost inevitably a group of peers, some of whom may have formerly lived as partners or boarders with the family. Sicilian immigrants did not respond to geographical mobility in ways theorists of modernization predict—they did not assign different roles to kin, neighbors and friends.[12] Instead, they gradually replaced the all-purpose neighbor of the Sicilian agrotown with the neighboring kinsman. (And since many immigrants had relatives in more than one American location, these small kin networks actually facilitated moves within the United States.)

As children began seeking work and the immigrant family settled down for a time in one neighborhood, its economic need for cooperation with other families diminished somewhat, but its idealization of a large social network did not. A neighborhood like Elizabeth Street housed growing numbers of families with working children through time; only a third of all families in 1905, they represented over half of Street families in 1925. These families enjoyed to the fullest the social possibilities inherent in the everyday tenement life described in the last chapter. For less mobile older families, the neighbors of similar age and family composition became again a ready source of social relationships.

In the street and cafe, immigrant men and children "capitalized" on their neighborhood, as Sicilian proverbs suggested. The street, yard, or cafe drew residents not from a single tenement (a group which continued to change, since young families shared tenements with less mobile older ones), but from all the tenements on a block or crossing. Because this was the case, an immigrant man or child could move about within the area, as many continued to do, without being removed from his usual street, yard, or cafe social groups.

Personal ties among neighbors may not have sustained a rich institutional life like that of the Jewish settlers east of the Bowery, but Elizabeth Street men did create formal and informal organizations that far surpassed Sicilian peasant localism. As in Sicily, there were not one, but many ways to build a social network around the family: peddler's markets, business partnerships, youth gangs, festival societies, *paese* clubs, funerary, and sickness or mutual benefit societies.[13] Festival societies left the most visible historical traces. Riis wrote, they "last as long as there is any profit in it," and he noted that the creation of a festival society on one block soon led to the formation of a rival society on the next.[14] Santa Rosalia, San Faro and San Calogero, along with many other Sicilian patrons, enjoyed Elizabeth Street celebrations. The formation of a mutual benefit or *paese* society, like those that in the 1930's joined in the *Unione Siciliano*, had Sicilian artisan precedents. And artisans seemed particularly active in these organizations. The unskilled also participated, as they had not always done in Sicily.[15] Unfortunately, we know little more about the social bases of the many networks Elizabeth Street men created. These organizations await their historian. Their existence tells us, however, that immigrant men had not forgotten the social possibilities that many Sicilian proverbs perceived in friendship and neighborliness.

Immigrant women, as chapter 6 showed, did not share these social possibilities with their husbands and children. A woman's immediate neighbors in the tenement continued to change kaleidoscopically, even when her own family stopped moving so frequently. And she saw less of the neighbors when her family occupied a better-equipped apartment in a new law tenement: No partner wives provided company in the kitchen, and housework could be performed indoors. Even in the 1920's when the proportion of less-mobile older families in Italian neighborhoods reached a peak, Caroline Ware found that families in buildings with shared water supplies were more likely to know each other than were those in new law tenements.[16]

Tenement restraints on women's activities were not without social consequences for the immigrant family. Immigrant women, like the family itself during its mobile years, probably depended on kin for social exchange. Particularly through women, kin played a central role in the family's social network despite the relative availability of neighbors during this phase. Immigrant families lived especially close to the wife's kin in 1905, as table 5–2 showed. Women may have turned specifically to their own blood relatives as they sought a solution to the troublesome problem of supervising their children's play. Unable to keep them under her own two eyes, the mother tried at least to guarantee them acceptable playmates and supervisors in the form of cousins or slightly older aunts or uncles. Families also continued to form malleable households with kin during those years when neighbors offered an alternative source of social ties. (Boarding of nonkin, however, declined among families settled in the United States more than fifteen years.)

Years later in Boston's West End, Herbert Gans found that neighborhood groups competed with the kin-dominated peer groups for men's loyalty, and that most men opted for the latter group when they married.[17] Even in the early twentieth century, married men on Elizabeth Street seemed to vascillate in their social loyalties. The last two chapters showed that men sometimes chose peer-group socializing in the kitchen-*salotto* over the neighborhood cafe, street corner, mutual benefit society, or *paese* club. Kin remained important to men, too, even when men had neighbors as an alternative. Kinship and localism helped keep Elizabeth Street socially fragmented as time passed. Men's neighborhood networks extended beyond the individual tenement, but they never united the street into a single community. In 1925 the distinction between the day laborers and building-trades artisans from Palermo province living on the northern blocks, and the fish peddlers and dock workers from towns around Sciacca living further south, still persisted, little-changed since 1905.

The importance of the kin-dominated peer group suggests that the social network of an older immigrant family reached only occasionally the size of an artisan's network in Sicily, although it usually surpassed in size that of a typical peasant. Immigrant families seemed satisfied with the size of their social networks; as chapter 5 noted, they rarely complained about their tenement social lives. Their satisfaction is not puzzling. An immigrant social network was "many-stranded" and semicorporate.[18] Kin were neighbors and came from the same town; often they shared a common occupation or workplace and belonged to the same mutual benefit, *paese*, or festival society. Furthermore, most members of a family-based network recognized most of the others as members of their own family's network. A peer group, then, had fluid but identifiable boundaries. Multistranded and semicorporate, the kin-dominated peer group was based on personal, emotional, and informal blood loyalties, rather than strictly on the instrumental and calculative ties that formed the larger Sicilian networks, of artisans, *civili* and *gabelloti.*

As chapter 5 suggested, older families rapidly faced a serious conflict between their social satisfaction and their unmet housing ideals. In 1905 this was a small group of families, and their decision to abandon Elizabeth Street attracted no attention. Twenty years later, as a majority of the population, these families behaved in ways that impressed social workers with the important role played by housing ideals in family decision-making. Although the average Elizabeth Street family in 1925 rented more than three rooms (compared to only 2.4 rooms in 1905), such a family was tempted, local professionals believed, by the call of better apartments and houses for purchase, especially homes in Brooklyn.[19]

Some families refused to abandon their neighborhoods or locally based peer groups to seek better housing. For example, Elizabeth Street families that remained in the Fourteenth Ward in 1925 had twice as many kin living in the area in 1905 as had the average immigrant family at that time. When slum renewal projects inquired about the plans of displaced renters, Italian immigrants in New York often indicated that they hoped to find housing nearby. A few actually moved together, in small groups, to apartments in nearby buildings.[20]

But many more families left Elizabeth Street, as both declining populations and local observers testified. (See Table B-1 in Appendix B.) The decisions and desires of the younger generation carried special weight in this new migration away from Elizabeth Street to the outlying boroughs.[21] While the older generation seemed to have achieved a delicate balance between social satisfaction and unmet housing ideals while their children remained unmarried, the younger generation was less patient with tenement apartments as housing. In 1925 young couples and families on Elizabeth Street rented an average of 3.3 rooms, more even than larger older families. Although younger families also may have appreciated neighborhood social life — their peer groups, too, had been built there — they insisted that they wanted a "better environment" in which to raise their children. That better environment included better housing, with baths, central heating, and — probably — accessible play space for children.[22]

Thus new migration chains led outward from Manhattan tenement neighborhoods to the outlying regions of Brooklyn, Queens and other areas of New York City. Only a minority of families moved because they had purchased a house, but all mobile families improved their housing (by paying much higher rents after they moved).[23] Mario Puzo in *The Fortunate Pilgrim* left one description of the chain typical of this new migration: a young couple with their young children, the immigrant parents, and the remaining unmarried older children.[24] Unlike the chains that linked Sicily and New York, these new chains were intergenerational and limited to the closest of kin. Thus, in its final years, a typical elderly immigrant family returned to a functioning social group much like the Sicilian *casa*. The newly forming neighborhods of New York's outlying boroughs were even more fragmented than were areas of first settlement. The peers, kin and nonkin, scattered; their contacts became visits rather than everyday interaction.[25] The large male neighborhood groups gradually dispersed, leaving behind only an institution — the San Calogero shrine and office on Elizabeth Street, for example, persists to this day, and San Calogero's feast continues to be celebrated around the corner. The former peasant family had moved, quite literally, from *cortile* to kinship localism in one generation.

The social cycle of a typical Elizabeth Street family differed only in degree from those of other immigrant colonies in American cities. Other forms of urban housing released Italian immigrants from old restraint as effectively as did the tenements. On the other hand, some urban American housing environments matched Sicilian housing ideals far better than the tenements of Elizabeth Street. Elizabeth Street had particularly high rents, which may have encouraged particularly high residential mobility and population turnover.[26] Even more important, low density-housing provided far better opportunities for homeowner ship than did Elizabeth Street. Such areas did not force older families and the emerging second generation to choose between their housing and their social ideals.[27] The social consequences are clear: Whereas Elizabeth Street was divided into many local and kin groups, St. Louis' "Hill" gradually became a single community. Whereas Elizabeth Street Sicilians moved from *cortile* to kinship localism in a single generation, families in low-density housing areas bought houses and forged a community that could, potentially at least, transcend the new loyalties of kinship.

The social structure of an immigrant colony like Elizabeth Street was not static; neither a relatively fixed hierarchy of discrete groups, nor a set of overlapping but relatively stable family-centered networks. Its resemblance to an agrotown in western Sicily was limited. Between 1905 and 1925 Elizabeth Street completed a social cycle, one closely tied to the cycle of thousands of immigrant nuclear families. In 1905 Elizabeth Street, with its preponderance of young families, was a rapidly changing kaleidoscope characterized by high mobility and considerable social experimentation in the formation of malleable households and peer groups. By 1915 the kaleidoscope had slowed; fewer new families arrived and a far higher proportion of families settled down as their children began earning wages. In 1915 Elizabeth Street more closely resembled a Sicilian agrotown socially than at any other time. Even in 1915, however, similarities between the two were limited by new environmental restraints imposed on women and by men's liberation from old restraints. Only ten years later the colony itself was coming apart, as immigrants organized the move to Brooklyn, rearranging their social networks in order to do so. Social change was particularly clear among Elizabeth Street residents, because of the area's high mobility, but other Italian colonies — whether of first or second settlement — also changed socially during settlement and growth. None were static urban villages.[28]

The Question of Class

Rudolph J. Vecoli has observed that historians see Italian immigrants as either *padrone* slaves or primitive rebels; nowhere are they portrayed as the class-conscious backbone of an emerging and organized immigrant working class.[29] There were *padrone* slave scandals on Elizabeth Street, especially in the 1880's and 1890's. And street residents undoubtedly participated in strikes that swept the garment industry, the building trades and the excavations of the subways 1905–1915. Unions, radical organizations, class-based (as opposed to ethnic-based) mutual benefit associations, however, attracted little attention from American observers of the colony or from the popular Italian-language press in New York.[30]

Historians are a long way from understanding the significance of class among immigrant workers. Chapter 4 showed that migration left untouched the important Sicilian distinction between artisanal and dirty-dependent work, but that life in the United States eliminated many of the social and economic differences that in Sicily separated the two occupational categories of artisan and peasant. In Sicily, social similarities between artisans and the *civile* rentiers were striking, as were differences

109

between artisan and peasant manual laborers. Not so in New York. There, both skilled and unskilled duplicated the work and leisure patterns, the family and social lives, of Sicily's artisans. Less happily, both groups—like the poorest Sicilian peasants—suffered unemployment and low incomes, moved about a great deal during their early years in the United States, and remained renters for long periods of time, sometimes permanently. Objectively seen, immigrants did increasingly form a single working-class rather than a simple or complex hierarchy of classes as in Sicily.

It is difficult to know whether immigrants chose to focus on the positive, and artisanlike, or on the negative and peasantlike, aspects of this objective condition. The experiences of Elizabeth Street Sicilians raise many more questions about immigrants' understanding of class than the evidence can answer. Sicilians had distinguished the rich from the poor, and found their relationship necessary if antagonistic. Many of the "poor" in Sicily were nevertheless property owners—*padroni* of simple one-room houses. And we do not know if Sicilians identified artisans with the "rich" or with the "poor." We know only that they glorified the artisan while casting a suspicious eye on the merchant. Furthermore, some Sicilian artisans, at the very time of emigration, were busy transforming their long experience with occupational cooperation into class consciousness. Of these Sicilian precedents only a preference for skilled work and a continued strong desire for property ownership were obvious among Elizabeth Street's residents.

Historians have offered several explanations for the weakness of working-class organization among immigrant workers. None explains adequately the experiences of Elizabeth Street's Sicilians. Americans have long assumed that social mobility (or the dream thereof) undermined class consciousness among immigrant workers. Considerable numbers of Sicilian immigrants did succeed, by their own standards, in improving the work they did, becoming the idealized skilled worker or the less idealized but socially similar petty merchant. Even more succeeded in behaving like artisans in their private family and social lives. And immigrant sons were even more likely than their fathers to become skilled workers. Social mobility, alone, however, cannot explain limited immigrant attention to the relations of the classes, for it was precisely Sicilian artisans who valued occupational cooperation and nurtured a developing class consciousness in the years preceding and overlapping mass migration from Sicily. If immigrant skilled workers failed to do so, an explanation lies elsewhere than in the experience of social mobility.

Stephan Thernstrom — who first discovered the remarkable propensity of the American poor to move about — believed that it was geographical mobility that undermined both class consciousness and organization among American workers.[31] Immigrant Sicilians certainly moved as often as other immigrants, at least during certain times of their lives. Yet many also settled down long enough in midfamily cycle to support a variety of ongoing formal male organizations. Some of these were probably class-based or occupation-based. Only further study of Italian-language union locals, labor clubs, or radical groups can reveal whether these groups drew on a different group of men than did, for example, a *paese* club, a street-corner youth gang, or a festival society. Attention to the work and leisure activities of particular groups of skilled workers and petty merchants might also reveal whether the immigrant man or son who became a skilled worker in the United States adopted or rejected the similarly Sicilian tradition of artisanal cooperation and activism.

Of all interpretations, Yans-McLaughlin's seems to offer the most promise for understanding immigrant class values. She argues that strong families and powerful kinship sentiments rendered many community institutions unnecessary and made immigrants particularly skeptical of class-based organization.[32] Yans-McLaughlin views familism as an important part of immigrant cultural baggage; indeed, it is an explanation for their emigration. In short, familism was a serious hindrance to immigrant cooperation and provided a cultural alternative to class consciousness.

Like Buffalo's Italians, Elizabeth Street Sicilians did live in family and kin-centered social worlds during much of their early and later years in the United States. Family-centered social networks may have placed limits on working-class organization as Yans-McLaughlin suggests. But it would be incorrect to explain such social fragmentation or family-centeredness as a straightforward reflection of Sicilian cultural values. Familism was not part of Sicilians' cultural baggage; neither did it cause some Sicilians to emigrate while others organized. If familism provided immigrants with a cultural alternative to organization this was a product of cultural change among the immigrant first-generation. In short, the question of class and its role in immigrant social life still lacks an answer.

Social and Cultural Change

Constance Cronin concludes her study of twentieth-century Sicilian emigrants in Australia by asking,

Have they changed? It is not really a difficult question because the respondents themselves answered it. In the public sector they are Australians and they so appear, but in private they are the Sicilians they have always been, living a Sicilian way of life and holding intact those Sicilian values, norms and behavior patterns which perpetuate their way of life in the face of intrusions from the outside.[33]

By "private" Cronin means "that part of one's life which is lived away from the scrutiny and direct control of society and its members"; she argues that in their food and housekeeping habits, in their friends and associates, and in their family and social values, immigrants to Australia remained the Sicilians "they have always been."[34]

Had a scholar in 1905 or 1915 troubled to ask Elizabeth Street residents Cronin's question, these immigrants, too, I suspect, would have announced themselves Sicilians faithful to the old ways. Recognizing that possibility, Virginia Yans-McLaughlin summarizes the experience of Buffalo's immigrants: "Socially" they had become urbanites, but culturally they remained "folk." In fact it was folk values that enabled them to adapt socially to the requirements of an urban industrial world.[35] We have seen that Elizabeth Street residents considerably changed their private family and social behavior as they adapted to a new physical environment. Had they remained culturally "folk" while doing so? Social behavior and cultural values, Yans-McLaughlin notes, were not mirror reflections of each other.[36] My analysis of social and cultural change among Elizabeth Street's Sicilians began with that assumption. My conclusions, however, differ: Elizabeth Street's Sicilians experienced fundamental cultural change during migration to and urban life in the United States.

Throughout this book the concept of match provided a way of analyzing variations in the relationship among cultural ideals, environmental possibilities, and actual social behavior. Where match was good, people behaved as they pleased, and their behavior reflected their ideals. Far more interesting were instances of poor match. Restraints forced people to become creative socially and culturally. Drawing upon existing ideals, they decided how to respond to restraints and how to interpret their own behavior. Faced with severe restraints, people could always respond in a number of ways, each with differing cultural implications. They could pick and choose among many ideals to justify their behavior, a source of cultural diversification. They could elaborate compensatory ideals. Or they could simply and practically refuse to acknowledge any discrepancy between their behavior and their ideals.

Environmental restraints and the linkages of ideals and behavior they often required can help us understand the process of cultural change as it was experienced by Sicilian immigrants. That process began in Sicilian agrotowns with peasants' social frustrations, and it continued, in New York, with immigrants' strong dislike of tenement housing. By examining the ways in which immigrants linked ideals and behavior, it is easy to see that immigrants could feel themselves completely Sicilian, "the Sicilians they have always been," despite the fact that they differed socially *and* culturally from their siblings and cousins still in Sicily.

Chapters 2 and 3 showed that Sicilians responded in a number of ways when they failed to achieve their ideals. Peasants lived cheerfully in houses that poorly matched many of their housing and their social ideals. At most, they expressed in their proverbs anxiety about the social problems posed by small one-room dwellings: Their concerns about doors, windows and eavesdropping, for example, were not shared by the owner of a *casa civile*, who could offer hospitality or enjoy an open window without violating his or her privacy.

The myth of male dominance, on the other hand, was a compensatory belief. It, too, was a value limited largely to peasant Sicilians, for it compensated male peasants for the exceedingly large discrepancy between their actual family role and the ideal models for fatherly behavior.

On Elizabeth Street, Sicilians perceived high rents and small dark rental housing as obstacles to living as they might wish or as they were accustomed to doing—as nonmobile homeowners with low housing costs. To achieve their economic and later their housing ideals, immigrant families moved about far more frequently than had Sicilians in agrotowns. Mobility influenced the ways in which immigrants pursued their social ideals, freed in so many other ways from the restraints imposed by Sicilian agrotowns. Anxieties about privacy and the compensatory myth of male dominance gradually disappeared as immigrants built new social networks in New York; appreciation of *parenti*, by contrast, increased as immigrants justified their new experiments in social behavior.

Immigrant families could not have formed malleable households or peer groups had they remained obsessed about wifely infidelity, the seduction of daughters, or the necessity of male supervision of female sexuality. Most boarders and a large proportion of boarding kin were, after all, young men. Yans-McLaughlin dismisses the possibility that these men represented a threat to the family, because friends or relatives were trusted and because their interaction with women fell under family or neighborly scrutiny.[37] Such scrutiny existed in Sicily as well—yet it was precisely cousins and godparents who were most feared as potential seducers. Why, then, did immigrants come to evaluate outsiders more positively, abandoning the worst misogyny of the myth of male dominance?

Since the myth of male dominance was largely a compensatory ideal, as Rogers argues, it had no function in the United States, where men fulfilled their role as ideal fathers. Immigrant families, like *civili* and artisans in Sicily, could quietly abandon the most virulent of their suspicions, making the malleable household possible. They could view the boarder or boarding kinsman as a potentially useful friend, not just as a sexually threatening man. I do not wish to imply that all anxiety about female character and sexuality or the belief in the necessity of male control disappeared overnight as fathers began returning nightly to their own families. They did not. The wage-earning daughter provided new fuel for this fire. But anxiety about the wife's chastity diminished as immigrant husbands and wives began to behave "properly."[38] Without this cultural change, experimentation with new social forms like the malleable household or the intimate peer group would not have been possible. Still, it should be obvious that immigrants did not change their values consciously in order to justify social experimentation. Cultural values and social behavior in this example were not mirror reflections; nor did one change to reflect the other.

Anthropologist George Foster calls the quiet form of cultural change described here "stripping down."[39] "Stripping down" occurred when immigrants dropped some of their cultural baggage overboard. The myth of male dominance was not the only aspect of Sicilian culture so jettisoned. In the United States, Sicilians (and perhaps other Italian immigrants) consistently justified the new social behaviors they developed to cope with rapid mobility through reference to only a limited number of Sicilian social ideals: the desirability of a social network and, most important, the positive aspects of kinship.

To justify their preference for peer-group socializing in the neighborhood over unachieved housing ideals, the older generation would refer to the importance of blood ties. To justify a move with the children to Long Island, parents could invoke a proverb about the benefits of cooperating with the kin. At the same time, emphasis on family solidarity may have helped compensate for the departure of the children's behavior from Sicilian ideals. This process of linking new behavior to some Sicilian ideals can, of course, only be inferred in the historical evidence. However, we do know, that immigrants' social values glorified what Leonard Covello and other writers since call *la famiglia*. The ideal l *famiglia*, as Covello described it, did not resemble Sicilian social ideals; *la famiglia* was a positively evaluated category which included all manner of closer and more-distant kin (plus a few fictive ones), one which demanded loyalty, emotional involvement, and mutual support among kinsman.[40] *La famiglia* was a product of migration and life in the United States.

As Sicilians defined new social ideals, blood ties became more culturally *and* socially central than they had been in Sicily. Kinship now differed categorically from other social ties. Furthermore, blood ties of many kinds were now unambiguously positive. Kinship became the immigrants' main tool for organizing a social network that more nearly replaced rather than surrounded the once jealously bounded nuclear family and the positively evaluated *casa*. Obviously, *la famiglia* has its cultural origin in Sicily. Nevertheless, this social ideal left out much that for Sicilians was important and useful: The warnings, the similarities between friendship and kinship, and the distinction between *parenti* and *casa* had disappeared.

It is tempting to hypothesize that "stripping down" also characterized Sicilian occupational and class values. Chapter 4 demonstrated that migration eliminated the "rich" as a significant group in immigrant society because so few *civili* migrated. It is equally easy to imagine that proverbial social lessons about the relations of rich and poor quietly disappeared along with the *civili*. But only further research on the social origins of immigrant *prominenti* and their ties to ordinary immigrants can reveal whether this was in fact the case.

In assessing match it was necessary to focus on what an environment made impossible. In studying cultural change it seems important to focus on what is left out as immigrants confront new restraints or begin to behave in new ways. Disappearing ideals help to explain how immigrants could depart from their cultural origins without—as Cronin's study shows—finding it necessary to emphasize that they did so. Still, it seems important to stress that the first generation was rapidly becoming Sicilian-American; they were not, as Yans-McLaughlin believes, socially changed but culturally still "folk."

Stripping down was neither a painful nor disorienting cultural process. Because they drew on some Sicilian ideals, immigrants did not experience fundamental family and social change as particularly wrenching. They made choices as the Sicilians "they had always been." The fact that they identified themselves as Sicilians—as at least some still do today—is, of course, important. But their Sicilian cousins, themselves departing from the shared cultural starting place, would notice the differences and find them impressive. *They* would call the immigrants *Americani*. And they would puzzle over who these people had actually become.

Both *Americani* and their Sicilian cousins eagerly changed their social behavior in the twentieth century, and both altered their ideals, too. However, the two groups evaluated culture change in very different ways. Unlike their cousins, *Americani* often seemed unable to accept that they had changed; they viewed cultural and social change negatively. Their Sicilian cousins did not. Thus the conservatism of the immigrant was not necessarily Sicilian in origin; more likely it was a product of the migration experience. Aware of the differences separating them from the people that *they* called "Americans," immigrant Sicilians saw in cultural change a threat to their identity: Inevitably perhaps, immigrant minorities view change with greater suspicion than their nonemigrant cousins who are spared that threat.

A resident of Sambuca who in 1980 had recently visited close relatives and *paesani* in Brooklyn and Chicago summed up for me his understanding of the cultural transformation of Sicilian into Sicilian-American. "Why," he asked of his recently migrated relatives, "do these *Americani* always accuse us of having abandoned the old ways? We are Sicilians, but we are proud to have changed. We are *evoluto*, but they . . . These *Americani*! Why, they seem to think that they are the only real Sicilians!"[41]

Appendix A: Social Ideals in Sicilian Proverbs

Friends (Amici)

La caritati 'n Curti è estinta, e l'amicizia è finta.
A l'amicizia nun cci voli tacca.
A li bisogni servinu l'amici.
A lu bisognu l'amicu pari.
'Ntra li bisogni si conuscinu l'amici.
L'amici si conuscinu 'n tempu di nicissità.
A lu to amicu avvìsacci lu beni.
Ama l'amicu tò cu lu viziu sò.
Amici di salutu cci nn'è assai.
Amici senza 'ntentu nun cci nn'è.
Amicizia 'ncutta, prestu nnimicizia.
Amicizia ricunciliata e minestra scarfata mai fòru boni.
Amicu di bon tempu e di putia, Nun è 'na bona e duci cu cumpagnia.
Amicu di gottu ti lass 'ntra un bottu.
Amici di gottu, tintu cui nn'ha troppu.
Amicu di tutti, amicu di nuddu.
Amicu d'occhi è nnimicu di cori.
Amicu fintu è veru tradituri.
Amicu fintu, nnimicu di morti, e guàrdati d'iddu.
Amicu tò, Spicchiali tò.
Chiddu è lu veru amicu chi 'un ti sparra.
Amicu vecchiu, è sempri amicu fidili.
Amicu vecchiu e casa nova.
Amicu vidiri, Pasqua fari.
Bisogna sèrviri l'amicu, ma nun cci mettiri di cuscenzia.
È bonu sèrviri l'amicu, ma nun cci vaja la cuscenza.
N'offenniri a Diu pri l'amicu.
Càncianu l'amici a tinuri di li cosi.

Canuscinu li 'nfilici, Quali su' li boni amici.
Càrzari, malatii e nicissitati, Schummògghianu lu cori di l'amici.
'Ntra càrzari, malatii e nicissitati, Si scròpinu l'amici cchiù fidati.
'Ntra càrciri e 'ntra tempi 'nfilici, Si scoprinu li veri e fàusi amici.
'N tempu di malatia e puvirtati, Si canusci lu cori di l'amici.
Chiddu è lu veru amicu chi 'un ti sparra.
Cu' ama l'amicu, nun cura dinari.
Cu' è veru amicu, nun guarda 'ntressu.
Cu' è riccu d'amici, è scarsu di guai.
Cu' ha bonu amicu a la citati, stà sicuru a lu casali.
Cu' havi un amicu, havi un tisoru.
Cui si fa un bon amicu, s'acquista un gran tisoru.
L'amicu fidili vali un tisoru.
Cui disprezza la sua vita pri serviziu di l'amicu, Si guadagna chidda di l'amicu.
Cui perdi un amicu, scinni un scaluni.
Ogni amicu chi si perdi, è un scaluni chi si scinni.
Quantu amici si perdinu, Tanti scaluna si scìnninu.
Cui sempri pigghia e mai duna, l'amicu l'abbannuna.
Cu lu *dammi* e *te'*, l'amicizia cc'è.
Lu dari e lu mannàri manteni l'amicizia.
Quannu cc'è lu *dammi* sulu, l'amicizia tocca duru.
Quannu l'amicizia cc'è, Eni cu lu *dammi* e *te'*; Quann' è cu lu *dammi* e *mu'*, Amicizia 'un cci nn'è cchiù.
Cu l'amicu tò pàrraci chiaru.
Di l'amici 'un ni nn'avemu abusari tantu assai.
Diu ti scanzi d'amici e nnimici, e di chiddi chi ti mancianu lu pani.
È bonu aviri amici a tutti banni.
L'amici sunnu boni in ogni chiazza: Cu'nun n'havi, si li fazza.
L'amici di luntanu si vasanu li manu.
Si vonnu beni l'amici luntanti.
L'amici nun sunnu mai suverchiu.
L'amici pri lu cciù sunnu 'ntrissati.
L'amici veri su' rari.
Si trovi amici, truvasti tisori, Ma avverti ca l'amici sunnu rari.
Amicu veru nun si trova mai.
L'amicizia 'ntra li picciriddi dura quantu l'acqua 'ntra pan . . . pin . . .
L'amicu certu si canusci 'ntra li cosi 'ncerti.
L'amicu nun servi pri 'na vota sula.
Sarva l'amicu pri n'àtra fiata.
L'amicu pri darreri si difenni, e mai davanti la sò facci.

L'amicu quannu duna chiddu chi ha, è nisciutu d'obbligu.
L'amicu si difenni a spata tratta, Binchì la vita a piriculu si metta.
Lu bonu amicu pri bonu amicu ti teni.
S'hai boni amici, tenitìlli forti.
Lu focu prova l'oru e l'avvirsità l'amicu.
Lu veru amicu ama a tutti tempi.
Megghiu lassari a li to' nnimici, chi aviri bisognu di to' amici.
Noci cchiù l'amicizia simulata chi la guerra scuperta.
'Ntra boni amici si perdi lu *no*.
'Ntra l'amici nun cc'è nè mio nè tò.
Nun canciàri l'amicu vecchiu pri lu novu.
Nun cc'è forma truvari un veru amicu: Cui voli amici assai, pròvanni
    pocu.
Voi amici assai? pròvanni pocu.
Nun diri tantu beni di l'amicu, chi quannu nni vo' diri mali nun si' crittu.
O amicu, o no.
Picca amici e boni; Chi quannu sunnu assai fannu ammuìnu.
Pri canusciri un amicu riali, Si cci havi a manciari 'na sarma di sali.
Cci voli sarmi di sali pri conusciri amici.
Avanti chi voi conusciri n'amicu, cci voi manciari 'na sarma di sali.
Quannu li misèrii se fèddanu, Tannu l'amici a manciari s'affùddanu.
Tannu l'amici nun s'affuddanu, Quannu li misèrii se fèddanu.
Quannu si voli sèrviri l'amicu, Si lassa jiri la robba a lu focu.
Quantu va n'amicu 'n chiazza 'un cci va cent'unzi 'ntra la tazza.
Vali chiù n'amicu 'n chiazza, Ca centu mila scuti 'n cascia.
Scarsi su' li cosi duci senza sali, Ma su' cchiù scarsi l'amici fidili.
S'havi bisognu cchiù di l'amicu, ca di lu pani chi si mancia.
Si 'ntra l'amici nun c'e ugualità, Pirfettu amuri nun ci sarrà.
Tannu l'amicu lu canuscirai, Quannu lu perdi e nun lu vidi cchiui.
L'amicu si conusci quannu si perdi.
Quannu si perdi l'amicu si chianci.
Tannu n'amicu si dici di cori, Quannu si perdi e 'un si pò cchiù aviri.
Unni cc'è radicata la malizia, Allignari 'un cci pò mai l'amicizia.
Cui nun sapi finciri d'essiri amicu, nun è feru nnimicu.
Tinta chidda mandra chi lu picuraru è amicu di li lupi.
Arraspa a lu tò amicu unni cci mancia.
Quali cunsigghiu di l'amici toi tu senti, tali cori ti farrai.
Amici siamu e li vurzi si cummàttinu.
Cu amici 'un ti ficari: Nun cci vinniri nè accattari.
N' accattari di l'amicu, nè di lu mircanti cumprari granu.
Vo' 'mmitari lu bonu amicu? Carni di vacca e ligna di ficu.

Cui va cridenza perdi l'amicu.
Cui fa cridenza vinni robba assai, Perdi l'amici e dinari 'n' ha mai.
Si voi perdiri l'amicu, facci cridenza.
Cui fa cridenza senz' aviri pignu, Perdi la robba, l'amicu e lu gnegnu.
Cui nun ha maritu, Nun ha nuddu amicu.
Cui di vecchia si 'nnamura, Amicizia pocu dura.
Amici e guàrdati.
Amici, e guardatinni di luntanu: Salutali e po' passa a manu a manu.
Amici, e passa arrassu.
Amici e megghiu e cavuli cu l'ògghiu.
Amicu cu tutti, e cunfidenti cu nuddu.
Amicu cu tutti e liali cu nuddu.
Cunti spissu, amicizia longa.
Di l'amicu fintu mi guarda Diu, Cà di lu nnimicu mi nni guardu iu.
Ognunu si guarda di l'amicu palisi, e no di l'occultu.
L'amicu nu è sempri amicu; so pò fari nnimicu.
Nun diri a lu tò amicu quantu sai; Pensa s'un jornu pri nnimicu l'hai.
Patti chiari, amici cari.
Patti chiari, amicizia longa.
Cu' havi dinari ed amicizia, Si teni 'ntra lu culu la giustizia.
A ogni gran Statu un nnimicu è troppu, e centu amici sunnu pocu.
Megghiu amicu cu lu latru, ca cu lu sbirru.
Megghiu amicu di lu sbirru ca di lu capitanu.
Amicu binificatu, Nnimicu dichiaratu.
La milizia havi stritt' amicizia cu la malizia.
Giustu dici lu muttu anticu: Cui perdi la libbirtà, perdi l'amicu.
Cui beni servi acquista amici, E cui mali parra si fa nnimici.
Cu' è amicu d'un jardinaru, E amicu d'un guranu.
Cui cadi 'n puvirtà, perdi l'amicu.
A li bisogni nun cc'è megghiu amici di li dinari.
A lu riccu mancanu amici?
Amici 'n quantitati ha l'omu riccu.
A lu tempu filici, si vidinu multi amici; A tempu di puvirtati, nun dicinu
      comu stati.
'Ntra tempi filici, si trovanu amici; 'Ntra li calamitati, nun vi spianu
      comu stati.
Amici poviri, amici pirduti.
Lu povir' omu è un amicu pirdutu.
Cu' havi pani campa filici, E cui nu nn'havi, perdi l'amici.
Li megghiu amici su' li dinari.

Nun cc'è cchiù càudu amicu di lu dinaru.
L'amicu è vulutu quann'havi dinari; Quannu nu nn'havi, 'un lu vonnu di li cavi.
Quannu frisca l'oricchia gritta, l'amica è stritta.
Megghiu perdiri l'amicu, Ca scattari lu viddicu.
Nun canciari l'amicu vecchiu pri lu novu.
Amicu chi finci, è comu lu carvuni; o t'ardi o tinci.
Stamu cchiù amici stannu luntanu.
Un veru amicu nun si pò pagari.
Va cchiù un bon amicu ca centu frati.
Si paganu li sbirri cuntanti e l'amici cu lu tempu.
Cui ti fa l'amicu, ti fa lu boja.
Robba d'amici, 'mmanu di latri.
Voi dispiàciri l'amicu? Metti purrazzi assai, ricotta pocu.

Parenti, *Including Particular Kin*

Lu datu a lu mannatu manteni lu parintatu.
Cu' havi parenti, havi turmenti.
Guerra tra nnimici, e amuri tra parenti.
Quannu lu carnizzeri vinni sapura, Signu ca vo' 'ntricciari parintela.
È cchiù vicinu lu denti di lu parenti.
Meggiu pri li me' denti, Chi pri li mei parenti.
Di zoccu sapi bonu a li mei denti, Affattu nun ni dugnu a li parenti.
Chiddi d'i' parenti, nun su'nenti; Chiddi di'i soru, sunnu d'oru.
Lu zitu cu zita vògghianu, Cà li parenti poi s'accordanu.
Lu zitu cu la zita mi si vogghia, Cà poi lu parintatu s'arricogghia.
Si vo' passari vita cuntenti, Statti luntanu di li to' parenti.
Cui cerca parenti, cerca corna.
Li megghiu parenti su' li spaddi.
Li megghiu sciarri su' 'ntra parenti.
Li sciarri 'ntra parenti cunsumanu li casi.
Li parenti su' parenti, e li strànii sempri su' strànii.
Li parenti di lu maritu, Su' àghiri comu l'acitu; Li parenti di la mugghieri, Su' duci comu lu meli.
Li parenti di la mugghieri, Su' sfinci cu lu meli; Li parenti di lu maritu, Su sfinci cu l'acitu.
Parenti di maritu, Sirpenti di cannitu.
Cu la stissa parintela, Cci nni voli cautela.
Cui parenti 'un arrispetta, Jorna laidi a lu 'nfernu aspetta.
Cui prestu nasci li denti, aspetta lu parenti.

Cugnati, spati.

Jènnari, sbirri; nori, grattalori.

Bona maritata, Senza soggira e cugnata.

Nun voli nè soggira nè cugnata.

Soggira e cugnati, Nun cci stati avvicinati.

Niputi, pùtali; zii, 'nzitali.

Nora, grattalora.

'Ntra l'anta e la paranta, Amaru chiddu ca la manu cci chianta.

Pensa e pensala beni, La soggira di tò mugghieri unni la teni?

Quannu mori la soggira, la nora chianci un pezzu e poi s'allissia li capiddi.

Quattru C su' piriculusi: Cucini, cummari, cugnati, e cammareri.

T'hai a guardari di li quattru C: Cucini, criati, cugnati e cummari.

Mali è dda casa chi havi dintra cucini, cugnati, cumpari e cunfissuri.

Si li parenti 'ntra d'iddi si cuntrastanu, mai ponnu essiri boni pr'àutru.

Soggira, cuteddu; nora grattalora.

Soggira e nora, jèttali fora.

Soggira e nora, mala parintela.

Soggira e nora, lu Signuri nni scanzi.

Soggira e nora, mancu di zuccaru è bona.

Soggira e nora scinnèru di lu celu sciarriati.

Soggiri e nori calàru sciarriannusi di lu Paraddisu.

Soggira e nora sempri stannu 'n guerra.

Quali nora voli bèniri la soggira?

Soggira e parrastra, Nè di crita nè di pasta.

Megghiu un tintu maritu chi 'na bona soggira.

Sciarra 'ntra parenti è cchiù accanita.

Sciarri 'ntra parenti sdisòlanu li casi.

Cui guarda fieru e 'nsirràgghia li denti, A Giuda ed a Cainu èni parenti.

Medicu nuveddu, ruina di parintatu.

Lu Jòviri di li parenti, Cu' 'un havi dinari si munna li denti.

Lu sonnu è parenti di la morti.

Cu' havi dinari, trova parenti.

Li veri parenti, Su' li dudici tari cu l'ali bianchi.

Lu poviru e lu malatu, Nun è vulutu di lu parintatu.

Lu puvirtà nun havi parenti.

'Ntra parenti e parenti, Guai pri cui nun havi nenti.

Picca e nenti, sù parenti.

Quannu lu riccu havi lu poviru pri parenti, Si cunsuma e nun fa nenti.

Li surci assimigghianu a li parenti.

Neighbors (Vicini)

Ortu e mulinu, Nun diri quantu renni a tò vicinu.
Si chianti cavuli 'ntr'Aprili, Lu tò vicinu si nni ridi.
Amari la sò vicina è gran vantaggiu, Spissu si vidi, e nun si fa viaggiu.
Addisia beni a li vicini, Cà si nni grassanu boni li gaddini.
Disia beni a lu tò vicinu, Cà lu tò è 'mpressu.
A la vicina, Nun cci fari tastari la cucina.
Nun addiccare la vicina a la cucina.
A li vicini toi nun dari peni.
Cu' havi la mala vicina, Havi la mala jurnata e la mala siritina.
Cu' havi lu malu vicinu, havi lu malu matinu.
Megghiu 'na mala matina, Chi 'na mala vicina.
Cu' havi vicini, havi spini.
Cui nun havi casa, nun havi vicini.
Di Diu e di li vicini, nun ti pò ammucciari.
Di tutti ti po'ammucciari, fora di lu vicinu.
Guardari nun ti poi di lu vicinu.
Lu vicinu è sirpenti, Si nun vidi, senti.
Lu vicinu t'è dintra.
Diu ti scanzi di malu vicinu, E di principianti di viulinu.
Diu nni scanza di malu vicinu, Di cavaleri, viddani, muli e mulinu.
Diu nni scanza di mali vicini, E di minzogni d'omu dabbeni.
Diu vi scanza di malu vicinu, Di principianti di viulinu, E di soru di
   parrinu, E di chiddi chi pàrranu latinu.
Fa capitali di lu tò vicinu.
Li vicini su' comu li catusa, si dùnanu acqua l'unu cu l'autru.
Vicini, vicenna.
Mala vicina, mala catina.
Nè mulu, nè mulinu, nè signuri pri vicinu, nè cumpari cuntadinu.
Tantu durassi la mala vicina, Quantu dura la nivi marzulina.
Vicini mei, spicchiali mei.
Voi stari 'n paci cu la vicina? Nun nèsciri piatta di la cucina.
Voi conusciri lu tò vicinu? rùmpicci un piattu.
E fu la riggina, E appi bisognu di la vicina!
'Un è tanta grossa la gaddina, Ch' 'un ha bisognu di la vicina.
Gatta chi mancia li so' gattini, Vidi chi voli far cu li so' vicini.
Pri lu pani e pri lu vinu, Si cància lu vicinu.
Mugghieri e runzinu, Pigghiali di lu vicinu.

Megghiu la munnizza di lu vicinu, chi la ricchizza di lu straniu.
Cui nni la sò casa si vota e gira, Nu 'nninga la vicina.
Diu ti scansi di figghia picchiusa, E di vicina 'nvidiusa.
Cui me torna, m'è vicinu.
Diu nni scanza di mali vicini, E di livata d'omini dabbeni.
La vigna di lu vicinu pari sempri chhiù carricata.
Ciumi, casteddi, monaci e pàrrini, Sunnu li mali vicini.
Rimiti, ciumi e 'nduvini, Su' li mali vicini.
Frati, ciumi e parrini, Su' tri mali vicini.
Quannu si' pri caminu, Nun diri mali di lu tò vicinu.
Cui si vanta, ha tristi vicini.
Cui s'arza matinu, gabba lu vicinu.
Quannu s'ardi la casa di lu tò vicinu, porta l'acqua a la casa tò.
Quannu s'abbrucia la casa di lu tò vicinu, porta l'acqua a la tua.
Quannu s'ardi lu tò vicinu, Lu tò mali è vicinu.
Dissi Betta a la vicina: Chiddu chi pari nun cci voli prova.
Di vicinu 'un ti pozzu vidiri, E di luntanu ti mannu a salutari.
Quannu la mamma si junci cu la figgia, La vicina s'arrassa centu migghia.
Tri su' li nnimici di l'omu: Cani, malu vicinu e lustru di luna.
La casa chiusa fa lu bonu vicinanzu.

Comparing Several Social Ties

Amicu di lu tò vinu, Nun l'aviri pri vicinu.
Amicu fàusu e lu malu vicinu, Ti fa vidiri lu munti pri chianu.
Amicu fàusu e malu vicinu, Jetta la petra e s'ammuccia la manu.
Amicu vicinu vali chhiù d' un parenti luntanu.
Cui perdi amici e cu' perdi parenti, Ma è cchiù tintu cu' perdi l'amanti.
L'amici su' cchiù di li parenti.
Fa beni prima a li parenti toi, Ddoppu a cui piaci di l'amici toi.
Meggiu prossimu vicinu chi parenti luntanu.
La vicinanza è menza parintela.
Lu malu vicinu è amicu fintu.
Lu primu parenti è lu vicinu.
Lu vicinu è lu veru parenti.
Tintu cu' havi lu malu vicinu, e tintu cu' è malu apparintatu.
Cu lu vìnniri e cumprari, 'Un cc'è amici nè cumpari.
'Ntr'amici e 'ntra parenti, 'N' accattari e 'un vìnniri nenti.
A tempu di favi, Nè parenti nè cummari.
A tempu di ficu, Nè parenti nè amicu.
A tempu di scattioli, Vegna cui voli; A tempu di racina, Nè parenti nè
vicina.

124

A tempu di racina e ficu, Nun cc'è nè parenti e mancu amicu.

A tempu di scattioli, Cci sunnu amici boni; A tempu di ficu, Nè parenti nè amicu.

Nè amici nè parenti, Pri li cosi chi sannu boni a li denti.

Amicu ch' 'un ti duna, e parenti ch' 'un ti 'mpresta, Fùjli tutti dui comu la pesta.

Amicu ch' 'un ti duna, parenti ch' 'un ti guarda, e mircanti ch' 'un ti 'mpresta, fùjli comu pesta.

Amicu ch' 'un ti giuva, Parenti ch' 'un ti duna, Nnimicu ch' 'un ti noci, Pàssali pri tutt'una.

Lu vidannu, fattu riccu, Nun canusci nè parenti, nè amicu.

Semu amici, e semu parenti sina chi voli Diu.

Bonu è l'amicu, bonu lu parenti, Amara dda casa chi nun havi nenti.

Mentri su' riccu, parenti ed amici.

Li veri amici e li veri parenti, Su' li quattru tari cu l'ali bianchi.

Lu poviru e l'assenti, Nun lu vonnu amici nè parenti.

A li parenti, nun fari nenti; A li vicini, comu li spini; A li cummari, nun tuccari.

Cu amici e cu parenti, nigòzii nenti.

Si lu parenti nun ti voli, E l'amicu nun ti coli, E lu mircanti nun ti 'mpresta, Fùjli comu pesta.

Appendix B: A Note on Method and Sources

Although the best studies of environmental change and social behavior trace a group of mobile families or individuals from one setting to another, some studies use a cross-sectional comparative method like that used in this study.[1] I chose to focus on Sicilian immigrants because I knew good local records existed in Sicily and because the nineteenth-century collections of folklorist Giuseppe Pitrè are practically without equivalent. Although Sicilians settled in many places in the United States, Elizabeth Street was the most distinctively Western Sicilian colony in the country; it was also the best-documented, probably because its tenement housing attracted considerable attention from housing reformers.[2] By focusing on the families and social networks of a relatively well-defined group of immigrants, I hoped to minimize the possibility that considerable cultural variation among south Italians rather than environmental change caused social variation on the two continents.[3]

All data on Elizabeth Street houses, households and occupational clusters presented in this book is based on linkage of ownership and housing records (1870–1930) and manuscript census data (1905, 1915, 1925) for the entire area.[4] This data also provided some information on migration chains in chapter 4. Table B-1 summarizes the numbers involved at each census date.

Table B-1. Elizabeth Street Housing and Population

	1905	1915	1925
Apartments	1826	1927	1828
Tenements	148	130	124
Families	1951	1807	1112
Households	1653	1765	1111
Population	8249	8846	6204

126

As far as it was possible, I identified the construction history, building type and ownership of any building occupied by at least one family in 1905, 1915 or 1925. *The Real Estate Record and Guide* listed cost, builder and owner of all buildings constructed after 1870. Reform literature described the construction and renovation of older buildings.[5] Bromley's Real Estate Atlases revealed the size and orientation of each building — allowing me to identify apartment size and floorplan in the extremely standardized tenement plans reproduced in reform literature. Individual blue prints for new law tenements and renovations after 1901 were available on microfilm from the New York City Bureau of Buildings, "Block and Lot Records." I also traced ownership for the years 1890–1930 in the "Conveyance Ledgers" in New York City's Hall of Records.

To identify potential *paesani*, I looked for persons listed in the census that bore distinctive patron saints names. I traced the names Ciro/a, Accursio/a, Rosalia, Calogero/a, Vito/a, Gerolamo/a, Gennaro/a, Rocco/a, Ignazio/a and Alfio/a, as well as the more common names Pietro, Angelo/a, and Domenico/a as controls, for the entire Fourteenth Ward, that is, on all the streets between Broadway and the Bowery, from Canal to East Houston Street.

Historians rightfully complain that the sources for the study of kinship patterns in the past are limited. Reconstitution of mobile families is difficult, and depends on good series of vital records — not always available in the United States. Census data, of course, does not identify kin, except within the household unit. I chose to do the best I could with census data, employing a naming pattern used almost without exception in Sicilian families. Sicilians named their children of each sex first after paternal then after maternal grandparents.[6] (See Figure B-1.) Married couples with children sharing common names, as this figure shows, often were kin.

To begin, I listed family and first names of 765 families living in two clusters of tenements along Elizabeth Street in 1905 (212, 214, 216 Grand Street, 358–60 Broome Street, 6, 16 and 22 Spring Street, 17 Prince Street, and 113, 117, 120, 123, 125, 126, 129, 147, 149, 151, 155, 157, 161, 163, 164, 168, 170, 230, 232, 233–35, 237, 238, 240, 241, 242, 243, 244, 245, 251, 259, 260, 261, 262, 264, 266, 269, 271, and 275 Elizabeth Street.) The tenements selected represented a variety of building types. Then I traced name combinations of the first four children in these families, comparing them to other families living on Elizabeth Street. Children with common first and last names were assumed to be cousins, the children of married brothers. When eldest sons and/or

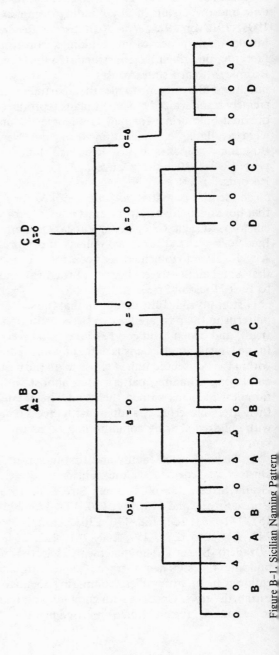

Figure B-1. Sicilian Naming Pattern

daughters in one family shared the names of second-eldest sons and/or daughters in another family, they too were assumed to be cousins, the children of married opposite-sex siblings. When second eldest children shared first names, they were assumed to be the children of married sisters. This method almost certainly underestimated kinship ties outside the household, especially ties linking families with no children or only one child of each sex. (Fortunately, these small families often lived in partner households, where census takers themselves identified kin ties.) Nevertheless it had the advantage of being a systematic method for analyzing more than a very limited number of families. And the degree of kin clustering it suggested was roughly similar to that revealed in studies of smaller numbers of reconstituted families.[7] Analysis of these 765 families provided data not only on kinship clustering, but on kin migration chains and residential mobility.

Notes

Notes to Introduction

1. This study employs a cross-sectional comparative method. Particularly rich demographic and folkloric sources first encouraged me to focus on Sicilian immigrants. This choice led in turn to Elizabeth Street. Appendix B discusses methods and sources more fully.

2. (Ithaca: Cornell University Press, 1977).

3. The literature of housing reform is rich, and it has already attracted considerable attention from historians. See, for example, Roy Lubove, *The Progressives and the Slums; Tenement House Reform in New York City, 1890–1917* (Pittsburgh: University of Pittsburgh Press, 1962) or more recently Anthony Jackson, *A Place Called Home: Low Cost Housing in Manhattan* (Cambridge, Mass.: M.I.T. Press, 1976). Two classic statements of material determinism are Jacob Riis, "The Making of Thieves in New York," *Century Magazine* 49 (1894): 109–116 and Ernest Poole, "The Lung Block," *Charities* 11 (1903): 193–99.

4. Besides Yans-McLaughlin, *Family and Community*, see James Borchert, *Alley Life in Washington* (Urbana: University of Illinois Press, 1980), John Bodnar, Roger Simon and Michael P. Weber, *Lives of Their Own: Blacks, Italians and Poles in Pittsburgh, 1900–1960* (Champaign: University of Illinois Press, 1981) and Judith E. Smith, "Our Own Kind: Family and Community Networks in Providence," *Radical History Review* 17 (1978): 99–120.

5. Herbert J. Gans, *The Levittowners* (New York: Pantheon, 1967), pp. 288–290; see also Herbert J. Gans, "Urbanism and Suburbanism Reconsidered," in *Neighborhood, City and Metropolis*, ed. R. Gutman and David Popenoe (New York: Random House, 1970).

6. Alan Lipman, "The Architectural Belief System and Social Behavior," *British Journal of Sociology* 20 (1969): 196.

7. The statement is usually attributed to Winston Churchill in a post-war debate on Britain's housing policy.

8. Louis Wirth, "Human Ecology," *Classic Essays on the Culture of Cities*, ed. Richard Sennett (New York: Appleton Century-Crofts, 1969), p. 177. See also William H. Ittelson, et al., *An Introduction to Environmental Psychology* (New York: Holt, Rinehart and Winston, 1974).

9. See the excellent bibliography in Nelson Foote, et al., *Housing Choices and Housing Constraints* (New York: McGraw-Hill, 1960). Introductions to the social-psychological proxemic studies are Robert Sommer, "Studies in Personal Space," *Sociometry* 22 (1959): 247–60; Sommer, *Personal Space: The Behavioral Basis of Design* (Englewood Cliffs: Prentice Hall, 1969); Sommer, "Man's Proximate Environment," *The Journal of Social Issues* 22 (1966): 59–70 and Edward T. Hall, *The Hidden Dimension* (New York: Doubleday, 1966).

10. William M. Michelson, *Environmental Choice, Human Behavior and Residential Satisfaction* (New York: Oxford University Press, 1976), p. 6.

11. Amos Rapoport, *House Form and Culture* (Englewood Cliffs: Prentice-Hall, 1969), p. 26.

12. William M. Michelson, *Man and His Urban Environment* (Reading, Mass.: Addison-Wesley, 1970), p. 26; see also Roger Barker, *Ecological Psychology* (Stanford: Stanford University Press, 1968); Christopher Alexander, "The Goodness of Fit and Its Sources," *Environmental Psychology: Man and His Physical Setting*, Harold Proshanski et al. New York: Holt, Rinehart and Winston, 1970), pp. 42–56.

13. Michelson, *Man and His Urban Environment*, pp. 30–31.

14. Michelson, *Environmental Choice*; Wendell Bell, "A Theory of Social Choice," in *The New Urbanization*, ed. Scott Greer (New York: St Martin's Press, 1968); Arnold S. Feldman and Charles Tilly, "The Interaction of Social and Physical Space," *American Sociological Review* 25 (1960): 877–83; Peter H. Rossi, *Why Families Move* (Glencoe, Ill.: The Free Press, 1955).

15. William Michelson, "Some Like it Hot: Social Participation and Environmental Use as Functions of the Season," *American Journal of Sociology* 76 (1971): 1072–83; Stephen Friedman and Joseph B. Juhasz, *Environments: Notes and Selections on Objects, Spaces and Behavior* (Monterey: Brooks/Cole, 1974); Women's Group on Public Welfare, "Effect of the Design of Temporary Prefabricated Bungalows on Household Routines," *The Sociological Review*, 2nd series, 43 (1951): 17–48. The Bibliography lists additional studies.

16. Dell Upton, "Ordinary Buildings: A Bibliographical Essay on American Vernacular Architecture," *American Studies International* 19 (1981): 69–70. See also Rapoport, *House Form and Culture*. Correcting Rapoport and Levi-Strauss, Demetrios Agememnon Phillippides, "The Vernacular Design Setting of Elymbos: A Rural Spatial System in Greece," unpublished Doctoral Dissertation, University of Michigan, 1973, p. 3, notes that spatial relationships — because of their permanence — may lag well behind changing social or cultural ideals.

17. Yans-McLaughlin, p. 23.

Notes to Chapter One

1. Constance Cronin, *The Sting of Change* (Chicago: The University of Chicago Press, 1970); Jeremy Boissevain, *Friends of Friends: Networks, Manipulators and Coalitions* (Oxford: Basil Blackwell, 1974); Anton Blok, *The*

Mafia of a Sicilian Village, 1860-1960 (New York: Harper and Row, 1974). For a popular Italo-American evaluation, see Vincent Teresa, "The Mafia Craze," repr. *A Documentary History of the Italian-Americans*, ed. Wayne Moquin (New York: Praeger, 1974).

2. Edward Banfield, *The Moral Basis of a Backward Society* (Glencoe, Ill.: The Free Press, 1958).

3. Roy A. Miller, "Are Familists Amoral? A Test of Banfield's Amoral Familism Hypothesis in a South Italian Village," *American Ethnologist* 1 (1974): 515-36; Sydel F. Silverman, "Agricultural Organization, Social Structure and Values in Italy: Amoral Familism Reconsidered," *American Anthropologist* 70 (1968): 1-20; J. Davis, "Morals and Backwardness," *Comparative Studies in Society and History* 12 (1970): 340-59; Anthony H. Galt, "Carnival on the Island of Pantelleria: Ritualized Community Solidarity in an Atomistic Society," *Ethnology* 12 (1973): 325-39; William Muraskin, "The Moral Basis of a Backward Sociologist: Edward Banfield, the Italians and the Italian-Americans," *American Journal of Sociology* 79 (1974): 1484-96.

4. Charlotte Gower Chapman, *Milocca, A Sicilian Village* (Cambridge, Mass.: Schenkman, 1971).

5. John W. Briggs, *An Italian Passage* (New Haven: Yale University Press, 1978), ch. 2; Peter Schneider, "Coalition Formation and Colonialism in Western Sicily," *Archives Européènes de Sociologie* 18 (1972): 255-67; Anton Blok, "Coalitions in Sicilian Peasant Society," in *Network Analysis: Studies in Human Interaction*, ed. J. Boissevain and J. Clyde Mitchell (The Hague: Mouton, 1973); Joseph Lopreato, "Social Stratification and Mobility," *American Sociological Review* 26 (1961): 585-96.

6. See Humbert S. Nelli's review of Yans-McLaughlin, *Family and Community*, in *Journal of American History* 66 (1979): 433.

7. Giuseppe Pitrè, *Proverbi Siciliani*, I-IV, Biblioteca delle Tradizioni Popolari Siciliane, vol. 8-11 (Palermo: Luigi Pedone Lauriel, 1880).

8. Ingeborg Weber-Kellermann, *Deutsche Volkskunde zwischen Germanistik und Sozialwissenschaft* (Stuttgart: Metzler, 1969), ch. 3; Hermann Bausinger, "Kritik der Tradition," *Zeitschrift für Volkskunde* 65 (1969): 232-50.

9. Salvatore Salomone-Marino, *Costumi e Usanze dei Contadini di Sicilia* (Palermo: Ando Ed., 1968), p. 27; see also Rudolf Schenda, "Statik und Dynamik der aktuellen Italienischen Volkskunde," *Zeitschrift für Volkskunde* 65 (1969): 251-63.

10. *The American Heritage Dictionary of the English Language.*

11. Giovanni Sprini, "Prefazione," *Proverbi Siciliani* I, (Palermo: Ed. il Vespro, 1978).

12. O.E. Moll, *Sprichwörter Bibliografie* (Frankfurt: V. Klostermann, 1958) summarizes the uses of proverbs.

13. Pitrè, *La Famiglia, la Casa, la Vita del Popolo Siciliano*, Biblioteca delle Tradizioni Popolari Siciliane, vol. 25 (Palermo: Libreria Internazionale A. Reber, 1913).

14. The proverbs' unceasing emphasis on the benefits of *casa* solidarity can be seen as a direct reflection of solidarity or as a sign of stress resulting from its absence. On the relation of ideal and reality, see chapter 3.

15. Dialect terminology is in Antonio Traina, *Vocabolario Siciliano-Italiano*, 2nd ed. (Palermo: Lorenzo Finnocchiare e Fiorenza Garazio, 1890). I agree with Rudolph M. Bell that a *casa* does not resemble a nuclear family, but I disagree with his conclusion that the nuclear family, therefore, had no social significance in rural Italy. As property-owner, it was the single most important unit of economic solidarity. See *Fate and Honor, Family and Village* (Chicago and London: University of Chicago Press, 1979), pp. 72–76.

16. Chapman, ch. 3.

17. Jane and Peter Schneider, *Culture and Political Economy in Western Sicily* (New York: Academic Press, 1976), pp. 14–16. Certificates of birth and marriage, local draft records and electoral lists also give occupations.

18. Ministero di Agricoltura, Industria e Commercio, Direzione Generale della Statistica, *Censimento della Popolazione del Regno d'Italia al 10 Febbraio, 1901* (Rome: Tip. Naz. di G. Bertero, 1902), vol. III; Sonnino, *passim*; see also *Atti della Giunta per l'Inchiesta Agraria e sulle Condizioni della Classe Agricola*, vol. 13, tome I and II, Relazione del Commissario Abele Damiani (Rome: Forzani Tip. del Senato, 1884–85), hereafter *Inchiesta Agraria*.

19. About a quarter of Sicilian sharecroppers were female; females were 14 percent of peasants cultivating their own lands and 8 percent of those working as agricultural laborers in 1901. See also Emmanuele Navarro della Miraglia, *Storielle Siciliane* (Palermo: Sellerio, 1974), p. 61; Douglas Sladen and Norma Lorimer, *Queer Things About Sicily* (London: Kegan Paul, Trench, Trübner, 1913), pp. 397–98; *Inchiesta Agraria, passim*; Pitrè, *La Famiglia*, p. 135–55; Giuseppe Giarrizzo, "La Sicilia e la Crisi Agraria," in *I Fasci Siciliani*, G. Giarrizzo, et al. (Bari: De Donato, 1975).

20. According to the *Inchiesta Agraria*, four towns in the provinces of Agrigento, Palermo and Trapani had "no" landowning peasants; 36 had "few" or "very few" and 64 had "many" or "very many." Census figures reported in *Inchiesta Parlamentare sulle Condizioni dei Contadini nelle Provincie Meridionali e nella Sicilia*, vol. 6, G. Lorenzoni, *Sicilia* (Rome: Tip. Naz. G. Bertero, 1910), p. 54; hereafter *Inchiesta Parlamentare*.

21. George Foster, "The Dyadic Contract: A Model for the Social Structure of a Mexican Peasant Village," *American Anthropologist* 63 (1961): 1173–92; Anthony H. Galt, "Re-thinking Patron-Client Relationships: The Real System and the Official System in Southern Italy," *Anthropological Quarterly* 47 (1974): 182–202.

22. Schneider and Schneider, pp. 117–18; Blok, *Mafia*, p. 91; see also Emilio Sereni, *Il Capitalismo nelle Campagne, 1860–1900* (Turin: Einaudi, 1968), pp. 134–41; Dennis Mack Smith, *Modern Sicily after 1713*, vol. 2 of *A History of Sicily* (New York: The Viking Press, 1968), pp. 343–44; Dennis Mack Smith, "The Latifundia in Modern Sicilian History," *Proceedings of the British Academy* 6 (1965): 85–124.

23. Orazio Cancila, "Variazioni e Tendenze dell'Agricoltura Siciliana a Cavallo della Crisi Agraria," in *I Fasci Siciliani*, Dollo et al. (Bari: De Donato, 1976); *Inchiesta Parlamentare*, p. 235.

24. Salvatore Francesco Romano, *Storia dei Fasci Siciliani* (Bari: Ed. Laterza, 1959), pp. 54-55; Schneider and Schneider, pp. 150-151; Peter Schneider, "Honor and Conflict in a Sicilian Town," *Anthropological Quarterly* 42 (1969): 130-31.

25. F. Brancato, *La Sicilia nel Primo Ventennio del Regno d'Italia* (Bologna: Dott. Cesare Zuffi, 1956), pp. 23-24; Navarro della Miraglia, pp. 10, 62, 114.

26. Sydel Silverman, "An Ethnographic Approach to Social Stratification: Prestige in a Central Italian Community," *American Anthropologist* 68 (1966): 899-921; Blok, *Mafia*, pp. 146-47, n.; Schneider and Schneider, pp. 87-89.

27. Comparing their field work to Pitrè's descriptions, Rudolf and Suzanne Schenda emphasize changes that have occurred in the last seventy years, *Eine Sizilianische Strasse* Tübingen: Drückerei Tübinger Chronik, 1965).

Notes to Chapter Two

1. These descriptions are drawn from the population registers (*fogli di famiglia*) of Sambuca di Sicilia. Only the names of families and each *cortile* are fictional.

2. Schneider and Schneider, pp. 14-16.

3. Giuseppe Bruccoleri, *l'Emigrazione Siciliana* (Rome: Coop. Tip. A. Manuzio, 1911).

4. See also Chapman, pp. 12-14.

5. Anton Blok, "South Italian Agrotowns," *Comparative Studies in Society and History* 11 (1969): 121-35.

6. Schneider and Schneider, pp. 13-14; *Inchiesta Agraria*, pp. 34-38.

7. Blok, *Mafia*, p. 46.

8. Francesco Renda, *l'Emigrazione in Sicilia* (Palermo: Tip. La Cartografica, 1963), p. 73.

9. Schneider and Schneider, p. 51.

10. Blok, "Agrotowns."

11. Giorgio Valussi, *La Casa Rurale nella Sicilia Occidentale*, Recerche sulle Dimore Rurali in Italia, vol. 24 (Florence: Leo S. Olschki, 1968), ch. 1-2.

12. Pitrè, *La Famiglia*, ch. 6; Valussi; Tina Storai de Rocchai, *Guida Bibliografica allo Studio dell'Abitazione Rurale in Italia*, Ricerche sulle Dimore Rurali in Italia, vol. 7 (Florence: Leo S. Olschki, 1968).

13. Emmanuele Navarro della Miraglia, *La Nana* (Bologna: Capelli, 1963), p. 22.

14. Valussi, pp. 36-38 and Figures 24, 32, 33, 37, 120 and 127.

15. "Catasto dei Fabbricati," 11 vol, Archivio Municipale, Sambuca di Sicilia.

16. Chapman, p. 15.

17. Navarro della Miraglia, *La Nana*, pp. 26-37.

18. Besides Pitrè, *La Famiglia,* see *Inchiesta Agraria passim*; Salomone-Marino, ch. 2.

19. Pitrè, *La Famiglia,* p. 76; Salomone-Marino, p. 55.

20. The best descriptions are fictional: Tomasi di Lampedusa, *Il Gattopardo* (Milan: Feltrinelli, 1976), pp. 106–107; Navarro della Miraglia, *La Nana.* See also C. Levi, *Fabbricati Civile di Abitazione* (Milan: Hoepli, 1910).

21. Pitrè, *La Famiglia,* pp. 36, 89; Giuseppe Pitrè, *Usi e Costumi, Credenze e Pregiudizi del Popolo Siciliano,* 1–4, Biblioteca delle Tradizioni Popolari Siciliane, vol. 14–17, (Palermo: Libreria L. Pedone Lauriel di Carlo Clausen, 1889), vol. 15, pp. 9–12; Salomone-Marino, p. 54; Chapman, p. 97; Caico, p. 50.

22. Pitrè, *La Famiglia,* pp. 34, 89.

23. Sonnino, p. 107.

24. Sladen and Lorimer, p. 80.

25. Leonard Covello, *The Social Background of the Italo-American School Child,* ed. Francesco Cordasco (Leiden: E.J. Brill, 1967), p. 73.

26. Antonio Mangano, "The Effect of Emigration Upon Italy, part 2," *Charities and the Commons* 19 (1908): 1478.

27. *Inchiesta Parlamentare,* p. 52.

28. Schneider and Schneider, p. 123.

29. Chapman, pp. 55–56; Salomone-Marino, p. 54; Valussi, p. 48.

30. Phyllis H. Williams, *South Italian Folkways in Europe and America* (New Haven: Yale University Press, 1938), p. 49.

31. Sonnino, p. 53.

32. William Agnew Paton, *Picturesque Sicily* (New York: Harper, 1898), pp. 181–82.

33. Lorenzo Bellini, *Guida Pratica ai Municipi per il Rilascio di Atti e Documenti in Uso Pubblico e Privato* (Suzzara: Tip. della Suzzarese, 1901), p. 478.

34. Sonnino, p. 11.

35. Four hundred *fogli* (each with at least one child living in the United States in 1921 or 1931) were analyzed for kin ties among the families listed. (*Fogli* gave complete names of father and mother for all persons listed, thus allowing identification of kin ties beyond the household.) In addition, the *fogli* often reported the new address of a child marrying and leaving the household. These methods identified the addresses of 200 parents/married daughter ties, 140 parents/married son ties, 70 ties between 2 married sisters, 90 ties between 2 married brothers and 80 between a married woman and her married brother. In analyzing the geographic location of the households so linked, I divided Sambuca into five sections of roughly equal size, more or less according to my own sense of which parts of town formed units, and generally choosing major streets as boundaries. All these units were quite small by American standards, easily traversed by foot in about five minutes. I chose this method because I do not believe that the parish (often mentioned as an important south Italian geographical unit in discussions

of *campanilismo*) had any meaning in Sambuca, a town where churches, with one or two exceptions, clustered along the centrally-located *corso* or an immediately parallel street.

36. Chapman, p. 131.

37. Chapman, p. 131.

38. Changes in property transmission did occur elsewhere in southern Italy: John Davis uncovered such a change in nineteenth-century Pisticci. There, families originally gave houses to sons, but as large numbers of young men migrated, fearful parents responded by giving more family property (including houses) to daughters. This made them more attractive as prospective brides in a disrupted marriage market. Davis, *Land and Family in Pisticci*, London School of Economics Monographs on Social Anthropology (New York: Humanities Press, 1973). See also Peter Loizos, "Changes in Property Transfer Among Greek Cypriot Villages," *Man* 10 (1975): 10.

39. Navarro della Miraglia, *La Nana*, p. 33.

40. "Sviluppo della Popolazione Italiana dal 1861 al 1961," *Annali di Statistica*, anno 94, serie VIII, vol. 17, pp. 260–61.

41. Pitrè, *La Famiglia*, p. 30.

42. Chapman, p. 130.

43. Bellini, p. 483.

44. Valussi, pp. 33, 48; unlike classic *mezzadria*, sharecropping in Sicily did not encourage father-son cooperation in stem-family households. See David I. Kertzer, "European Peasant Household Structure: Some Implications from a Nineteenth Century Italian Community," *Journal of Family History* 2 (1977): 333–49; Carlo Poni, "Family and 'Podere' in Emilia-Romagna," *The Journal of Italian History 1 (1978): 201*–34.

45. Jane and Peter Schneider, "The Reproduction of the Ruling Class in Sicily, 1860-1920," unpublished paper, p. 29.

46. Chapman, p. 13.

47. Caico, p. 30.

48. Luigi Villari, *Italian Life in Town and Country* (New York: G.P. Putnam's Sons, 1902), pp. 109–10.

49. Valussi, p. 38.

50. Chapman, p. 13.

51. Pitrè, *La Famiglia*, p. 77 and photograph, p. 87. See also Giuseppe Cocchiara, *La Vita e l'Arte del Popolo Siciliano nel Museo Pitrè* (Palermo: F. Ciuni Libraio, 1938), p. 23.

52. Pitrè, *La Famiglia*, p. 92; Salomone-Marino, pp. 55–56.

53. Navarro della Miraglia, *La Nana*, p. 27.

54. Pitrè, *Proverbi*, I, p. 217; Giuseppe Cocchiara, *Il Folklore Siciliano* (Palermo: S.F. Flaccovio, 1957), vol. 1, p. 15.

55. Lizabeth A. Cohen, "Embellishing a Life of Labor: An Interpretation of the Material Culture of American Working-Class Homes, 1885-1915," *Journal of American Culture* 3 (1980): 752–55; H. Plath, "Elendswohnungen in der Altstadt

Hannover, um 1933," *Zeitschrift für Volkskunde* 68 (1972): 61–89; Lee Rainwater, "Work and Identity in the Lower Class," in *Planning for a Nation of Cities*, ed. Sam Bass Warner (Cambridge, Mass.: The M.I.T. Press, 1966), pp. 105–123. Here I directly contradict Yans-McLaughlin, who believes that south Italians had no equivalent of "the home ideal," *Family and Community*, p. 223.
56. Chapman, p. 130.
57. Pitrè, *Proverbi*, vol. I, p. 216.
58. Pitrè, *Proverbi*, vol. IV, p. 221.
59. Pitrè, *Proverbi*, vol. I, pp. 216, 226.
60. (Harmondsworth: Penguin Books, 1970), p. 27.

Notes to Chapter Three

1. Michelson, *Environmental Choice*, p. 27; see also Margret Tränkle, *Wohnkultur und Wohnweisen*, Untersuchungen des Ludwig-Uhland Instituts der Universität Tübingen (Tübingen: Tübinger Vereinigung für Volkskunde, 1972).
2. Lewis Henry Morgan, *Houses and House-Life of the American Aborigines* (Washington: Government Printing Office, 1881).
3. Characteristically vague is John W. Dodd, *Everyday Life in Twentieth Century America* (New York: G.P. Putnam, 1965). An attempt at definition, albeit not useful to historians, is Hans Peter Thurn, "Grundprobleme eines sozialwissenschaftlichen Konzepts der Alltagskultur," *Kölner Zeitschrift für Soziologie und Sozialpsychologie* 30 (1978): 47–59.
4. An Italian example of this approach is Guido Vincelli, *Una Comunità Meridionale* (Turin: Taylor Torino, 1958).
5. Emmanuel L. Ladurie, *Montaillou: The Promised Land of Error*, trans. Barbara Bray (New York: Random House, 1979).
6. Navarro della Miraglia, *Storielle Siciliane*, p. 74.
7. Giuseppe Pitrè housed a considerable artifact collection in what is now the Museo Pitrè, Parca Favorita, Palermo.
8. Robert F. Berkhofer, *A Behavioral Approach to Historical Analysis* (New York: The Free Press, 1969), ch. 5–6.
9. Sonnino, p. 12.
10. Pitrè, *Usi e Costumi*, vol. III, p. 105; Navarro della Miraglia, *Storielle Siciliane*, p. 111.
11. Blok, *Mafia*, pp. 43–44.
12. Sonnino, pp. 31–32.
13. Salomone-Marino, p. 63.
14. Douglas Sladen, *Sicily, the New Winter Resort* (New York: E.P. Dutton, 1907), p. 178.
15. "Sicilian Mountain Peasants," Arthur Stanley Riggs, "Inexhaustible Italy," *National Geographic* 30 (1916): 357.
16. Celena A. Baxter, "Sicilian Family Life," *Family* 14 (1930): 82.

17. Chapman, p. 32; Salomone-Marino, p. 258; Rudolf and Susanne Schenda, *Eine Sizilianische Strasse*, pp. 25–26.
18. Interview with Pasquale Maggio, March 11, 1977. See also K. Jaberg and J. Jud, *Sprach–und Sachatlas Italiens und der Südschweiz* (Zofingen: Ringier, 1933), map 873.
19. Pitrè, *La Famiglia*, pp. 87–88.
20. Chapman, p. 21.
21. Covello, p. 161; Cronin, pp. 93–94.
22. Chapman, p. 131.
23. Chapman, p. 62.
24. Chapman, p. 62.
25. Chapman, p. 38; Salomone-Marino, p. 298.
26. Navarro della Miraglia, *La Nana*, p. 24; Pitrè, *La Famiglia*, pp. 212–228.
27. Salomone-Marino, p. 63.
28. Pitrè, *La Famiglia*, p. 41; *Usi e Costumi*, vol. III, pp. 108–109; Sladen, p. 125.
29. *Inchiesta Agraria*, tome 2, p. 117; Paul Scheuermeier, *Bauernwerk in Italien und in der italienischen und rätromanischen Schweiz* (Bern: Verlag Stämpfli, 1956), p. 84.
30. Scheuermeier, pp. 60–61; Jud and Jaberg, map. 931.
31. Chapman, p. 15; Pitrè, *Proverbi*, II, p. 287.
32. Chapman, p. 54.
33. Covello, p. 131.
34. Schenda and Schenda, p. 53.
35. Chapman, p. 54.
36. Chapman, pp. 56–57.
37. Navarro della Miraglia, *Storielle Siciliane*, p. 4.
38. Navarro della Miraglia, *La Nana*, pp. 41–73; Sladen, p. 275; Douglas Sladen, *In Sicily* (London: Sands and Co., 1901), vol. 1, pp. 46–47.
39. Baxter, p. 82; see also Istituto Nazionale di Economia Agraria, Monografie di Famiglie Agricole, vol. 4, Taddei-Ledda, *Contadini Siciliane* (Rome: S.A. Tip. Operaia, Romano, 1933), pp. 38–39.
40. Dr. Alexander Rumpelt, *Sicilien und die Sicilianer*, 2nd. ed. (Berlin: Allgemeiner Verein für Deutsche Literatur, 1902), pp. 38–39.
41. Pitrè, *Usi e Costumi, vol. II, p. 53–58*.
42. Cronin, p. 82.
43. Pitrè, *Usi e Costumi*, vol. II, p. 170; Cronin, p. 89; Cocchiara, *La Vita*, p. 85.
44. Sladen, *In Sicily*, vol. 1, pp. 46–47; Schneider and Schneider, *Culture*, p. 15.
45. Enrico Loncao, *Considerazioni sulla Genesi ed Evoluzione della Borghesia in Sicilia* (Palermo: Tip. Coop. fra gli Operai, 1899), pp. 210–14.
46. Chapman, p. 14; Pitrè, *La Famiglia*, pp. 87–88; for a slightly later period, Taddei-Ledda, pp. 31–32.
47. Baxter, p. 83.
48. Pitrè, *Proverbi*, vol. III.

49. Chapman, pp. 21–23; Pitrè, *La Famiglia*, p. 138; *Inchiesta Agraria*, tome 2, p. 641; Taddei-Ledda, p. 90; see also Davis, appendix VI.

50. Chapman, p. 32.

51. Chapman, pp. 21–24; Valussi, pp. 67–68; Blok, *Mafia*, p. 23. Seasonal changes described in J.M. Houston, *The Western Mediterranean World* (London: Longmans, Green and Co., 1964), pp. 15–35; Renée Rochefort, *Le Travail en Sicile* (Paris: Presse Universitaires, 1961), p. 87.

52. Pitrè, *Proverbi*, vol. II, p. 4; Sonnino, pp. 45, 51; Salomone-Marino, p. 172; Salvatore Francesco Romano, *La Sicilia nell'Ultimo Ventennio del Secolo XIX* (Palermo: Industria Grafica Nazionale, 1958), p. 154.

53. Pitrè, *La Famiglia*, pp. 135–156; Taddei-Ledda, p. 12; *Inchiesta Agraria*, passim, for example, tome 2, pp. 216, 266; Cocchiara, *La Vita*, pp. 56–57.

54. Pitrè, *Proverbi*, vol. IV, p. 4.

55. Sonnino, pp. 11–12; Blok, *Mafia*, pp. 46–47.

56. Sonnino, p. 11.

57. Blok, *Mafia*, pp. 48–49.

58. Alfonso di Giovanna, *Inchiostro e Trazzere* (Sambuca: Ed. La Voce, 1979), p. 52; Cronin, p. 64; Blok, *Mafia*, p. 47; Wilhelm E. Mühlmann and Roberto J. Llaryora, *Strummula Siciliana; Ehre, Rang und Soziale Schichtung in einer Sizilianischen Agro-Stadt* (Meisenheim am Glan: Anton Hain, 1973).

59. Chapman, p. 32.

60. Chapman, p. 15; Sereni, p. 155; Pitrè, *La Famiglia*, p. 80; Taddei-Ledda, p. 63.

61. Pitrè, *La Famiglia*, p. 89; Sonnino, p. 53; William Seymour Monroe, *Sicily, the Garden of the Mediterranean* (Boston: L. C. Page, 1909), p. 120.

62. Navarro della Miraglia, *La Nana*, p. 23; Sladen and Lorimer, p. 85.

63. Chapman, pp. 60, 62; Navarro della Miraglia, *La Nana* p. 24; William Foote Whyte, "Sicilian Peasant Society," *American Anthropologist* 46 (1944): 69–70.

64. Navarro della Miraglia, *La Nana*, pp. 63–65.

65. Chapman, p. 14; Giovanni Verga, *Tutte le Novelle*, 2 vols. (Milan: Mondadori, 1942), I, p. 24; Covello, p. 88.

66. For symbolic significance of doors and windows, see Otto Friedrich Bollnow, *Mensch und Raum* (Stuttgart: W. Kohlhammer, 1963), pp. 154–56.

67. *Inchiesta Agraria*, tome 1, p. 467. Leonard Covello, *The Heart is the Teacher* (New York: McGraw-Hill, 1958); see also Covello, *Social Background*, p. 93.

68. Pitrè, *Proverbi*, vol. II, p. 414.

69. Pitrè, *La Famiglia*, pp. 30, 36; Salomone-Marino, p. 44.

70. Navarro della Miraglia, *Storielle Siciliane*, pp. 130–31; Sladen and Lorimer, pp. 397–98; Chapman, pp. viii–ix, 46.

71. John Davis, "Town and Country," *Anthropological Quarterly*, 42 (1969): 171–185.

72. Pitrè, *La Famiglia*, p. 80; Taddei-Ledda, p. 63.

73. Chapman, pp. 111–12; Sereni, p. 155; Rumpelt p. 40.

74. Taddei-Ledda, p. 63; Covello, *Social Background*, p. 179; Benedetto Rubino and Giuseppe Cocchiara, *Usi e Costumi, Novelle e Poesie del Popolo Siciliano* (Palermo: Remo Sandron, 1924), p. 34; Giovanni Verga, *Little Novels of Sicily* (New York: Thomas Selzer, 1925), p. 63.

75. Sladen, *Sicily*, p. 178; Davis, *Land and Family*, p. 72; Sladen and Lorimer, p. 82; Giovanni Verga, *The House by the Medlar Tree* (New York: Grove Press, 1953), pp. 22–23, 97.

76. Navarro della Miraglia, *Storielle Siciliane*, p. 73.

77. Chapman, p. 129.

78. Chapman, p. 46; Navarro della Miraglia, *Storielle Siciliane*, p. 4.

79. "Female Forms of Power and the Myth of Male Dominance: A Model of Female/Male Interaction in Peasant Society," *American Ehnologist* 2 (1975): 727–56.

80. Pitrè, *La Famiglia*, pp. 30, 36; Cronin, p. 76.

81. Verga, *The House*, p. 78.

82. Asked to give a reference address to the local draft authorities in the 1870's and 1880's, young men universally gave the name of their *cortile*, not a street address (although these existed). Yans-McLaughlin, p. 264, argues that community for ordinary Italians was not a place, but a "spiritual, emotional or blood tie." Obviously, I disagree.

83. Chapman, pp. 12, 39; Williams, p. 41.

84. p. 152; see also Rubino, p. 16.

85. Sladen, *Sicily*, p. 35.

86. Chapman, pp. 39, 60; Peter Schneider, "Honor and Conflict," pp. 148–49; Jane Schneider, "Of Vigilance and Virgins: Honor, Shame and Access to Resources in Mediterranean Societies," *Ethnology* 10 (1971): 3–22.

87. Briggs, ch. 2; di Giovanna, p. 52; Christian Giordano, *Handwerker und Bauernverbände in der Sizilianischen Gesellschaft*, Heidelberga Sociologica, 14 (Tübingen: J.C.B. Mohr, 1975), App. 1.

88. Schneider and Schneider, "Reproduction," p. 28.

89. Schneider and Schneider, *Culture*, p. 9; Blok, *Mafia*, p. 179.

90. di Giovanna, pp. 28–29; Schneider and Schneider, *Culture*, pp. 156–58.

Notes to Chapter Four

1. Ministero di Agricoltura, Industria e Commercio, *Statistica della Emigrazione Italiana* (Rome: 1878–79, 1881–1897, 1900–15.)

2. Renda, *l'Emigrazione*, p. 42; Robert F. Foerster, *The Italian Emigration of Our Times* (Cambridge, Mass.: Harvard University Press, 1924), p. 48.

3. Walter Laidlaw, ed., *Population of the City of New York, 1890–1930* (New York: Cities Census Committee, 1932).

4. U.S. Senate, *Report on Conditions of Women and Child Wage-Earners in*

the United States, Men's Ready-Made Clothing (Washington: Government Printing Office, 1911), p. 261; *Immigrants in Cities*, p. 175.

5. John S. MacDonald, "Some Socioeconomic Emigration Differentials in Rural Italy, 1902–13," *Economic Development and Cultural Change* 7 (1958): 55–72; "Agricultural Organization, Migration and Labour Militancy in Rural Italy," *The Economic History Review*, 2nd series, 16 (1963): 61–75; J.S. and Leatrice MacDonald, "Institutional Economics and Rural Development: Two Italian Types," *Human Organization* 23 (1964): 113–18.

6. Yans-McLaughlin, pp. 109–10; Josef J. Barton, *Peasants and Strangers* (Cambridge, Mass.: Harvard University Press, 1975), pp. 28–31.

7. MacDonald, "Institutional Economics," pp. 117–18; "Agricultural Organization," pp. 72–73.

8. John S. MacDonald and Leatrice D. MacDonald, "Italian Migration to Australia: Manifest Functions of Bureaucracy versus Latent Functions of Informal Networks," *Journal of Social History* 3 (1970): 248–76, suggest that Sicilian culture also changed over time. Their earlier articles characterize Sicilians as a culturally transitional group; here the MacDonalds group Sicilians with other parts of the familist "Deep South."

9. John S. MacDonald and Leatrice D. MacDonald, "Chain Migration, Ethnic Neighborhood Formation, and Social Network," *Milbank Fund Quarterly* 42 (1964): 82–97.

10. Ministero di Agricoltura, Industria e Commercio, *Statistica della Società di Mutuo Soccorso* (Rome: 1873, 1878, 1885) and *Le Società di Mutuo Soccorso in Italia* (Rome: Tip. G. Bertero, 1906). See also Briggs, ch. 2. For fuller analysis of the relationship of protest and migration in western Sicily, see my "Migration and Peasant Militance: Western Sicily, 1880–1910", *Social Science History* (forthcoming).

11. Renda, *l'Emigrazione*, p. 42.

12. *Statistica della Emigrazione Italiana avvenuta nell' Anno 1888*, pp. 145–147.

13. For example, *Statistica della Emigrazione, 1900–1905*.

14. Francesco Renda, *I Fasci Siciliani, 1892–94* (Turin: Einaudi, 1977), ch. 8.

15. "Lista della Leva," 1868–1935, Sambuca di Sicilia.

16. Jane and Peter Schneider, "The Demographic Transition in Sicily, Progress Report on a Local Level Case Study," unpub. paper, Table 4.

17. Francesco DeStefano and Francesco Luigi Oddo, *Storia della Sicilia dal 1860 al 1910* (Bari: Laterza, 1963), pp. 119–21; Jürg K. Siegenthaler, "Sicilian Economic Change Since 1860," *The Journal of European Economic History* 2 (1973): 368–69; 374–76.

18. Renda, *I Fasci*, ch. 2.

19. Cancila, "Variazioni," and Giarizzo, "La Sicilia."

20. *Inchiesta Parlamentare*, p. 125; *Inchiesta Agraria*, tome 2, pp. 253, 266.

21. Yans-McLaughlin; more generally, see Charles Tilly and Harold C. Brown, "On Uprooting, Kinship and the Auspices of Migration," *International*

Journal of Comparative Sociology 8 (1967): 139–164; Harvey M. Choldin, "Kin ship Networks in the Migration Process," *International Migration Review* ` (1973): 167–75; Robert E. Bieder, "Kinship as a Factor in Migration," *Journal o Marriage and the Family* 35 (1973): 429–39.

22. MacDonald and MacDonald, "Chain Migration."
23. Yans-McLaughlin, p. 96.
24. U.S. Senate, Reports of the Immigration Commission, *Immigrants i Cities* (Washington: Government Printing Office, 1911), vol. 2, Table 372.
25. Robert Coit Chapin, *The Standard of Living Among Workingmen' Families in New York City* (New York: Charities Publication Committee, 1909)
26. Yans-McLaughlin, pp. 62–63.
27. Richard N. Juliani, "American Voices, Italian Accents," *Italian American* 1 (1974): 1–25; Franc Sturino, "Family and Kin Cohesion Among South Italia Immigrants in Toronto," *The Italian Immigrant Woman in North America*, ed Betty Boyd Caroli, Robert F. Harney and Lydio F. Tomasi (Toronto Multicultural History Society of Ontario, 1978).
28. Cronin, pp. 24–25.
29. Briggs, pp. 69–94, quoted material, p. 75.
30. Giuseppe Pitrè, *Feste Patronali in Sicilia*, Biblioteca delle Tradizion Popolari Siciliane, vol. 21 (Turin-Palermo: Carlo Clausen, 1900) and Pitrè, *Pro verbi*, vol. III, "Nazioni, Paesi, Città.
31. Briggs, pp. 5–7; Yans-McLaughlin, pp. 26–27.
32. Briggs' immigrants resemble artisans; Yans-McLaughlin's peasants.
33. Robert M. Lichtenberg, *One-Tenth of a Nation: Natural Forces in th Economic Growth of the New York Region* (Cambridge, Mass.: Harvard Univer sity Press, 1960).
34. Briggs, pp. 3–4; Barton, pp. 91–94.
35. Luciano John Iorizzo, *Italian Immigration and the Impact of the Padron System* (New York: Arno Press, 1980); *Little Italies in North America*, ed. Rober F. Harney and J. Vincenza Scarpaci (Toronto: The Multicultural History Societ of Ontario, 1981).
36. *Immigrants in Cities*. An exaggeration. South Italians working in the gar ment trade almost always claimed to have worked in the production of garment in southern Italy before migration—claims which must be regarded with mor than a little skepticism.
37. Humbert S. Nelli, *The Business of Crime* (New York: Oxford Universit Press, 1976), pp. 27, 37.
38. Mabel Hurd Willett, *The Employment of Women in the Clothing Trade* Columbia University Studies in History, Economics and Public Law, 16 (Nev York: Columbia University Press, 1902); *Women and Child Wage-Earners*; U.S 62nd. Congress, 2nd. Session, Senate Document no. 633, Reports of the Im migration Commission, *Report on Immigrants in Industries, Part 6, Clothin Manufacturing* (Washington: Government Printing Office, 1911).
39. Willett, map. opp. p. 258.

40. Covello, *The Heart*, and Garibaldi M. Lapolla, *The Grand Gennaro* (New ork: Vanguard, 1935) provide examples of artisans who never re-achieve heir old skilled work, and of men without training who transform themselves in- o artisans or merchants.

Notes to Chapter Five

1. Jacob Riis, *Ten Years War* (Boston: Houghton Mifflin, 1900), pp. 53–61.
2. See *The Peril and Preservation of the Home* (Philadelphia: George W. acobs, 1903), p. 34.
3. I followed Robert E. Park and Herbert A. Miller, *Old World Traits Transplanted* (New York: Harper and Bros., 1921), map opp. p. 146 and defined Elizabeth Street as the area bounded on the north by E. Houston, and on the outh by Grand—including the north side of Broome and the south side of E. Houston (between Mott and Elizabeth), as well as the north and south sides of Spring and Prince (between Mott and Elizabeth) and the south side of Prince be- ween Elizabeth and the Bowery. For the Fourteenth Ward, see James Ford, *Slums and Housing* (Cambridge, Mass.: Harvard University Press, 1936), Part 1; ra Rosenwaike, *Population History of New York City* (Syracuse: Syracuse University Press, 1972), ch. 3.
4. Real Estate Record Association, *A History of Real Estate Building and Ar- hitecture in New York City during the Last Quarter of a Century* (New York: Real Estate Record Association, 1898), p. 51.
5. New York State Assembly, Tenement House Committee, *Report* (Albany: ames Lyon, 1895), Map 2.
6. *The Tenement House Problem*, ed. Robert de Forest and Lawrence Veiller New York: McMillan, 1903), p. 102; hereafter, *The Tenement House Problem*.
7. *The Tenement House Problem*, p. 204.
8. *The Tenement House Problem*, Appendix IX.
9. *Immigrants in Cities*, p. 228. Average income of $519 was reduced to the ower figure because the sample used in that study contained higher proportions of skilled workers than did the Elizabeth Street population.
10. *Immigrants in Cities*, Table 66.
11. Lillian Betts, "The Italian in New York," *University Settlement Studies* 1 1905–06): 98.
12. Betts, *"The Italian in New York,"* p. 98.
13. New York State Factory Investigating Commission, *Second Report* Albany: The Argus Company, 1912), vol. 4, p. 1556.
14. Riis, *Ten Years War*, p. 24; Lillian Betts, "Italian Peasants in a New Law Tenement," *Harper's Bazaar* 38 (1904): 805.
15. Betts, "Italian Peasants," p. 803.
16. John Modell and Tamara K. Hareven, "Urbanization and the Malleable Household: An Examination of Boarding and Lodging in American Families," *Journal of Marriage and the Family* 35 (1973): 467–79. Boarding practices are

described in Chapin; Louise Bolard More, *Wage Earners' Budgets*, Greenwic House Series of Social Studies, 1 (New York: Henry Holt 1907); Louise C. Oder crantz, *Italian Women in Industry* (New York: Russell Sage Foundation, 1919)

17. Robert Harney, "Boarding and Belonging," *Urban History Review*, 1978

18. Boarding provided food and housing for less than 10 percent of a yearly in come of $350. In contrast, sharing a two-room apartment required somewha over 10 percent for housing alone. About 20 percent of New York's south Italia male wage earners over age eighteen earned less than $400 a year, *Immigrants i Cities*, p. 224. I assumed that boarders fell disproportionately in this group.

19. *Immigrants in Cities*, pp. 59, 64; New York State Factory Investigatin Commission, *Fourth Report* (Albany: J.B. Lyon, 1915), vol. 4, pp. 1547, 1549

20. Betts, "Italian Peasants," p. 807.

21. Betts, "Italian Peasants," p. 802; *The Tenement House Problem*, p. 437

22. Pietro di Donato, *Three Circles of Light* (New York: Julian Messne 1960), p. 5; see also Betts, "The Italian," p. 94.

23. Jacob A. Riis, *The Children of the Poor* (New York: Charles Scribner Sons, 1908), p. 12.

24. Williams, pp. 42–43, 47; New York City AICP, *74th Annual Repor* (1917): 14; New York City Tenement House Department, *Second Report* (Nev York: Martin B. Brown Press, 1907), plate 24; New York State Factory In vestigating Commission, *Second Report*, vol. 2, p. 681, and *Fourth Report*, vol 4, opp. p. 1540.

25. Chapin, pp. 71, 202, 240. New York State Welfare Conference, *Report o the Special Committee on the Standard of Living* (New York: New York Stat Welfare Conference, 1907), p. 129. Typical photos are New York State Factor Investigating Commission, *Preliminary Report* (Albany: The Argus Co., 1912) vol. 2, "Laight Street." See also Lewis Hines, "Photographic Documents," uni no. 1, picture 1, New York Public Library.

26. Lapolla, p. 304; New York State Factory Investigating Commission *Fourth Report*, vol. 4, p. 1547; Williams, p. 48.

27. More, pp. 48–59. The Immigration Commission, questioning families tha had been in New York more than ten years, found that 80 percent of the souther Italians had lived the entire time in one neighborhood, *Immigrants in Cities*, p 243. In a much later survey of Italian garment workers leaving the Lower Eas Side, Leo Grebler found that the average family had lived twenty-one years there in an average 3.2 apartments, *Housing Market Behavior in a Declining Are* (New York: Columbia University Press, 1952), p. 247. See also James Ford, p 658; Fred L. Lavanburg, *What Happened to 386 Families Who Were Compelle to Vacate Their Slum Dwellings to Make Way for a Large Housing Project* (Nev York: Fred L. Lavanburg Foundation, 1933), p. 5.

28. Averages are from a sample of real estate properties advertised in *Bolletin della Sera*, 1905–1910.

29. Harry M. Shulman, *Slums of New York* (New York: Albert and Charle Boni, 1938), p. 195.

Notes to Chapter Six

1. Patrick Watson, *Fasanella's City* (New York: Ballantine Books, 1973), p. 33.
2. Watson, p. 33.
3. Covello, *The Heart*, p. 22.
4. "The Big Flat," New York AICP, *43rd Annual Report* (1886): 46.
5. Betts, "Italian Peasants," p. 804.
6. Mary E. Richmond, *The Good Neighbor in the Modern City* (Philadelphia: J.B. Lippincott 1908), pp. 120–21.
7. Betts, "Italian Peasants," p. 803; *Women and Child Wage-Earners*, p. 262; Lapolla, *Grand Gennaro*, p. 151.
8. New York State Factory Investigating Commission, *Fourth Report*, vol. 4, p. 1800.
9. Florence Nesbitt *Household Management* (New York: Russell Sage Foundation, 1918), p. 121.
10. Mabel Kittredge, "Home-Making in a Model Tenement," *Charities* 15 (1905): 180.
11. Pianos were commonly advertised in the *Bolletino della Sera* in the early years of the century; three male "music teachers" lived on Elizabeth Street in 1905; see also Shulman, p. 8.
12. Mario Puzo, *The Fortunate Pilgrim* (New York: Lancer, 1964), pp. 188–89.
13. Shulman, p. 105.
14. "The Coal Situation in New York," *Charities* 9 (1902): 357.
15. Betts, "Italian Peasants," p. 804.
16. *Women and Child Wage-Earners*, p. 251.
17. Annie S. Daniel, "The Wreck of the Home, How Wearing Apparel is Fashioned in the Tenements," *Charities* 14 (1905): 629; New York State Factory Investigating Commission, *Second Report*, vol. 4, p. 1524; Betts, "Italian Peasants," p. 804; Elizabeth Watson, "Homework in the Tenements," *Survey* 25 (1911): 776; Lewis Hines, "Photographic Documents of Social Conditions," Unit no. 1, picture 34, New York Public Library.
18. Betts, "The Italian," p. 99.
19. Nesbitt, p. 136.
20. New York State Factory Investigating Commission, *Fourth Report*, vol. 2, p. 695; Shulman, p. 180.
21. "The Cost of Living," *The Charities Review* 9 (1899): 238.
22. Antonio Mangano, "The Italian Colonies of New York City," in *Italians in the City*, p. 21.
23. Betts, "Italian Peasants," p. 804.
24. New York AICP, Bureau of Public Health and Hygiene and New York City Department of Health, Bureau of Child Hygiene, *Flies and Diarrheal Disease* (New York: AICP, n.d. 1915?), p. 10.
25. Betts, "The Italian," p. 94.
26. Betts, "Italian Peasants," p. 805.

27. Works Progress Administration, Federal Writers Project of the City of New York, *The Italians of New York, a Survey* (New York: Random House, 1938), p. 205.

28. Betts, "Italian Peasants," p. 807.

29. Riis, *Ten Years War*, p. 110.

30. Covello, *The Heart*, p. 36.

31. Daniel, p. 625; Hines, "Photographic Documents," Unit 2, no. 40.

32. Daniel, p. 624; New York State Factory Investigating Commission, *Second Report*, vol. 4, pp. 1546–1547.

33. New York State Factory Investigating Commission, *Second Report*, vol. 2, p. 69; vol. 4, p. 1553; *Women and Child Wage-Earners*, p. 230; Riis, *The Children of the Poor*, pp. 20, 92, 96; New York State Factory Investigating Commission, *Preliminary Report*, pp. 88–89; New York State Department of Labor, *Seventh Annual Report of the Commissioner of Labor, 1907* (Albany: J.B. Lyon, 1908), p. 161; New York State Assembly, Tenement House Committee, *Report*, p. 160.

34. New York State Assembly, Tenement House Committee, *Report*, pp. 154–58.

35. Shulman, p. 14; Federal Writers Project, p. 53.

36. Chapin, p. 115. This scavenging was regarded as work, not stealing. "Punish the Real Offender and Not the Child," *Charities* 12 (1904): 858.

37. Daniel, pp. 624–25.

38. New York State Assembly, Tenement House Committee, *Report*, pp. 154–158.

39. Thomas Jesse Jones, *The Sociology of a New York City Block*, Columbia University Studies in History, Economics and Public Law, 21 (New York: Columbia University Press, 1904), p. 124; Betts, "Italian Peasants," p. 804.

40. Chapin, pp. 138–39.

41. *The Tenement House Problem*, p. 294.

42. New York State Assembly, Tenement House Committee, *Report*, p. 20; Nesbitt, pp. 104–105.

43. Chapin, p. 240.

44. New York State Factory Investigating Commission, *Fourth Report*, vol. 4, p. 1800.

45. New York State Welfare Conference, p. 14; Williams, p. 61.

46. Covello, *The Social Background*, p. 295; see also Jo Pagano, *Golden Wedding* (New York: Random House, 1943), pp. 12–13.

47. Betts, "Italian Peasants," p. 803; Mabel Hyde Kittredge, *The Home and its Management* (New York: The Century Co., 1917), pp. 17–19. See also, "Coal Situation in New York," pp. 357, 388.

48. Betts, "Italian Peasants," p. 803; Sophonisba P. Breckinridge, *New Homes for Old* (New York: Harper and Brothers, 1921), p. 59.

49. Betts, "Italian Peasants," p. 803.

50. *Women and Child Wage-Earners*, p. 252; New York City Tenement House Department, *First Report*, p. 109; *The Tenement House Problem*, p. 437; Lapolla, pp. 19, 51.

51. *The Tenement House Problem*, pp. 387, 430.

52. New York City Tenement House Department, *Sixth Report* (New York: M.B. Brown, 1911), photo, p. 15. New York City Tenement House Department, *First Report*, pp. 107, 113; "Calendar of Photographic Negatives of the New York City Tenement House Department," (Compiled by Lilian Zwyns and Sylvia Szmuk for the New York Public Library, Local History and Genealogy Division), photo 169.

53. *The Tenement House Problem*, p. 431; Covello, *Social Background*, p. 39.

54. More, p. 218.

55. Italian American Directory Company, *Gli Italiani negli Stati Uniti* (New York: Italian American Directory Co., 1906), pp. 73-75.

56. *Immigrants in Industries*, p. 388.

57. *Immigrants in Industries*, p. 388.

58. *Women and Child Wage-Earners*, p. 245; *Immigrants in Industries*, pp. 385-88.

59. *Women and Child Wage-Earners*, pp. 228, 242; Willett p. 81; New York State Factory Investigating Commission, *Second Report*, vol. 2, p. 698.

60. New York State Factory Investigating Commission, *Fourth Report*, vol. 1, p. 250.

61. Daniel, p. 625; New York State Assembly, Tenement House Committee, *Report*, p. 153.

62. New York AICP, *68th Annual Report* (1911): photo, n.p.; see also Ford, photo, p. 464; *Immigrants in Industries*, p. 385.

63. Mary Sherman, "Manufacturing Foods in the Tenements," *Charities and the Commons* 15 (1906): 669, 672; "Calendar of Photographic Negatives," no. 46, 187, 343, 345, 768, and 773.

64. Sherman, p. 669.

65. George M. Price, *Tenement House Inspector* (New York: The Chief, 1910), p. 93; New York State Factory Investigating Commission, *Fourth Report*, vol. 2, pp. 315-323, 336; Mary Brown Sumner, "A Strike for Clean Bread," *Survey* 24 1910): 486; New York Commission on the Congestion of Population, *Report* New York: Lecouver, 1911), p. 123.

66. Edward Ewing Pratt, "Industrial Causes of Congestion of Population, New York City," Unpublished doctoral dissertation, Columbia University, 1911, p. 138; for a later period, see Lavanburg, p. 5.

67. *Women and Child Wage-Earners*, pp. 390, 392 reports far higher proportions of married women workers than do census listings. Compare Thomas Kessner and Betty Boyd Caroli, "New Immigrant Women at Work: Italians and Jews in New York City, 1880-1905," *Journal of Ethnic Studies* 5 (1978): 19-32, to the papers by Miriam J. Cohen and Virginia Yans-McLaughlin in

Sex, Class and the Woman Worker, ed. Milton Cantor and Bruce Laurie (Westport: Greenwood, 1977). Census takers varied considerably in recording married women's work, especially piece work done at home. Riis reported large numbers of sweated workers in the Astor tenements, *Ten Years War*, p. 112, but census takers listed few in those buildings.

68. Betts reported even higher rates—80 percent, "Italian Peasants," p. 804.
69. Pratt, p. 140.
70. *Women and Child Wage-Earners*, p. 252; New York State Factory Investigating Commission, *Second Report*, vol. 2, p. 693, vol. 4, pp. 1508, 1544.
71. Betts, "The Italian," p. 94; Betts, "Italian Peasants," p. 804.
72. New York State Factory Investigating Commission, *Second Report*, vol. 1, p. 109; Puzo, p. 7; Riis, *How the Other Half Lives*, New York: Charles Scribner's Sons, 1907), p. 57.
73. New York State Assembly, Tenement House Committee, *Report*, p. 93; *The Tenement House Problem*, pp. 19, 314.
74. New York State Assembly, Tenement House Committee, *Report*, p. 18.
75. As the garment district moved north and west towards Penn Station in the 1920's, fewer Lower East Side sons found work there, while daughters began to travel longer distances to work, Lavanburg, p. 5.
76. Jacob A. Riis, *The Battle with the Slum* (New York: MacMillan, 1902), photo, p. 32, pp. 38, 32; New York City AICP *41st Annual Report* (1884): 53.
77. *Immigrants in Cities*, p. 205.
78. Caroline F. Ware, *Greenwich Village, 1920–30* (Boston: Houghton Mifflin, The Riverside Press, 1935), p. 150.
79. More, p. 14. Architects call this a "fixed feature" space.
80. *The Tenement House Problem*, p. 430.
81. Betts, "Italian Peasants," p. 803; Betts, "The Italian," p. 92.
82. *The Tenement House Problem*, p. 428; New York City Tenement House Department, *Second Report*, p. 33; J.W. Sullivan, *Tenement House Tales of New York* (New York: Henry Holt, 1895), p. 362.
83. *The Tenement House Problem*, p. 430; Riis, *Battle With the Slum*, p. 32.
84. *Women and Child Wage-Earners*, p. 262; Daniel, photo p. 626.
85. Henry R. Mussey, " 'Fake' Installment Business and its Consequences," *Charities* 19 (1903): 236.
86. Schenda and Schenda, p. 21.
87. Betts, "Italian Peasants," p. 804.
88. Betts, "The Italian," p. 94.
89. Betts, "The Italian," p. 94; *The Tenement House Problem*, p. 414; Nesbitt p. 121. See photos, Ann Novotny, *Strangers at the Door* (Riverside, Conn. Chatham Press, 1971), p. 85; Oscar Handlin, *A Pictorial History of Immigration* (New York: Crown Publishers, 1972), pp. 227–28; Italian American Directory Company, p. 10; "Mulberry Bend from 1897–1958," *Saturday Evening Post* Aug. 2, 1958, pp. 34–35.
90. "The Poor in Summer," *Scribner's Magazine* 39 (1901): 269.

91. *Women and Child Wage-Earners*, p. 262; New York City Tenement House Department, *Third Report* (New York: Martin B. Brown Press, 1908), plate 14; Handlin, p. 229; Ford, photo, p. 382 (probably Jewish children).

92. New York City Tenement House Department, *First Report*, p. 114, *Second Report*, p. 33; Lapolla, p. 7; Angelo Patri, *A Schoolmaster of the Great City* (New York: MacMillan, 1917), p. 123.

93. Kittredge, p. 180; New York State Factory Investigating Commission, *Second Report*, vol. 2, p. 695; Shulman, p. 13; New York City Tenement House Department, "Prints Made from Glass Negatives," New York Public Library, Local History and Genealogy Division, no. M-14; Watson, p. 776.

94. Patri, p. 4; Irvin L. Child, *Italian or American, the Second Generation in Conflict* (New Haven: Yale University Press, 1943), p. 25; William Foote Whyte, *Street Corner Society, The Social Structure of an Italian Slum* (Chicago: The University of Chicago Press, 1943); Herbert J. Gans, *The Urban Villagers* (New York: The Free Press, 1962).

95. Dorothy Reed, "Leisure Time of Girls in a 'Little Italy,' " Unpublished Doctoral dissertation, Columbia University, 1932, pp. 44, 50; Ware, p. 145; Lillian D. Wald, *The House on Henry Street* (New York: Henry Holt, 1915), p. 96.

96. Riis, *How The Other Half Lives*, p. 60.

97. "Social Map of the Lower East Side," p. 2; Lapolla, p. 41; Wald, pp. 72-73; Jones, p. 45; Konrad Bercovici, *Around the World in New York* (New York: D. Appleton-Century, 1938), p. 125.

98. More, p. 203; Lapolla, p. 41; ;Bercovici, p. 125; Covello, *The Heart*, p. 26; Child, p. 25.

99. Williams, p. 62.

100. Berkovici, p. 131; Reed, p. 33.

101. Wald, p. 196.

102. Jones, p. 34; Mangano, p. 21; *The Tenement House Problem*, p. 204.

103. Watson, p. 777.

104. Covello, *The Heart*, p. 46; Edward Corsi, *In the Shadow of Liberty: The Chronicle of Ellis Island* (New York: MacMillan, 1935), p. 15; Lapolla, p. 104; Antonino Marinoni, *Come ho 'Fatto' l'America* (Milan: Athena, 1932), p. 138.

105. Marinoni, p. 139.

106. Marinoni, p. 138.

Notes to Chapter Seven

1. Beginning with Rudolph Vecoli's criticisms of Oscar Handlin in "*Contadini* in Chicago: A Critique of *The Uprooted*," *Journal of American History* 51 (1964-65): 404-417.

2. Ware, p. 174.

3. Smith, pp. 112-14. See also Judith Smith, "Italian Mothers, American Daughters," in *The Italian Immigrant Woman in North America*, p. 213.

4. Williams, p. 47; Ware, p. 179; Chapin, pp. 25, 87; More, pp. 175-76.

5. Furniture advertisements in *Bolletino della Sera* called bedroom suites a *corredo*, that is, the Italian term for movable dowry items. The occasionally haphazard nature of the immigrant marriage market is obvious in some ora histories. See, for example, Sharon Strom, "Italian-American Women and Theii Daughters in Rhode Island: The Adolescence of Two Generations, 1900-1950," in *The Italian Immigrant Woman in North America*, p. 195. In contrast, Yans McLaughlin argues that children gladly contributed to family savings for a house — and grasped only much later, at the parents' death, that homeownership provided them neither a first step toward middle-class status nor material security for their own new families, *Family and Community*, p. 177.

6. Patri, p. 123.

7. Gans, ch. 4.

8. More, pp. 16-17; Mussey, p. 240.

9. Mangano, "Italian Colonies," p. 21.

10. New York State Factory Investigating Commission, *Second Report*, vol. 4 p. 1524.

11. Daniel p. 629.

12. Eugene Litwack and Ivan Szelenyi, "Primary Group Structures and Thei Functions: Kin, Neighbors and Friends," *American Sociological Review* 3 (1965): 465-81; see also my article, "Sicilians in Space: Environmental Change and Family Geography," *Journal of Social History* 16 (1982): 53-66.

13. Mangano, p. 35; Riis, *How the Other Half Lives*, p. 177; More, p. 42; Ber covici, pp. 132-33; Betts, "The Italian," p. 95; Shulman, p. 25.

14. Riis, *Children of the Poor*, pp. 25-26; Mangano, p. 35.

15. The sons of shoemakers, for example, dominated the membership of Sam buca's *paese* society, "La Nascente Federazione delle Società Siciliane," *Corrier Siciliano*, March 7, 1931.

16. Ware, p. 104.

17. Gans, p. 53.

18. Boissevain, p. 32.

19. Grebler, p. 239; Ware, p. 225; Gwendolyn Hughes Berry, *Idleness and th Health of a Neighborhood: A Social Study of the Mulberry District* (New York AICP, 1933), p. 5.

20. Lavanburg, p. 5.

21. John G. Gebhart, *The Health of a Neighborhood: A Social Study of th Mulberry District* (New York: AICP, 1924), p. 5.

22. Grebler, p. 223. The term "environment" is, of course, ambiguous. Walte Firey believed that the younger generation sought a better *social* environment; b leaving the ghetto, they declared their American identities and rejected foreig associations, *Land Use in Central Boston* (New York: Greenwood Press, 1968) p. 222. Having carried a baby, shopping bags and stroller up and down the stair of an urban walk-up, I am inclined to believe that the second generation was jus as interested in a physical environment that better matched their needs an

childrearing preferences. In areas of lower-density housing like Brooklyn, mothers could hope to supervise their children carefully, an important Sicilian goal.

23. Grebler, p. 233; Ware, p. 30. Only one of five families moving bought a home.

24. Puzo, pp. 285–86.

25. Interesting although idiosyncratic memories of the years immediately following the move to Queens are in Vincent Panella, *The Other Side, Growing Up Italian in America* (Garden City: Doubleday, 1979).

26. Yans-McLaughlin dismisses high rates of mobility in her account of immigrant social life, blaming inaccurate sources (census listings and city directories) for failing to record many families, *Family and Community*, p. 79. Her interpretation stands in clear contrast to Humbert Nelli, *The Italians in Chicago* (New York: Oxford University Press, 1970), pp. 44–54. My own interpretation more closely resembles Nelli's. Although census listings and directories may overstate mobility, a wide variety of impressionistic sources—from both within and without the immigrant population—confirm high rates of mobility. Other immigrant Italians actually were only slightly less mobile than Elizabeth Street residents, see Howard P. Chudacoff, *Mobile Americans* (New York: Oxford University Press, 1972).

27. See, for example, Gary Mormino, "The Hill Upon a City: The Evolution of an Italian-American Community in St. Louis, 1882–1950," in *Little Italies in North America*, pp. 141–64.

28. Most of the essays collected in *Little Italies in North America* emphasize evolution over time, rather than describing one archetypical form of immigrant social structure. All, however, give *prominenti* a large role in immigrant social life, perhaps because of the definition of colony that all essays share (p. 5). See my review of this volume, *International Labor and Working-Class History* 22 (1982): 95–97.

29. "Italian American Workers, 1880–1920: *Padrone* Slaves or Primitive Rebels?" in *Perspectives on Italian Immigration and Ethnicity*, ed. S. M. Tomasi (Staten Island: Center for Migration Studies, 1977), pp. 24–49.

30. See George Pozzetta, "The Mulberry District of New York City: The Years Before World War One," in *Little Italies in North America*, pp. 7–40.

31. Stephan Thernstrom and Peter Knights, "Men in Motion: Some Data and Speculations on Urban Population Mobility in Nineteenth Century North America," *Journal of Interdisciplinary History* 1 (1970): 7–35.

32. *Family and Community*, ch. 4.

33. Cronin, pp. 267–68.

34. Cronin, pp. 166–67.

35. *Family and Community*, p. 23.

36. *Family and Community*, p. 20. My own understanding of culture change was very much influenced by Social Science Research Council, Summer Seminar on Acculturation, 1953, "Acculturation: An Exploratory Formulation,"

American Anthropologist 56 (1954): 973–1002 and Edward H. Spicer, "Spanish-Indian Acculturation in the Southwest," *American Anthropologist* 56 (1954): 663–84.

37. *Family and Community*, p. 205.

38. Yans-McLaughlin seems to concur, *Family and Community*, ch. 8.

39. Stripping down produced a Spanish "conquest culture," *Culture and Conquest* (Chicago: Quadrangle Books, 1960), p. 10.

40. The first discussion of *la famiglia* is Covello, *The Social Background*, based on interviews with New York Italians and their children. Although emphasizing the importance of kinship in Italy, Paul Campisi offers an alternative interpretation of the immigrant family, one that stresses increased nuclearity and individualism, "Ethnic Family Patterns: The Italian Family in the United States," *American Journal of Sociology* 53 (1948): 443–49. Most recent studies, including Yans-McLaughlin, depend heavily on Covello, especially for his analysis of European family patterns. The most recent general analysis of the immigrant *la famiglia* is Lydio F. Tomasi, *The Italian American Family*, The Italian in America Education Series, no. 113 (Staten Island: Center for Migration Studies, 1982). The Sicilian *la famiglia* is analyzed in Richard Gambino, *Blood of My Blood* (Garden City: Doubleday, 1974). Humbert Nelli provides an interesting sidelight to the growing importance of kinship among immigrants when he notes that in the 1930's criminal syndicates abandoned earlier terms for their associations and began organizing themsleves in and calling themselves families, *The Business of Crime*, p. 258.

41. August 8, 1980; the informant wished to remain anonymous. His views were confirmed by others in Sambuca. *Evoluto*, as he used it, means "advanced" and refers to a positive process of change, much as does "evolution." Sicilians today use *evoluto* to distinguish between those with strong material, occupational or cultural ties to the modern economy (mainly through migration to northern Europe) or to the state (through party membership, patronage, higher education, or employment) and those involved in subsistence agriculture or locally based social networks. People in Sambuca found it puzzling that emigrants boast of their high standard of living while rejecting modernity as Sicilians define it. The fact that Sambuca is a town with strong leftist traditions may contribute to these tensions between Sicilians and *Americani*. Can an *Americano* see a young Communist as a "real Sicilian?"

Notes to Appendix B

1. Michelson, *Environmental Choice* and Daniel M. Wilner, et al., *The Housing Environment and Family Life* (Baltimore: The Johns Hopkins Press, 1962) traced families from one setting to another. Cross-sectional comparisons are Michael Young and Peter Willmott, *Family and Kinship in East London* (London: Routledge and Kegan Paul, 1957) and Willmott and Young, *Family and Class in a London Suburb* (London: Routledge and Kegan Paul, 1960), or Sylvia

F. Fava, "Contrasts in Neighboring: New York City and a Suburban County," in *The Suburban Community*, ed. William Dobriner New York: G.P. Putman's Sons, 1958).

2. Willett, p. 99; Antonio Stella, "The Effects of Urban Congestion on Italian Women and Children," repr. in *The Italians in the City: Health and Related Needs*, ed. Francesco Cordasco (New York: Arno Press, 1975); Robert E. Park and Herbert A. Miller, *Old World Traits Transplanted* (New York: Harper and Bros., 1921), map opp. p. 146.

3. Leonard Covello, *The Social Background*, ch. 6; see also Bruno Ramirez, "Italian Immigrants in Rural and Small Town America: A Conference Report," *International Labor and Working Class History*, no. 21 (Spring, 1982): 77.

4. New York State manuscript census listings for Manhattan are available in the New York County Clerk's Office.

5. Besides the volumes by Ford and *The Tenement House Problem*, see New York City Health Department, *The Tenement House Problem in New York* (New York: W.P. Mitchell, 1887).

6. Pitrè, *Usi e Costumi*, vol. 2, p. 162.

7. Smith, "Our Own Kind," pp. 105–10.

Bibliography

Sicily and Migration

Unpublished

Atti di Nascita. Archivio Comunale. Sambuca di Sicilia.
"Catasto dei Fabbricati." Archivio Comunale. Sambuca di Sicilia.
"Fogli di Famiglia." Archivio Comunale. Sambuca di Sicilia.
"Lista della Leva." 1868–1935. Archivio Comunale. Sambuca di Sicilia.
Schneider, Jane and Peter. "The Demographic Transition in Sicily, Progress Report on a Local Level Case Study."
— — —. "The Reproduction of the Ruling Class in Sicily, 1860–1920."
Weber, Karl E. "Materialien zur Soziologie Siziliens." Inaugural Dissertation zur Erlangung der Doktorwürde der Philosophischen Fakultät der Ruprecht-Karl Universität im Heidelberg, 1966.

Published

Banfield, Edward C. *The Moral Basis of a Backward Society*. Glencoe, Ill.: The Free Press, 1958.
Baxter, Celena A. "Sicilian Family Life." *Family* 14 (1930): 82–88.
Bell, Rudolph M. *Fate and Honor, Family and Village*. Chicago and London: The University of Chicago Press, 1979.
Bellini, Lorenzo. *Guida Pratica ai Municipi per il Rilascio di Atti e Documenti in Uso Pubblico e Privato*. Suzzara: Tip. della Suzzarese, 1901.
Bieder, Robert E. "Kinship as a Factor in Migration." *Journal of Marriage and the Family* 35 (1973): 429–39.
Blok, Anton. *The Mafia of a Sicilian Village, 1860–1960*. New York: Harper and Row, 1974.
— — —. "South Italian Agrotowns." *Comparative Studies in Society and History* 11 (1969): 121–35.
Boissevain, Jeremy. *Friends of Friends, Networks, Manipulators and Coalitions*. Oxford: Basil Blackwell, 1974.

— — — and J. Clyde Mitchell, ed. *Network Analysis: Studies in Human Inter-action*. The Hague: Mouton, 1973.

Brancato, F. *La Sicilia nel Primo Ventennio del Regno d'Italia*. Bologna: Dott. Cesare Zuffi, 1956.

Bruccoleri, Giuseppe. *l'Emigrazione Siciliana, Caratteri ed Effetti Secondo le Più Recenti Inchieste*. Rome: Coop. Tip. A. Manuzio, 1911.

Caico, Louise. *Sicilian Ways and Days*. London: John Long, 1910.

Carpi, Leone. *Delle Colonie e dell' Emigrazione d'Italiani all' Estero*. Milan: Tip. Ed. Lombarda, 1874.

Chapman, Charlotte Gower. *Milocca, a Sicilian Village*. Cambridge, Mass.: Schenkman, 1971.

Choldin, Harvey M. "Kinship Networks in the Migration Process." *International Migration Review* 7 (1973): 163–75.

Cocchiara, Giuseppe. *Il Folklore Siciliano*. 2 vol. Palermo: S.F. Flaccovio, 1957.

— — —. *La Vita e l'Arte del Popolo Siciliano nel Museo Pitrè*. Palermo: F. Ciuni Libraio, 1938.

Coletti, Francesco. *Dell'Emigrazione Italiana*. Milan: Ulrico Hoepli, 1912.

Cronin, Constance. *The Sting of Change*. Chicago: The University of Chicago Press, 1970.

Davis, John. *Land and Family in Pisticci*. London School of Economics Mono-graphs on Social Anthropology, 48. New York: Humanities Press, 1973.

— — —. "Morals and Backwardness." *Comparative Studies in Society and History* 12 (July, 1970): 340–59.

— — —. "Town and Country." *Anthropological Quarterly* 42 (1969): 171–85.

De Stefano, Francesco and Francesco Luigi Oddo. *Storia della Sicilia dal 1860 al 1910*. Bari: Laterza, 1963.

di Giovanna, Alfonso. *Inchiostro e Trazzere*. Sambuca: La Voce, 1979.

di Lampedusa, Tomasi. *Il Gattopardo*. Milan: Feltrinelli, 1976.

Dollo, Corrado et al. *I Fasci Siciliani*. Bari: De Donato, 1976.

Foerster, Robert M. *The Italian Migrations of Our Times*. Cambridge, Mass.: Harvard University Press, 1919.

Foster, George M. "The Dyadic Contract: A Model for the Social Structure of a Mexican Peasant Village." *American Anthropologist* 63 (1961): 1173–92.

Galt, Anthony H. "Carnival on the Island of Pantelleria: Ritualized Community Solidarity in an Atomistic Society." *Ethnology* 12 (1973): 325–39.

— — —. "Rethinking Patron-Client Relationships: The Real System and the Official System in Southern Italy." *Anthropological Quarterly* 47 (1974): 182–202.

Giarrizzo, Giuseppe et al. *I Fasci Siciliani*. Bari: De Donato, 1975.

Giordano, Christian. *Handwerker und Bauernverbände in der Sizilianischen Gesellschaft*. Heidelberger Sociologica 14. Tübingen: J.C.B. Mohr, 1975.

Houston, J.M. *The Western Mediterranean*. London: Longmans, Green and Co., 1964.

Italy. *Atti della Giunta per l'Inchiesta Agraria e sulle Condizioni della Classe*

Agricola. Vol. 13, Tome I and II. Relazione del Comm. Abele Damiani. Rome: Forzani Tip. del Senato, 1884–85.

— — —. *Inchiesta Parlamentare sulle Condizioni dei Contadini nelle Provincie Meridionali e nella Sicilia.* Rome: Tip. Naz. di Giovanni Bertero, 1910.

Italy. Ministero di Agricoltura, Industria e Commercio, Dir. Generale della Statistica. *Censimento della Popolazione del Regno d'Italia al 10 Febb. 1901.* Rome: Tip. Naz. di G. Bertero, 1902.

— — —. *Statistica degli Scioperi Avvenuti in Italia.* Rome: 1884–1903.

— — —. *Statistica della Società di Mutuo Soccorso.* Rome: 1873, 1878, 1885.

— — —. *Le Società di Mutuo Soccorso.* Rome: Tip. Naz. di G. Bertero, 1906.

— — —. *Statistica della Emigrazione Italiana.* Rome: 1878–79, 1881–1915.

Jaberg, K. and J. Jud. *Sprach und Sachatlas Italiens und der Südschweiz.* Zofingen: Ringier, 1933.

Juliani, Richard N. "American Voices, Italian Accents." *Italian-Americana* (1974): 1–25.

Kertzer, David I. "European Peasant Household Structure: Some Implications from a Nineteenth-Century Italian Community." *Journal of Family History* 2 (1977): 333–349.

Levi, C. *Fabbricati Civili di Abitazione.* Milan: Hoepli, 1910.

Loizos, Peter. "Changes in Property Transfer Among Greek Cypriot Villages." *Man* 10 (1975): 503–504.

Loncao, Enrico. *Considerazioni sulla Genesi ed Evoluzione della Borghesia in Sicilia.* Palermo: Tip. Coop. fra gli Operai, 1899.

Lopreato, Joseph. "Social Stratification and Mobility." *American Sociological Review* 26 (1961): 585–96.

MacDonald, J.S. "Agricultural Organization, Migration and Labour Militancy in Rural Italy." *The Economic History Review,* 2nd Ser. 16 (1963): 61–75.

— — —. "Some Socio-Economic Emigration Differentials in Rural Italy, 1902–1913." *Economic Development and Cultural Change* 7 (1958): 55–72.

MacDonald, John S. and Leatrice D. MacDonald. "Chain Migration, Ethnic Neighborhood Formation and Social Networks." *Milbank Memorial Fund Quarterly* 17 (1964): 82–97.

— — —. "Institutional Economics and Rural Development: Two Italian Types." *Human Organization* 23 (1964): 113–18.

— — —. "Italian Migration to Australia: Manifest Functions of Bureaucracy versus Latent Functions of Informal Networks." *Journal of Social History* 3 (1970): 248–76.

Mack Smith, Dennis. *A History of Sicily,* 2 vol. New York: The Viking Press, 1968.

— — —. "The Latifundia in Modern Sicilian History." *Proceedings of the British Academy* 6 (1965): 85–124.

Mangano, Antonio. "The Effect of Emigration upon Italy." *Charities and the Commons* 19 (1908): 1475–86.

Miller, Roy A. "Are Familists Amoral? A Test of Banfield's Amoral Familism Hypothesis in a South Italian Village." *American Ethnologist* 1 (1974): 515–536.

Monroe, Will Seymour. *Sicily, the Garden of the Mediterranean.* Boston: L.C. Page, 1909.

Mühlmann, Wilhelm E. and Roberto J. Llaryoro. *Klientschaft, Klientel und Klientelsystem in einer Sizilianischen Agro-Stadt.* Tübingen: Paul Siebeck, 1968.

— — —. *Strummula Siciliana; Ehre, Rang und Soziale Schichtung in einer Sizilianischen Agro-Stadt.* Meisenheim am Glan: Anton Hain, 1973.

Muraskin, William. "The Moral Basis of a Backward Sociologist: Edward Banfield, The Italians and the Italian-Americans." *American Journal of Sociology* 79 (1974): 1484–96.

Navarro della Miraglia, Emmanuele. *La Nana.* Bologna: Capelli, 1963.

— — —. *Storielle Siciliane.* Palermo: Sellerio, 1974.

Paton, William Agnew. *Picturesque Sicily.* New York: Harper and Brothers, 1898.

Pitrè, Giuseppe. *Biblioteca delle Tradizioni Popolari Siciliane.* Vol. 25: *La Famiglia, la Casa, la Vita del Popolo Siciliano.* Palermo: Libreria Internazionale A. Reber, 1913.

— — —. Vol. 21. *Feste Patronali in Sicilia.* Turin and Palermo: Carlo Clausen, 1900.

— — —. Vol. 8–11. *Proverbi Siciliani.* Palermo: Luigi Pedone Lauriel, 1880.

— — —. Vol. 14–17. *Usi e Costumi, Credenze e Pregiudizi del Popolo Siciliano.* Palermo: Libreria L. Pedone Lauriel di Carlo Clausen, 1889.

Poni, Carlo. "Family and *Podere* in Emilia-Romagna." *The Journal of Italian History* 1 (1978): 201–234.

Renda, Francesco. *l'Emigrazione in Sicilia.* Palermo: Tip. la Cartografica, 1963.

— — —. *I Fasci Siciliani, 1982–94.* Turin: Einaudi, 1977.

Riggs, Arthur Stanley. "Inexhaustible Italy." *National Geographic* 30 (1916).

Rochefort, Renée. *Le Travail en Sicile.* Paris: Presse Universitaire de France, 1961.

Rogers, Susan Carol. "Female Forms of Power and the Myth of Male Dominance: A Model of Female/Male Interaction in Peasant Society." *American Ethnologist* 2 (1975): 727–56.

Romano, Salvatore Francesco. *La Sicilia nell'Ultimo Ventennio del Secolo XIX.* Parte 2. Storia della Sicilia Post-Unificazione. Palermo: Ind. Grafica Nazionale, 1958.

— — —. *Storia dei Fasci Siciliani.* Bari: Laterza, 1959.

Rubino, Benedetto and Giuseppe Cocchiara. *Usi e Costumi, Novelle e Poesie del Popolo Siciliano.* Palermo: Remo Sandron, 1924.

Rumpelt, Dr. Alexander. *Sicilien und die Sicilianer.* Berlin: Allgemeiner Verein für Deutsche Literatur, 1902.

157

Salomone-Marino, Salvatore. *Costumi e Usanze dei Contadini di Sicilia.* Palermo: Ando, 1968.

Schenda, Rudolf. "Statik, und Dynamik der Aktuellen Italienischen Volkskunde." *Zeitschrift für Volkskunde* 65 (1969): 251–263.

— — — and Suzanne Schenda. *Eine Sizilianische Strasse.* Tübingen: Drückerei Tübinger Chronik, 1965.

Schneider, Jane. "Family Patrimonies and Economic Behavior in Western Sicily." *Anthropological Quarterly* 42 (1969): 109–25.

— — —. "Of Vigilance and Virgins: Honor, Shame and Access to Resources in Mediterranean Societies." *Ethnology* 10 (1971): 1–24.

Schneider, Jane and Peter. *Culture and Political Economy in Western Sicily.* New York: Academic Press, 1976.

Schneider, Peter T. "Coalition Formation and Colonialism in Western Sicily." *Archives Européènes de Sociologie* 18 (1972): 255–67.

— — —. "Honor and Conflict in a Sicilian Town." *Anthropological Quarterly* 42 (1969): 130–54.

Scheuermeier, Paul. *Bauernwerk in Italien und der Italienischen und Rätromanischen Schweiz.* Bern: Verlag Stämpfli, 1956.

Sereni, Emilio. *Il Capitalismo nelle Campagne, 1860–1900.* Turin: Einaudi, 1968.

Siegenthaler, Jürg K. "Sicilian Economic Change Since 1860." *The Journal of European Economic History* 2 (1973): 363–415.

Silverman, Sydel F. "Agricultural Organization, Social Structure, and Values in Italy: Amoral Familism Reconsidered." *American Anthropologist* 70 (1968): 1–20.

— — —. "An Ethnographic Approach to Social Stratification: Prestige in a Central Italian Community." *American Anthropologist* 68 (1966): 899–921.

Sladen, Douglas. *In Sicily.* 2 Vol. London: Sands and Co., 1901.

— — —. *Sicily, the New Winter Resort.* New York: E.P. Dutton, 1907.

Sladen, Douglas and Norma Lorimer. *Queer Things About Sicily.* London: Kegan Paul, Trench, Trübner, 1913.

Somogyi, Stefano. *Bilanci Demografici dei Comuni Siciliani dal 1861 al 1961.* Palermo: Università di Palermo, Istituto di Scienze Demografiche, 1971.

Sonnino, Sidney. *I Contadini in Sicilia.* Vol. 2. Inchiesta in Sicilia. Florence: Vallecchi, 1974.

Storai de Rocchi, Tina. *Bibliografia allo Studio dell'Abitazione Rurale in Italia.* Vol. 7. Ricerche sulle Dimore Rurali in Italia. Florence: Leo S. Olschki, 1968.

Sviluppo della Popolazione Italiana dal 1861 al 1961. Annali di Statistica. Anno 94, Serie 8, vol. 17.

Tilly, Charles and Harold C. Brown. "On Uprooting, Kinship and the Auspices of Migration." *International Journal of Comparative Sociology* 8 (1967): 139–64.

Taddei-Ledda, *Contadini Siciliani.* Vol. 4. Monografie di Famiglie Agricole. Rome: S.A. Tip. Operaio Romano, 1933.

Traina, Antonio. *Vocabolario Siciliano-Italiano.* 2nd. Ed. Palermo: Lorenzo Finnocchiare e Fiorenza Garazio, 1890.

Verga, Giovanni. *The House by the Medlar Tree.* New York: Grove Press, 1953.

— — —. *Little Novels of Sicily.* New York: Thomas Seltzer, 1925.

— — —. *Maestro Don Gesualdo.* Harmondsworth: Penguin Books, 1970.

— — —. *Tutte le Novelle.* 2 Vol. Milan: A. Mondadori, 1942.

Villari, Luigi. *Italian Life in Town and Country.* New York: G.P. Putnam's Sons, 1902.

Vincelli, Guido. *Una Comunità Meridionale.* Turin: Taylor Torino, 1958.

Whyte, William Foote. "Sicilian Peasant Society." *American Anthropologist* 46 (1944): 65-74.

Immigrant Italians

Unpublished

"Block and Lot Records." New York City Bureau of Buildings. City Hall.

"Conveyance Ledgers." 1890-1916 and 1917-1930. New York City Hall of Records.

Hines, Lewis Wickes. "Photographic Documents of Social Conditions." Local History and Genealogy. New York Public Library.

New York City Tenement House Department. "Prints Made From Glass Negatives." Local History and Genealogy. New York Public Library.

New York State. Manuscript Census, 1905, 1915, 1925. New York County Clerk's Office.

Pratt, Edward Ewing. "Industrial Causes of Congestion of Population in New York City." Ph.D. Dissertation. Columbia University, 1911.

Reed, Dorothy. "Leisure Time of Girls in a 'Little Italy.' " Ph.D. Dissertation. Columbia University, 1932.

Zwyns, Lilian and Sylvia Szmuk. "A Calendar of Photographic Negatives of the New York City Tenement House Department, 1902-1914." Local History and Genealogy. New York Public Library.

Maps, Newspapers and Journals

Bromley, George W. and Walter S. Bromley. *Atlas of the City of New York, Borough of Manhattan.* Philadelphia: 1891, 1902, 1915, 1922, with corrections through October 1925.

"Social Map of the Lower East Side." *New York Times.* April, 3, 1910.

Bolletino della Sera. 1905-15.

Corriere Siciliano. 1931-1933.

Real Estate Record and Guide. 1870-1920.

Published

Barton, Josef J. *Peasants and Strangers.* Cambridge, Mass.: Harvard University Press, 1975.

Bercovici, Konrad. *Around the World in New York.* New York: D. Appleton-Century, 1938.

Berry, Gwendolyn Hughes. *Idleness and the Health of a Neighborhood, a Social Study of the Mulberry District.* New York: Association for Improving the Condition of the Poor, 1933.

Betts, Lillian. "The Italian in New York." *University Settlement Studies* 1 (1905–1906): 90–105.

— — —. "Italian Peasants in a New Law Tenement." *Harper's Bazaar* 38 (1904): 802–805.

Bodnar, John, Roger Simon and Michael P. Weber. *Lives of Their Own: Blacks, Italians and Poles in Pittsburgh, 1900–1960.* Champaign: University of Illinois Press, 1981.

Borchert, James. *Alley Life in Washington.* Urbana: University of Illinois Press, 1980.

Breckinridge, Sophonisba P. *New Homes for Old.* New York: Harper and Brothers, 1921.

Briggs, John W. *An Italian Passage.* New Haven: Yale University Press, 1978.

Campisi, Paul J. "Ethnic Family Patterns: The Italian Family in the United States." *American Journal of Sociology* 53 (1948): 443–49.

Cantor, Milton and Bruce Laurie, ed. *Sex, Class and the Woman Worker.* Westport Conn.: Greenwood Press, 1977.

Caroli, Betty, Robert F. Harney and Lydio F. Tomasi, ed. *The Italian Immigrant Woman in North America.* Toronto: Multicultural History Society of Ontario, 1978.

Chapin, Robert Coit. *The Standard of Living Among Workingmen's Families in New York City.* New York: Charities Publication Committee, 1909.

Charity Organization Society of the City of New York. Committee on Housing. *Forty Years of Housing.* New York: Charity Organization Society, 1938.

Child, Irvin L. *Italian or American, the Second Generation in Conflict.* New Haven: Yale University Press, 1943.

"The Coal Situation in New York." *Charities* 9 (1902): 356–58.

Cohen, Lizabeth A. "Embellishing a Life of Labor: An Interpretation of the Material Culture of American Working-Class Homes, 1885–1915." *Journal of American Culture* 3 (1980): 752–75.

Chudacoff, Howard. *Mobile Americans.* New York: Oxford University Press, 1972.

Cordasco, Francesco, ed. *Italians in the City: Health and Related Social Needs.* New York: Arno Press, 1975.

— — — and Eugene Buccioni, ed. *The Italians, Social Backgrounds of an Immigrant Group.* Clifton: Augustus Kelly, 1974.

Corsi, Edward. *In the Shadow of Liberty: The Chronicle of Ellis Island.* New York: MacMillan, 1935.

"The Cost of Living." *The Charities Review* 9 (1899): 237–38.

Covello, Leonard. *The Heart is the Teacher.* New York: McGraw-Hill, 1958.

———. *The Social Background of the Italo-American School Child.* Francesco Cordasco, ed. Leiden: E.J. Brill, 1967.

D'Angelo, Pascal. *Son of Italy.* New York: MacMillan, 1924.

Daniel, Annie S. "The Wreck of the Home, How Wearing Apparel is Fashioned in the Tenements." *Charities* 14 (1905): 624–29.

de Forest, Robert and Lawrence Veiller, ed. *The Tenement House Problem.* New York: MacMillan, 1903.

de Donato, Pietro. *Christ in Concrete.* New York: Bobbs-Merrill, 1937.

———. *Three Circles of Light.* New York: Julian Messner, 1960.

Denison, Lindsay. "The Black Hand." *Everybody's Magazine* 19 (1908): 293–95.

Firey, Walter. *Land Use in Central Boston.* New York: Greenwood Press, 1968.

Ford, James. *Slums and Housing.* 2 vol. Cambridge, Mass.: Harvard University Press, 1936.

Foster, George. *Culture and Conquest.* Chicago: Quadrangle Books, 1960.

Gabaccia, Donna. "Sicilians in Space: Environmental Change and Family Geography." *Journal of Social History* 16 (1982): 53–66.

Gambino, Richard. *Blood of my Blood.* Garden City: Doubleday, 1974.

Gans, Herbert J. *The Urban Villagers.* New York: The Free Press, 1962.

Gebhart, John C. *The Health of a Neighborhood: A Social Study of the Mulberry District.* New York: New York Association for Improving the Condition of the Poor, 1924.

Gilder, Richard Watson. "The Housing Problem—America's Need of Awakening." *The American City* 1 (1909): 34.

Grebler, Leo. *Housing Market Behavior in a Declining Area: Long Term Changes in Inventory and Utilization of Housing on New York's Lower East Side.* New York: Columbia University Press, 1952.

Handlin, Oscar. *A Pictorial History of Immigration.* New York: Crown Publishers, 1972.

Harney, Robert F. and J. Vincenza Scarpaci, ed. *Little Italies in North America.* Toronto: Multicultural History Society of Ontario, 1981.

Harney, Robert F. "Boarding and Belonging." *Urban History Review* (1978).

Italian American Directory Company. *Gli Italiani negli Stati Uniti.* New York: Italian American Directory Company, 1906.

Jones, Thomas Jesse. *The Sociology of a New York City Block.* Columbia University Studies in History, Economics and Public Law, 21. New York: Columbia University Press, 1904.

Kessner, Thomas. *The Golden Door.* New York: Oxford University Press, 1977.

——— and Betty Boyd Caroli. "New Immigrant Women at Work: Italians and Jews in New York City, 1880–1905." *Journal of Ethnic Studies* 5 (1978): 19–32.

Kittredge, Mabel Hyde. *The Home and its Management* New York: Century, 1917.

— — —. "Homemaking in a Model Flat." *Charities* 15 (1905): 176–81.

Laidlaw, Walter, ed. *Population of the City of New York, 1890–1930*. New York: Cities Census Committee, 1932.

Lapolla, Garibaldi. *The Grand Gennaro*. New York: Vanguard, 1935.

Lavanburg, Fred L. *What Happened to 386 Families Who Were Compelled to Vacate their Slum Dwellings to Make Way for a Large Housing Project*. New York: Fred L. Lavanburg Foundation, 1933.

Lichtenberg, Robert M. *One Tenth of a Nation: Natural Forces in the Economic Growth of the New York Region*. Cambridge, Mass.: Harvard University Press, 1960.

Marinoni, Antonio. *Come ho 'Fatto' l'America*. Milan: Athena, 1932.

Modell, John and Tamara K. Hareven. "Urbanization and the Malleable Household: An Examination of Boarding and Lodging in American Families." *Journal of Marriage and the Family* 35 (1973): 467–79.

More, Louise Bolard. *Wage Earners' Budgets*. Greenwich House Series of Social Studies, 1. New York: Henry Holt, 1907.

Moquin, Wayne, ed. *A Documentary History of the Italian-Americans*. New York: Praeger, 1974.

"Mulberry Bend from 1897–1958." *Saturday Evening Post*. Aug. 2, 1958: 34–53.

Mussey, Henry R. " 'Fake' Installment Business and its Consequences." *Charities* 10 (1903): 236–44.

Nelli, Humbert S. *The Business of Crime*. New York: Oxford University Press, 1976.

— — —. *The Italians in Chicago*. New York: Oxford University Press, 1970.

Nesbitt, Florence. *Household Management*. New York: Russell Sage Foundation, 1918.

New York Association for Improving the Condition of the Poor. *Annual Report*. New York: 1890–1920.

New York Association for Improving the Condition of the Poor and New York City Department of Health. Bureau of Child Hygiene. *Flies and Diarrheal Disease*. New York: Association for Improving the Condition of the Poor, n.d.

New York City Commission on the Congestion of Population. *Report*. New York: Lecouver, 1911.

New York City. Health Department. *The Tenement House Problem in New York*. New York: W.P. Mitchell, 1887.

New York City. Tenement House Department. *Report*. New York: 1903–1931.

New York State. Assembly. Tenement House Committee. *Report*. Albany: James B. Lyon, 1895.

New York State. Department of Labor. *Seventh Annual Report of the Commissioner of Labor, 1907*. Albany: James B. Lyon, 1908.

New York State. Factory Investigating Commission. *Preliminary Report of the Factory Investigating Commission*. 3 vol. Albany: Argus, 1912.

— — —. *Reports*. Albany: 1912–1915.

New York State. Industrial Commission. *Report on Manufacturing in Tenements Submitted to Commission to Examine the Laws Relating to Child Welfare.* New York: Department of Labor, 1924.

New York State. Welfare Conference. *Report of the Special Committee on the Standard of Living, 1907.* New York: New York State Welfare Conference, 1907.

Novotny, Ann. *Strangers at the Door.* Riverside, Conn.: Chatham Press, 1971.

Odencrantz, Louise C. *Italian Women in Industry.* New York: Russell Sage Foundation, 1919.

Pagano, Jo. *Golden Wedding.* New York: Random House, 1943.

Panella, Vincent. *The Other Side, Growing Up Italian in America.* Garden City: Doubleday, 1979.

Park, Robert E. and Herbert A. Miller. *Old World Traits Transplanted.* Americanization Series. New York: Harper and Brothers, 1921.

Patri, Angelo. *A Schoolmaster of the Great City.* New York: MacMillan, 1917.

Poole, Ernest. "The Lung Block." *Charities* 11 (1903): 193–99.

Price, George M. *Tenement House Inspector.* 2nd. ed. New York: The Chief, 1910.

"Punish the Real Offender and Not the Child." *Charities* 12 (1904): 858–59.

Puzo, Mario. *The Fortunate Pilgrim.* New York: Lancer Books, 1964.

Real Estate Record Association. *A History of Real Estate, Building and Architecture in New York During the Last Quarter of a Century.* New York: Real Estate Record Associaton, 1898.

Richmond, Mary E. *The Good Neighbor in the Modern City.* Philadelphia: J.B. Lippincott, 1908.

Riis, Jacob. *The Battle with the Slum.* New York: MacMillan, 1902.

— — —. *The Children of the Poor.* New York: Charles Scribner's Sons, 1908.

— — —. "The Clearing of Mulberry Bend." *Review of Reviews* 12 (1895): 172–78.

— — —. "The Making of Thieves in New York." *Century Magazine* 49 (1894): 109–116.

— — —. *How The Other Half Lives.* New York: Charles Scribner's Sons, 1907.

— — —. *The Peril and Preservation of the Home.* Philadelphia: George W. Jacobs, 1903.

— — —. *Ten Years War.* Boston: Houghton Mifflin, 1900.

Rosenwaike, Ira. *Population History of New York City.* Syracuse: Syracuse University Press, 1972.

Sherman, Mary. "Manufacturing Foods in the Tenements." *Charities and the Commons* 15 (1906): 668–72.

Shulman, Harry M. *Slums of New York.* New York: Albert and Charles Boni, 1938.

Smith, Judith E. "Our Own Kind: Family and Community Networks in Providence." *Radical History Review* 17 (1978): 99–120.

Social Science Research Council. Summer Seminar on Acculturation 1953.

"Acculturation: An Exploratory Formulation." *American Anthropologist* 56 (1954): 973–1002.

Spicer, Edward H. "Spanish-Indian Acculturation in the Southwest." *American Anthropologist* 56 (1954): 663–84.

Stevenson, Robert Alston. "The Poor in Summer." *Scribner's Magazine* 30 (1901): 259–77.

Sullivan, J.W. *Tenement House Tales of New York.* New York: Henry Holt, 1895.

Sumner, Mary Brown. "A Strike for Clean Bread." *Survey* 24 (1910): 483–88.

Thernstrom, Stephan and Peter Knights. "Men in Motion: Some Data and Speculations on Urban Population Mobility in Nineteenth Century North America." *Journal of Interdisciplinary History* 1 (1970): 7–35.

Tomasi, Lydio F. *The Italian American Family.* The Italian in America Education Series, 113. Staten Island: The Center for Migration Studies, 1982.

Tomasi, S.M., ed. *Perspectives on Italian Immigration and Ethnicity.* New York: The Center for Migration Studies, 1977.

United States. Bureau of the Census. *Twelfth Census, 1900, Special Reports, Occupations.* Washington: Government Printing Office, 1904.

United State Senate. *Report on Conditions of Women and Child Wage Earners in the United States, Men's Ready Made Clothing.* Washington: Government Printing Office, 1911.

— — —. Senate. Reports of the Immigration Commission. *Immigrants in Cities.* Washington: Government Printing Office, 1911.

— — —. Senate. Reports of the Immigration Commission. *Immigrants in Industries, part 6, Clothing Manufacturing.* Washington: Government Printing Office, 1911.

United States. Works Progress Administration. Federal Writers Project of the City of New York. *The Italians of New York, a Survey.* New York: Random House, 1938.

Van Kleeck, Mary. *Artificial Flower Makers.* New York: Survey Associates, 1913.

Vecoli, Rudolph J. "*Contadini* in Chicago: A Critique of *The Uprooted.*" *Journal of American History* 51 (1964–65): 404–417.

Wald, Lillian. *The House on Henry Street.* New York: Henry Holt, 1915.

Ware, Caroline F. *Greenwich Village, 1920–1930.* Boston: Houghton Mifflin, the Riverside Press, 1935.

Watson, Elizabeth. "Home Work in the Tenements." *Survey* 25 (1911): 772–81.

Watson, Patrick. *Fasanella's City.* New York: Ballantine, 1973.

Whyte, William Foote. *Street Corner Society, The Social Structure of an Italian Slum.* Chicago: University of Chicago Press, 1943.

Willett, Mabel Hurd. *The Employment of Women in the Clothing Trade.* Columbia University Studies in History, Economics and Public Law, 16. New York: Columbia University Press, 1902.

Williams, Phyllis H. *South Italian Folkways in Europe and America.* New Haven: Institute of Human Relations, Yale University Press, 1938.

Woods, Robert A. et al. *The Poor in Great Cities.* New York: Charles Scribner's Sons, 1895.

Yans-McLaughlin, Virginia. *Family and Community, Italian Immigrants in Buffalo, 1880-1930.* Ithaca: Cornell University Press, 1977.

Environment and Behavior

Barker, Roger. *Ecological Psychology.* Stanford: Stanford University Press, 1968.

Belcher, John C. and Pablo B. Vazquez-Calcerrada. "Cross-Cultural Approach to the Social Functions of Housing." *Journal of Marriage and the Family* 34 (1972): 750-61.

Bell, Wendell and M.T. Force. "Urban Neighborhood Types and Participation in Formal Associations." *American Sociological Review* 21 (1956): 25-35.

Blake, Robert et al. "Housing Architecture and Social Interaction." *Sociometry* 19 (1956): 133-39.

Bollnow, Otto Friedrich. *Mensch und Raum.* Stuttgart: W. Kohlhammer, 1963.

Dobriner, William, ed. *The Suburban Community.* New York: G.P. Putnam's Sons, 1958.

Fava, Sylvia Fleis. "Suburbanism as a Way of Life." *American Sociological Review* 21 (1956): 34-37.

Feldman, Arnold S. and Charles Tilly. "The Interaction of Social and Physical Space." *American Sociological Review* 25 (1960): 877-83.

Foote, Nelson N. et al. *Housing Choices and Housing Constraints.* New York: McGraw-Hill, 1960.

Forman, Robert and Theodore Caplow. "Neighborhood Interaction in a Homogeneous Community." *American Sociological Review* 15 (1950): 357-66.

Friedman, Stephen and Joseph B. Juhasz. *Environments: Notes and Selections on Objects, Spaces and Behavior.* Monterey: Brooks/Cole, 1974.

Gans, Herbert J. *The Levittowners.* New York: Pantheon, 1967.

Greer, Scott, ed. *The New Urbanization.* New York: St. Martin's Press, 1968.

Guest, Avery M. "Neighborhood Life Cycles and Social Status." *Economic Geography* 50 (1974): 228-43.

– – –. "Patterns of Family Location." *Demography* 9 (1972): 159-71.

Gutman, R. and David Popenoe, ed. *Neighborhood, City and Metropolis.* New York: Random House, 1970.

Hall, Edward T. *The Hidden Dimension.* New York: Doubleday, 1966.

Harrington, Molly. "Resettlement and Self Image." *Human Relations* 18 (1968): 115-37.

Herlyn, Ulfert. *Wohnen im Hochhaus.* Stuttgart: Karl Krämer, 1970.

Ittelson, William H. et al. *An Introduction to Environmental Psychology.* New York: Holt, Rinehart and Winston, 1974.

Lipman, Alan. "The Architectural Belief System and Social Behavior." *British Journal of Sociology* 20 (1969): 190-204.

Madge, Charles. "Private and Public Spaces." *Human Relations* 3 (1950): 187-99.

Martin, Walter T. "The Structuring of Social Relationships Engendered by Suburban Residence." *American Sociological Review* 21 (1956): 446-53.

Meyer-Ehlers, Grete. *Wohnung und Familie.* Stuttgart: Deutsche Verlags-Anstalt, 1968.

Michelson, William M. *Environmental Choice, Human Behavior and Residential Satisfaction.* New York: Oxford University Press, 1974.

– – –. *Man and His Urban Environment.* Reading, Mass.: Addison-Wesley, 1970.

– – –. "Some Like it Hot: Social Participation and Environmental Use as Functions of the Season." *American Journal of Sociology* 76 (1971): 1072-83.

Mogey, J.M. *Family and Neighbourhood.* Oxford: Oxford University Press, 1956.

– – –. "Residence, Family and Kinship: Some Recent Research." *Journal of Family History* 1 (1976): 95-103.

Morgan, Lewis Henry. *Houses and Houselife of the American Aborigines.* Washington: Government Printing Office, 1911.

Morris, R.N. and John Mogey. *The Sociology of Housing.* London: Routledge and Kegan Paul, 1965.

Porteous, J. Douglas. *Environment and Behavior, Planning and Everyday Life.* Reading, Mass.: Addison-Wesley, 1977.

Proshansky, Harold, et al. *Environmental Psychology: Man and His Physical Setting.* New York: Holt, Rinehart and Winston, 1970.

Rapoport, Amos. *House Form and Culture.* Englewood Cliffs: Prentice-Hall, 1969.

Ross, H. Lawrence. "Uptown and Downtown: A Study of Middle Class Residential Areas." *American Sociological Review* 30 (1965): 255-59.

Rossi, Peter H. *Why Families Move.* Glencoe, Ill.: The Free Press, 1955.

Sennett, Richard, ed. *Classic Essays in the Culture of Cities.* New York: Appleton Century-Crofts, 1969.

"Social Policy and Social Research in Planning." Special Issue. *Journal of Social Issues* 7 (1951).

Sommer, Robert. "Man's Proximate Environment." *The Journal of Social Issues* 22 (1966): 59-70.

– – –. *Personal Space: The Behavioral Basis of Design.* Englewood Cliffs: Prentice-Hall, 1969.

– – –. "Studies in Personal Space." *Sociometry* 22 (1959): 247-60.

Tränkle, Margret. *Wohnkultur und Wohnweisen.* Untersuchungen des Ludwig-Uhlands Instituts der Universität Tübingen, 32. Tübingen: Tübinger Vereinigung für Volkskunde, 1972.

Upton, Dell. "Ordinary Buildings: A Bibliographical Essay on American Vernacular Architecture." *American Studies International* 19 (1981): 57–75.

Willmott, Peter and Michael Young. *Family and Class in a London Suburb.* London: Routledge and Kegan Paul, 1960.

Wilner, Daniel M. et al. *The Housing Environment and Family Life.* Baltimore: The Johns Hopkins Press, 1962.

Wohlwill, Joachim F. and Daniel H. Gerson. *Environment and the Social Sciences: Perspectives and Applications.* Washington: American Psychology Association, 1972.

Women's Group on Public Welfare. "Effect of the Design of Temporary Pre-Fabricated Bungalows on Household Routines." *The Sociological Review* 43 (1951): 17–48.

Yancey, William L. "Architecture, Interaction and Social Control, The Case of a Large-Scale Public Housing Project." *Environment and Behavior* 3 (1971): 3–22.

Young, Michael and Peter Willmott. *Family and Kinship in East London.* London: Routledge and Kegan Paul, 1957.

— — —. *The Symmetrical Family.* New York: Pantheon, 1973.

Index

Agriculture: 8–9, 13–14, 56–57; contracts, 24, 57; household, 55; seasonal cycle of, 41–42, 44; and workplace, 13, 18 34, 42–43. *See also* Grapes; Wheat; Work.

Agrigento: 12, 22.

Agrotown: xv, xx, 13–14, 42; everyday life, 37–45; housing, 18–21, 30–32; land use, 13, 14–16, 18; residential patterns, 24–32; social life, 45–51.

Airshaft: 71, 99.

Alleys: 14, 16, 68.

Americani: 116, 152n.

Amici: See Friends and Friendship.

Animals: 38, 42, 93; stalls, 18, 29, 30.

Apartment: 68, 71; and household structure, 75–77; size, 68, 77, 81, 107; as woman's workplace, 95–96.

Architecture, vernacular: xx.

Artisans, xx, 5–6, 7, 44; housing of, 23, 25, 27, 30, 74; leisure of, 43; and migration, 56, 61–62; and social change, 98, 101, 109–11; social networks of, 49–51. *See also* Family; Work.

Balcony: 21.

Banfield, Edward: 1, 7, 10.

Barton, Josef: 62.

Basement: 68, 93, 94.

Bastards: *See* Illegitimacy.

Bed: 29, 30, 82.

Betts, Lillian: 75, 76, 77, 86, 87, 92, 96.

Block: land use on, 68, 72; social life, 80, 105.

Boarding: 27–28, 71, 80–82, 104, 158n; of kin, 59, 81, 101, 106; and the "myth of male dominance," 113–14. *See also* Household, malleable.

Boissevain, Jeremy: 10.

Briggs, John: 60, 61, 62, 100.

Brothers: 5, 26, 59, 79.

Budgets: 22, 24, 75, 92, 103.

Building trades: 22, 42, 79, 93, 106, 109.

Burgisi: See Peasant, landowning.

Cadaster: 18, 22, 23, 24, 25.

Cafe: 43, 94, 97, 105, 106.

Calogero, Saint: 61, 79, 105, 108, 127.

Campagna: 13–14, 42–43, 50.

Campanilismo: 60, 149–50n. *See also* *Paesani*; Localism.

Casa (family): 4, 25. 26, 32, 48, 102, 147n; immigrant, 79, 102, 108, 115; and migration, 59, 60.

Casa (house): 12, 32, 46; *civile*, 21, 27, 29–30, 33.

Census: Italian, 6, 23, 27; New York State, 54, 63, 75, 77, 78, 92, 94, 126, 127, 129, 148–49.

Chain migration: 55, 58–60, 60–61, 79, 103, 108, 126.

Chapin, Robert: 91, 92.

Chapman, Charlotte Gower: 1, 5, 25, 26, 27, 28, 48, 50.

Childrearing: in New York: 82, 92, 96–97, 98, 101, 102, 106; in Sicily: 43, 46, 48, 51.

Children: family role, 27, 101–2; and housing, 13, 21–22, 23, 25, 104; and work, 22, 43, 91–92, 94, 95, 98, 101. *See also*; Leisure; Sons; Daughters; Childrearing.

Chimneys: 39, 44, 96.

Churches: 18, 42, 72.

City hall: 18, 56.

City planning: xvi, 72.

Civili: 5, 6–7, 8–9, 25, 43; leisure, 43,

49–50; and migration, 61, 62, 115; social life, 48, 49–50, 50–51, 107, 109. *See also: Casa civile*; Family.
Class: 3, 5–6, 6–7, 8, 50–51, 61–62, 109–10; consciousness, 51, 55, 56, 109, 110–11, 115; and everyday life, 37, 40. *See also* Housing.
Client: *See* Patrons and Patronage.
Clubs: *civile*, 43, 50; immigrant, 105, 111; workers, 51.
Clustering: xix; kinship, 25–26, 79, 104, 106, 126, 127–29, 135n; occupational, 25, 78; *paesani*, 79.
Coffee: 92, 103.
Community: xvi, 1, 50, 154n; immigrant, 55, 60, 106, 108, 111.
Competition: 1, 4, 8–9, 32, 102; immigrant, 83; and migration, 58.
Cooking: 38–39, 41, 91, 92, 95.
Cooperation: 1 4, 9, 82, 104; and migration, 57, 58; among women, 47, 103–04. *See also* Family Solidarity.
Copare: See Godparents.
Coresidence: *See* Household.
Corona: 13, 42, 43.
Cortile: 16–17, 44, 45, 80, 82; social life, 25–26, 33–34, 44, 48, 49.
Cousins, 4, 28, 113.
Covello, Leonard: 22, 114.
Covivenza: See Household, nonfamily.
Cronin, Constance: 111, 112, 115.
Cultural change: xxi, 1, 10, 60, 111–13, 114–16.

Daniel, Annie S.: 75.
Daughters: 4, 46, 97, 113; and housing, 22, 23, 26, 77, 79; work of immigrant, 91, 94, 98, 114.
Decoration of home: 29–30, 82–83.
"Deep South": 55, 155n.
De Forest, Robert: xvi.
Dockworkers: 79, 106.
Doors: 18, 21, 71, 76; symbolism of, 45–46, 47.

Eating: 38, 40, 92; and family solidarity, 28, 29, 81, 82; and privacy, 27, 30, 75. *See also* Food.
Elizabeth Street: 54, 65, 66, 126, 143n. *See also* Housing; Population; Tenement Neighborhood.
Environment: and behavior, xvi–xx; and everyday life, 42, 43–44, 93, 95, 96, 98–99; and residential patterns, 34,

76–77, 83–84. *See also* Match: Restraints.
Everyday life: 35; and housing, xix–xx, 45–46, 98–99; agrotown, 37–45; and social life, 45, 47–50, 99, 103–107; tenement, 87–97.

Factions: 50, 51.
Factories: 63, 72, 94, 95. *See also* Work.
Familism, amoral: 1, 3, 4, 10, 49; and migration, 55, 56–57; and class-consciousness, 111.
Family and Community: xv, 3.
Family: xvi, xviii–xix, 9, 32; among artisans, 46, 49–50, 114; among *civili*, 49–50, 114; among immigrants, xx, 100–02, 108, 112, 114–15; and migration, 58–59; among peasants, 34, 42, 45–46, 150n; reconstitution, 25, 127; roles, 3–4, 34, 40–41, 46–47, 49, 91; size, 33, 77, 129; solidarity, 4, 22, 45, 81, 82, 101–02, 133n, 150n. *See also Casa* (family); *Famiglia*; Nuclear Family; Household; Kinship.
Faro, Saint: 105.
Fasanella, Ralph: 86–87, 98.
Fasci Siciliani: 55, 56.
Fathers: 4, 9, 21, 32, 102; discrepancy between real and ideal roles, 46, 47, 51, 101, 113; immigrant, 98, 100, 114.
Festival societies: 50, 105.
Feudalism: 7, 8, 14.
Fire escapes, 71, 95, 96.
First settlement: 66, 77, 103, 108, 109.
Fishermen: 61, 78.
Floors: 18, 38, 45, 92–93.
Fogli di famiglia: 24–25, 28, 33, 135n.
Folklore: 2, 130n.
Food: 38, 39, 42, 92, 96; and migration, 57.
Foster, George: 114.
Fortunate Pilgrim: 108.
Fountains: 14, 18; and social life, 44, 48.
14th Ward: 66–67, 72, 94, 97; housing in, 67, 71, 75, 77.
Friends and friendship: ideals, xvi, 3, 4–5, 10; and chain migration, 59, 60; and Sicilian social network, 48; and immigrant social network, 103, 104, 105, 114, 115. *See also Paesani*.
Fuel: 39, 82, 91, 92.
Furniture: 29–30, 82–83, 102, 150n. *See also* Bed; Table.

Gabelloti: 8, 43, 50.
Gangs: 50, 105.
Gans, Herbert: 102, 106.
Garbage: 38, 93, 96.
Garment making: 6, 44, 63–64, 103–04, 109; concentration of immigrant women in, 62; and residential choice, 78, 92, 94–95, 144, 148; seasons in, 93–94.
Generations: first, xxi, 103, 111, 115; second, 107, 108, 150n. *See also* Peers and Peer Groups.
Godparents (fictive kin): 4, 5, 28, 113–14, 115.
Gossip: 9, 48, 58.
Grapes: 8, 41, 42, 43, 56.
Guild: 50.
Guests: *See* Hospitality.

Hallways: 68, 71, 76: and social life, 97, 98–99; as workplace, 95, 96.
Hearth: 18, 19, 32.
Homeownership: 12, 74; and residential mobility, 32, 33, 113; in New York, 74, 84, 102, 108, 126; in Sicily, 21–23, 32.
Honor: *See* Respect.
Hospitality: 10, 29, 30, 49; in New York, 83, 97, 103, 104.
House: *See Casa* (house); Housing.
Households: 27, 126; malleable, 80–83, 103, 104, 106, 113–14; nonfamily, 28, 81; nuclear family, 27–28, 30, 77, 82, 92; partner, 28–29, 75–77, 82, 92; stem family, 28, 29, 136n. *See also* Boarding.
Housework: *See* Work.
Housing: xv–xx; in agrotowns, xx, 18–21; class differences in, 21, 26–27, 29–30, 49, 77, 78; costs, 22, 24, 74–75, 84, 108; low density, 107, 108; reform, xvi, 71, 127; supply, 25, 66. *See also* Environment and Behavior; Ideals; Tenements; Tenement Neighborhoods.
Husbands: 46–47, 49.

Ideals: xv, xix–xx, 84–85, 100, 112–116; and behavior, 45, 49, 51–52, 80, 98, 101, 102; family, 3–4, 28, 80–81, 82, 114–15; historical study of, 2–3, 10; housing, 12–13, 21, 25, 32, 74, 107, 108; kinship, 4–5, 114–15; and migration, 55, 59; occupational, 5–6, 7, 61–62, 64; social, xv, 4–5, 7–8, 9–10, 83, 84.
Illegitimacy: 6, 28.

Immigration Commission: 54, 63, 95.
Income: 22, 24, 40; immigrants', 75, 81, 84, 98, 103, 110, 144n.
Individualism: 100–02.
Instrumental relationships: 5, 9, 47, 48, 102, 107.
Irish immigrants: 67.
Italian immigrants: in Brooklyn, 61, 66, 107, 108; in Buffalo, xv, xxi, 58, 63, 111, 112; in New York, 56, 63, 66–67, 107; in other locations, 56, 60, 63, 67, 106, 107, 108, 111.

Jewish immigrants: 83, 105.

Kin and kinship: xv, 111, 127–28; and migration, 54, 58–60; and immigrant social network, 60, 78, 79, 81, 103, 104, 106–07, 108, 114–15. *See also* Clustering: Ideals; *Famiglia*.

Labor unions: 49, 55, 109, 111.
Laborers: 5, 8, 2, 24; and migration, 61, 62, 64; and immigrant residential patterns, 79, 81. *See also* Work.
Land use: 13–18, 71–72.
Landlords: 24, 74.
Landownership: 5–6, 8–9, 23. *See also* Peasants.
Latifondo (large estate): 13, 37, 44.
Laundry: 44, 71, 93, 96.
Leisure: xx, 34, 35, 42, 43, 50; of immigrant children, 91, 96–97, 98, 101; of immigrant men, 97, 105, 110; women's, 97.
Le Roy Ladurie, Emmanuel: 35.
Lifestyle: 35.
Little Italies: 53–54, 66, 108.
Localism: 48, 49, 105, 108. See also *Campanilismo*.
Lofts: 18, 30, 71.

MacDonald, J.S.: 55, 58.
Maestro don Gesualdo: 33.
Mafia: 49, 50.
Mangano, Antonio: 103, 104.
Manual work: *See* Laborers: Work.
Marriage: 22, 23, 48, 102, 150n, 150n.
Massaro/a: 6.
Masseria: 37.
Match: xviii, xx; in Sicily, 12, 13, 51; in New York, 66, 74, 84, 87; in other cities, 108.
Material determinism: xvi, 66, 83.

Matriarchy: 4, 49, 231.
Merchants: 5, 6; and migration, 61; in
New York, 63, 78–79, 92, 94. *See also*
Artisans.
Michelson, Williams: xviii.
Migration: 55; selective, 54, 61, 63, 64;
Sicilian, 53–54, 55–57; and immigrant
social structure, 54, 57–61, 62. *See
also* Chain Migration.
Mills: 13, 18.
Milocca: 1, 5, 25–26.
Miseria: 51.
Mobility: geographic, 111, 114; occupa-
tional, 64; residential, 32–34, 77–78,
144n; social, 8–9, 56, 110; and social
life, 84–85, 104, 108–09. *See also*
Migration.
Montaillou: 35.
Mothers: 4, 21, 22, 46–47; immigrant, 98,
101, 102.
Mutual benefit society: 50, 51, 57, 105.
Myth of male dominance: 49, 113–14.

Naming patterns: 61, 127–29.
Navarro della Miraglia, Emmanuele: 12,
35–36; *passim*, 14–18, 25–26, 29–30,
43–48, 50.
Neighbors and neighborhood: 25–26,
78–80; ideals, 3, 4–5, 13; and immigrant
social network, 84–85, 98–99, 103–06,
107–08; and migration, 59, 60; and
Sicilian social network, 34, 48, 49. *See
also* Clustering.
Networks, social: 35; class differences,
49–51; ideals, 9, 51–52; immigrant,
103–07, 108–09, 111, 115; and mobility,
57, 107–08; women's, 48–49, 105–06.
See also Chain Migration.
New York: 62–63, 64, 66; housing regula-
tion, 71.
Nuclear family: 1; immigrant, 80, 82–83,
100–02; and migration, 58–59; Sicilian,
3–4, 27–28, 30, 45–46.
Nulla osta: 56.

Occupational categories: immigrant,
62–64, 109–10; and migration, 61–62,
64; in Sicily, 5–7.
Orphans: 18, 28.

Padrone: 5, 7. *See also* Patrons and
Patronage.
Paesani: 59, 60, 60–61, 80, 127. *See also
Campanilismo*; Clustering.

Paese: 13.
Paese clubs: 105.
Palermo: 2, 60.61, 79, 106.
Parenti: See Kin and Kinship.
Parents: 101–02.
Parish: 135–36.
Parrini: See Godparents.
Participant observation: 36.
Patriarchy: 4, 49, 50. *See also* Myth of
Male Dominance.
Patrons and patronage: 10, 48, 50–51;
immigrant, 62, 109. *See* also *Padrone*.
Patron saints: 50, 61, 105, 127.
Peasants: 5–6; housing, 25, 27, 30, 34, 45;
landowning, 6–7, 9, 23, 133n; leisure,
42; and migration, 55, 56–57, 61–62,
63; social networks of, 47–49, 51. *See
also* Family; Work.
Peddlers: *See* Merchants.
Peers and peer groups: 102–03, 104,
106–07, 113–14.
Piano nobile (second floor): 12, 21, 45.
Piazza: 14, 18; and social life, 42, 43, 97.
Pitrè Giuseppe: 2–3, 25, 61; *passim*,
32–48.
Play: *See* Leisure.
Population: agrotown, 6, 13; Elizabeth
Street, 57, 58, 107, 126 *table*; 14th
Ward, 66–67; New York, 54, 66.
Poverty: and migration, 55, 57; "the
poor", 7, 51; and social life, xvi, 40,
87, 103.
Pratt, Edward: 94.
Primitive rebels: 109.
Privacy: 29–30, 45, 49; immigrant, 75,
76–77, 81, 82, 113.
Prominenti: 62, 115, 151n.
Property: *amore della robba*, 8; and
class, 5–6, 40; and marriage, 21–22, 23,
102, 133n, 136; social relations as, 7, 9.
See also Homeownership; Landowner-
ship.Proverbs: 2–3, 41.
Public garden: 18, 56.
Pushcart markets: 63, 72, 78.
Puzo, Mario: 86, 108.

Railroad flat: 68–71.
Rapoport, Amos: 83.
Reciprocity: 7–8, 9, 48, 58.
Renovations: 71
Rents and renting: in New York, 74–75,
75–76, 108; and residential mobility,
32–33, 77, 83–84; in Sicily, 24, 27,
28, 32; subletting, 75.

Residential choice: xviii-xix, 12–13, 21–22, 78.
Residential patterns; xix, 34, 83. *See also* Clustering; Households; Residential Mobility.
Residential satisfaction: xviii; immigrant, 84–85, 98, 99, 107; in Sicily, xx, 21, 32, 51–52.
Respect: 9, 48, 50, 58.
Restraints, environmental: xviii; and cultural change, 1122–13; and immigrant women, 95, 98–99, 106; and immigrant residential patterns, 77, 81, 108; and peasants, 34, 42, 44, 49, 51.
Riis, Jacob: xvi, 65–66, 75, 76, 105.
Rogers, Susan Carol: 49.
Roof: 18, 32; and social life, 89–99; as workplace, 95, 96.
Rooms: back, 71; bath, 71, 108; bed, 18, 30, 82; good (best, front), 44, 71, 83, 95; kitchen, 18, 71, 75, 81–83, 95–96, 97; *salotto*, 29–30, 82–83; *soggiorno*, 30, 82.
Rosalia, Saint: 61, 105, 127.

Salomone-Marino, Salvatore: 2.
Saloon: *See* Tavern.
Salvdenajo: 22.
Sambuca di Sicilia: example of typical agrotown, 14–18; housing in, 18–21, 33; migration from, 59–60, 61, 63; representativeness of, 12; social life in, 25, 26, 50–51.
Santa Margherita Belice: 61.
Scavenging: 42, 91.
Schneider, Jane and Peter: 10, 50.
Schools: 39, 46, 51; in New York, 91, 94, 101, 102.
"School sinks:" 71, 93.
Sciacca: 61, 79, 106.
Seasons: in New York, 93–94; in Sicily, 41–42.
Second settlement: 66, 109.
Segregation, residential: *See* Clustering.
Servants: 6, 27, 40, 44, 93.
Sexuality: 4, 46, 49, 51, 113–14.
Shoemakers: 51, 56, 93.
Shops and shopping: 18, 43, 44; in New York, 72, 96.
Sicilians: everyday life of, 37–45; Family life of, 3–4, 27–28, 46–48, 49–50; social life of, 45–52. *See also* Ideals: Migration.
Sidewalks: 95, 99.

Sisters: 59, 79.
6th Ward: 66.
Sleeping: 30, 75, 77, 81, 83.
Smith, Judith: 100.
Social change: xv, xx–xxi, 100–09; and cultural change, 326.
Social interaction: xx, 12, 34, 35, 45, 99.
Social organization of migration: 170. *See also* Chain Migration.
Socialism: 51, 55, 56.
Sonnino, Sidney, 13, 24, 25.
Sons: and housing, 22, 23, 30, 81; and work, 46, 91, 94, 101–02.
Spinning: 6.
Stevenson, Robert A.: 96.
Staircases: 68, 69; and women's work, 96, 99.
Streets: 14, 66, 97, 98, 105; Bowery, 66, 72; Broadway, 71; Canal, 78; *Corso*, 14, 15, 25; E. Houston, 54, 78, 79, 95; 14th, 94; Kenmare, 72; Mott, 79, 95; Mulberry, 66; Prince, 78, 79, 95; Spring, 78.
Strikes: 55, 56, 109.
"Stripping down": 114–15.

Table: 28, 30, 47.
Tavern: 43, 63, 97.
Ten Years War: 65.
Tenement House Problem: 72.
Tenements: 67–78, 71; barracks, 67, 68; dumbbells, 68–69, 76; front, 68; new law, 68, 71, 76, 84, 105, 127; old law, 68; rear, 68, 77.
Tenement neighborhood: xv, xvi; economy of, 62–64; everyday life in, 91–97; housing in, 67–71; land use in, 66–67, 71–72; residential patterns of, 75–83; social life of, 84–85, 102.09.
Theaters: 18, 56, 97.
Thernstrom, Stephan: 111.
Toilets: 21, 68, 71, 93.
Truancy: 91.
Turnialettu: 82.

Unemployment: 42, 93, 103, 110.
Urban renewal: 72, 107.

Vacancy rates: 77.
Vecoli, Rudolph: 109.
Veiller, Lawrence: xvi.
Verga, Giovanni: 33, 35; *passim*, 46–49.
Vicini: *See* Neighbors and Neighborhood.

Viddani: 6, 7.
Visiting: *See* Hospitality.
Voluntary association: and familism, 1; in
    New York, 105; in Sicily, 49, 50, 51,
    55, 56.

Wages: 76, 101, 102, 109. *See also* In-
    come.
Walls: 18, 23, 93.
Ware, Caroline: 95, 105–06.
Water supply: 14, 44, 48; in New York,
    68, 69, 93, 95, 105–06.
Weaving: 44, 48.
Wheat: 8, 13, 37, 41, 43; and migration,
    56.
Widowers: 23, 28.
Wives: 4, 46, 113–14.
Williamsburgh bridge: 72.
Windows: 18, 44, 68, 71; and social life,
    98, 99; symbolism of, 45, 49.
Wirth, Louis: xviii.
Wohnweisen: 35.
Women: family roles of, 4, 46–47, 96–97;
    seclusion of, 47–48, 96, 98–99. *See also*

Childrearing; Garment making; Leisure;
    Work.
Work: agricultural, 37, 42, 43, 64;
    artisanal, 39, 40, 42, 43, 44; factory,
    63–64, 91–92, 93; New York house-
    hold, 92–93, 95–96; professional, 43,
    62, 92; Sicilian household, 38, 40,
    43–44; and Sicilian ideals, 5–6; skilled,
    63, 110; unskilled, 64, 110; white collar,
    62, 92; women's, 6, 64, 92, 94, 147n,
    147–48.
Working-class: 51, 55, 62; in New York,
    110–11.
Workplaces: agricultural, 13, 42–43; the
    bottega (workshop), 18, 30, 43; and
    family life, 34, 42, 43, 98; the house,
    44, 94, 95–96; and Sicilian ideals, 13,
    74; and social life, 34, 46, 98–99; in
    tenement neighborhoods, 71–72, 94–96.

Yans-McLaughlin, Virginia: xv, 55, 100;
    passim, xxx–3, 111–15.
Yards: 93, 95, 96, 97, 102, 105.

Zone of transition: 71, 74.